The War at Troy

THE WAR
AT TROY

What Homer Didn't Tell

By *Quintus of Smyrna*
Translated, and with an Introduction and
Notes, by Frederick M. Combellack

BARNES
&NOBLE
BOOKS
NEW YORK

To C.R.B.C.

Contents

The War at Troy

***

Introduction

HOMER's *Iliad* is the real introduction to Quintus' *The War at Troy*. Homer's audience was intimately familiar with the Troy Story, and therefore not bothered by the fact that the *Iliad* ended before the story was complete. By the same token, Quintus' audience was familiar with the *Iliad*, and therefore not bothered by the fact that Quintus begins where Homer ends, with the death of Hector. Troy continued to resist for some months after this disaster, and this concluding phase of the war at Troy was an especially active one for both Greeks and Trojans. The events of these months included some of the most popular and famous of the whole Troy Story. The fiery splendor of Greek literature had sunk low by Quintus' time, and neither Quintus nor any of his contemporaries was able to rekindle it, but sad stories of the deaths of kings have enjoyed a long popularity, and during the centuries that have elapsed since Quintus wrote many readers have found his sequel to the *Iliad* a useful and interesting addition to the vast literature dealing with the greatest story of the ancient world.

The time and place of Quintus are almost as obscure as those of Homer, even though Quintus, unlike Homer, has included in his poem a scrap of autobiography. After calling upon the Muses in Book Twelve to name for him all those who entered the wooden horse, Quintus continues thus: "You put all song in my heart, before the down was spread over my cheeks. I was pasturing my fine sheep in the plains of Smyrna, three times as far from the river Hermus as one can hear a man shouting. It was by a temple of Artemis, in the garden of Zeus the Deliverer, on a hill neither particularly low nor very high" (307–13). Unfortunately, these few lines have produced much learned controversy about how they are to be interpreted, and there have been efforts to convince us that they are meant to be taken metaphorically, not literally. The sheep, for instance, are not actually sheep, but students in a school, and Quintus is not a shepherd, but a teacher. Or, again, the sheep are here, not because Quintus was literally a shepherd, but because he wants to connect himself with Hesiod, who in his *Theogony* tells of his encounter with the Muses when he was pasturing his sheep on Mt. Helicon. And Smyrna is mentioned, not because Quintus lived there, but because he wants to connect himself with Homer, and one ancient tradition located Homer's birthplace there. Many scholars, however, have been prepared to take Quintus' words at their face value, and it has even been pointed out that Quintus' statement that his sheep were "fine" is confirmed by reports of modern travelers about the unusually fine quality of the sheep in the neighborhood of Smyrna. There is still a good deal of doubt about the significance of the sheep, but the prevailing view today is that we may well accept as a fact the connection of Quintus with the city of Smyrna in Asia Minor, and he is ordinarily called today, as he was called by the Byzantine Tzetzes, Quintus of Smyrna, a name which also appears on some of the Quintus manuscripts. (The name "Quintus Calaber," which is found on some manuscripts and has also been used in modern times, arose because Cardinal Bessarion in about the middle of the fifteenth century discovered in the monastery of St. Nicholas near Otranto in Calabria the manuscript of Quintus which reintroduced him to the modern world.)

Quintus' date is also quite uncertain, and advocates have been

4

found for a date as early as Homer himself and as late as the sixth century after Christ. For many scholars a date in the fourth century after Christ has seemed most likely, and some writers have felt it fitting to guess that Quintus may have been inspired to produce his poem by the efforts of the Emperor Julian (A.D. 361–63) to restore paganism in the Roman Empire. The poem, then, would have been produced in the sixties of the fourth century.

The evidence for Quintus' date is all internal and reduces itself essentially to two sorts. In the first place, there are various stylistic criteria. The comparative study of the metrical technique of Greek hexameter poets, for instance, seems to put Quintus earlier than Nonnus, who produced his long epic on Dionysus in, probably, the fifth century after Christ. Some scholars, again, have tried to draw useful conclusions from a study of literary influences on or by a number of late Greek writers whose dates are less uncertain than that of Quintus. In the second place, two passages in Quintus' poem have been thought relevant to the problem of his date. A passage in Book Six has ordinarily been interpreted as a reference to gladiatorial combats: "The Atreussons in the center kept turning this way and that, just like boars or lions in a great enclosure on that day when lords collect people and huddle them cruelly together, preparing evil death from the strong wild beasts, and the beasts inside the enclosure devour whatever slaves come close to them; so the Atreussons in the center kept killing men who rushed at them" (531–37). This passage has meant for some readers that Quintus wrote before the Emperor Theodosius (A.D. 379–95) greatly mitigated the cruelty of the gladiatorial games. Köchly was reminded of a passage in Ammianus Marcellinus describing the fondness of the Emperor Valentinian (A.D. 365–75) for a pair of wild bears which had torn many slaves to pieces. The other relevant lines are in a speech by the prophet Calchas in Book Thirteen: "Stop hurling your cruel arrows and destructive spears at Aeneas. It is decreed for him by the splendid plan of the gods to go from Xanthus to the broad stream of the Tiber. There he shall fashion a sacred city, an object of wonder for future generations, and he shall himself be lord of a widespread people.

The stock born of him shall thereafter rule all the way from the rising to the setting sun" (334–41). For dating purposes, the significant detail in these lines is the absence of Constantinople. It has been argued that Quintus would not have spoken so expansively of Rome if he had written after the foundation of Constantinople as the eastern capital of the Empire (A.D. 324). The latest scholar to devote himself to Quintus, F. Vian, argues for a date in the third century. Vian, however, is rather more confident than I should be of the alleged imitations of Quintus by Nonnus and others and alleged imitations of Oppian by Quintus.

In sum, the evidence at our disposal is inadequate to support any certain conclusions about Quintus' date. If we say he probably lived in the third or fourth century after Christ, we are going about as far as we justifiably can. We may note that this Greek poet has a Latin name, but we are not in a position to draw from this fact any significant conclusions about him or his background.

Quintus' poem is referred to in some scholia on line 220 of the second book of the *Iliad* and is also mentioned by the Byzantine Homeric scholar Eustathius in the introduction to his vast Commentary on Homer. In these references, the poem is called "The Things after Homer" or, as we might say, "What Homer Didn't Tell." Similar titles appear in some of the manuscripts of Quintus. We do not know what title Quintus himself gave to his work. It is actually, of course, a sequel, not to Homer, but to the *Iliad*.

The poem of Quintus is our only extant literary work giving a connected account of the events of the Trojan War which took place between the death of Hector and the departure of the Greek army from Troy. It is not accidental that these events occur between the portion of the Troy Story narrated in Homer's *Iliad* and that narrated in his *Odyssey*. The purpose of Quintus' work is obvious: it is designed as a supplement to Homer's works. Indeed, there are a few manuscripts of Homer which contain Quintus' poem between the *Iliad* and the *Odyssey*. The present existence of this supplement, the fact that it is one of the comparatively few works of Greek literature to survive the collapse of the ancient world, is evidence enough that Quintus succeeded in his aim and found readers in late antiquity, the Middle Ages, and the Renaissance who were interested in such an addition to Homer's poems.

Indeed, there is every reason to believe that readers at all times have been interested in the general kind of information that Quintus has provided. We like to know what finally happened in a story which has aroused our interest and what was the ultimate fate of the characters to whom we have been introduced. Moreover, among the great literary works of the world, the *Iliad* seems rather especially to call for such a supplement. Many readers, from the greatest classical scholars to the most uninformed neophyte, have felt that the *Iliad* is incomplete. It does not finish what it has begun and ends, for example, when Achilles is still alive and Troy is still uncaptured. Quintus' poem gives us an account of what happened to Achilles and to Troy and tells us many other things besides. There is no likelihood that Homer and his original audience felt any incompleteness in his *Iliad*, since almost certainly everybody knew the whole story of which the *Iliad* is a part. But a supplement has a special appeal for many modern readers who may be somewhat vague about just what happened in the Trojan War.

The main episodes in the last months of the Trojan War were the following: the fatal enterprises of Penthesileia, Queen of the Amazons, and Memnon, King of Ethiopia, who came to help Troy and met their deaths at the hands of Achilles; the death of Achilles and the funeral games held in his honor; the contest between Aias and Odysseus for Achilles' splendid armor, the victory of Odysseus, and the resultant suicide of Aias; the theft of the Palladium (an old statue of Athena) from Troy by Odysseus (Quintus gives a number of lines to this episode in his strange report of Hera's conversation with her handmaids after Paris' death in Book Ten, but he does not narrate it as one of the events of his poem); the bringing of Achilles' son Neoptolemus from Scyros and his victory over Eurypylus, who had come to help Troy; the bringing of Philoctetes from Lemnos to help the Greeks; the death of Paris; the wooden horse; the capture and sack of Troy.

These events were dealt with in a series of three early Greek epic poems: the *Aethiopis*, by Arctinus of Miletus; the *Little Iliad*, usually attributed to Lesches of Mitylene; and the *Sack of Troy*, also by Arctinus. The dates of these authors are unknown, but the probability is that they produced their works in the seventh century B.C. The poems themselves are lost, except for a few scraps, and indeed it appears likely that they were unknown to Quintus fifteen hundred years ago, although a number of scholars have maintained that they were among Quintus' sources. We owe our knowledge of the contents of these poems primarily to a group of short prose summaries which have survived.

It is these episodes, of course, which form the story of Quintus' poem. The mere recital of them also reveals one of the basic differences between Quintus' work and the two poems of his great predecessor Homer: this is a chronicle poem, not a poem with a carefully constructed plot dealing with the Wrath of Achilles or the Man of Many Devices. Quintus' method is to relate his various events in sequence, surrounding them with persistent battle scenes, and adorning them with a rich abundance of similes. Different characters assume prime importance in the different episodes, and a few characters have some importance throughout the poem, but there is no figure who in his importance to the story is even remotely comparable to Achilles in the *Iliad* or Odysseus in the *Odyssey*. It is, in short, a heroic poem without a hero. If there is anything comparable to a hero, it is not a person at all, but the doomed city of Troy, which we see full of grief and terror at the poem's beginning and a shattered, smoking ruin at its end. But Quintus abandons even this heroic image before the end of his poem in order to give us a few glimpses of the Greeks' disastrous return home.

Quintus' debt to Homer is obvious, vast, and pervasive. What he owes to other sources is far less easy to determine. The uncertainties in this realm of speculation may be illustrated by a single example: in 1850 the distinguished German Hellenist Hermann Köchly published his important edition of Quintus. The problem of sources was discussed at length in the Latin "Prolegomena" to this edition, and Köchly's conclusion was that he found no traces of great learning and wide reading in Quintus and that, apart from Homer, the only poets Quintus had read carefully were Hesiod and Apollonius of Rhodes. The latest important contributions to Quintus have been made by F. Vian, who has published a book on the manuscript tradition, a volume of "Recherches," and the first volume of a new edition. Nearly half of the volume of "Recherches" is given to three chapters on Quintus' sources, and Vian has returned to the subject in the Introduction to his new edition of the poem. Vian finds in Quintus "une large culture" and is certain that he used the Greek tragedians and drew upon much in Hellenistic literature besides the *Argonautica* of Apollonius of Rhodes. When experts of this standing come to such different conclusions, we may again feel that we are faced with a problem which our evidence does not enable us to solve. A most important aspect of the problem, and a factor that contributes much to its insolubility, is that nearly all the Greek literature produced in the millennium separating Quintus from Homer has been lost. We cannot, therefore, even guess what ones among these lost works Quintus may have read and used.

In addition to poets whom Quintus might have found useful, there were also available to him handbooks of mythology. Besides possible Greek sources, there was also in existence, of course, a rich assortment of works in Latin, the most obviously useful for Quintus' purposes being Virgil's *Aeneid*. Ovid's *Metamorphoses*, too, deals with the conflict between Aias and Odysseus for the arms of Achilles, one of Quintus' episodes. There has been spirited debate on the question of Quintus' possible use of Latin literature and, again, no agreement. Vian has made a vigorous case for the theory that Quintus was not influenced by Latin literature and that many of the similarities that have been stressed are probably due to the use of the same Greek model.

Quintus' way of beginning his poem is very different from Homer's. There is no invocation of the Muse, no indication of just what his theme is to be. He is informal and almost prosaic; he begins as one might now begin a prose narrative. He does have two features in common with Homer: both poets make clear in their first few lines that their poems will deal with aspects of the Troy Story, and both poets tell us immediately at what point in the Trojan War they will begin their tale. Quite probably the informality and abruptness of Quintus' opening are due to the fact that he is producing a sequel. In a sense he (and we) might feel that this is not the beginning of a poem, but book xxv of the *Iliad*. Both Homer and Quintus can also count on audiences who know the story; so preliminary background for events, characters, and locale can be dispensed with. Quintus was, indeed, probably sensible to leave out anything corresponding to Homer's "Wrath" and "Man," because he has no such unified theme.

The central importance of Troy to his story is made clear at once by the way he underlines her weakness in three contrasts: Achilles and Hector, the lion and the cows, the bold Greek without and the fearful Trojans within, their minds haunted by recollections of earlier disasters. Finally, in line seventeen there is the foreshadowing of the blazing town.

Within the first few pages of his poem, Quintus reveals some of the further differences between himself and Homer. Homer is eager to get his story under way and his reader interested in it. Quintus devotes most of his first pages to literary adornment, and very little happens. The whole of the first book of the *Iliad* is without similes; Quintus gives us five similes in the first hundred lines— indeed the similes take up nearly a third of these lines. Quintus even feels a need for three similes within the first fifty lines, and two of the three are "doublets," both drawn from the same sphere and both designed to illustrate the same thing: Penthesileia's pre-eminence among her attendants is like that of (1) the moon among the stars and (2) the Dawn among the Hours. Such a piling up of similes reminds one of the number and variety of similes which Homer uses in describing the marshalling of the Greek army just before his Catalogue in the second book of the *Iliad*.

Homer likes catalogues of names—the Nereids and the Phaeacians, for instance—but he gets us interested in his story before he produces any. Quintus has barely begun before he devotes five lines to a catalogue of the Amazons who accompanied Penthesileia. Possibly Tennyson was right in saying that Quintus tells his story "somewhat lazily." To be sure, Quintus' un-Homeric technique in the use of catalogue and simile may be, like his abrupt, informal opening lines, the result of his feeling that this is not the beginning. Twenty-four books of the *Iliad* have come just before.

This sort of explanation, however, will not apply to Quintus' desire to describe in some detail Penthesileia's appearance (as he later describes the appearance of other characters) or his tendency to indulge in occasional quiet moralizing, as when he says that the Furies always haunt sinners (31–32) and that good hope often softens misery (72–73). The only one of his characters whom Homer describes is Thersites, in the second book of the *Iliad*. Homer now and then includes sententious remarks, but he usually puts them into the mouths of his characters and very seldom preaches at us in his own person. Quintus' practice is just the reverse: he gives only a few of his truisms to his characters and reserves most of them for himself.

The early pages of the poem also display some of Quintus' merits. He makes good use of some of Homer's motifs for similes, and the Homeric flavor of his lines is heightened by frequent Homeric formulas. On the other hand, he uses occasional words and phrases which have a good epic sound but which do not occur in Homer. Some of them do not occur elsewhere in extant Greek literature, and some of these may be Quintus' own invention. He shows skill in noting contrasting qualities in his characters. Penthesileia's beauty, for example, has in it something terrible as well as glorious (57), and her face shows strength as well as grace (61). More elaborate, and less common, is the complicated simile illustrating contrasting facets of the narrative by contrasting facets of the simile. Desiring to show us Priam simultaneously cheered by the arrival of Penthesileia and melancholy because of his dead sons, Quintus compares him to a man who has recovered his sight after illness but still has a dreadful pain in his eyes (71–85).

Quintus' cast of characters is basically the same as Homer's. Three of the *Iliad's* important personages are killed in the course of that poem: Sarpedon, Patroclus, and Hector. On the other hand, in Quintus five new leaders appear at Troy after Hector's death: Penthesileia, Memnon, and Eurypylus come to help Troy; Neoptolemus and Philoctetes are added to the Greek command.

The Homeric characters in Quintus are scarcely changed. Nestor is still the old man eloquent. Odysseus is still the man of diplomacy and ingenuity. It is he who plays the leading role in restoring Philoctetes to the army and in bringing Neoptolemus, Achilles' son, from Scyros; he suggests the stratagem of the wooden horse and the device of the roof of shields in the attack on the wall. In his journeys to get Philoctetes and Neoptolemus, Odysseus is associated with Diomedes, just as he is in the scouting expedition related in the tenth book of the *Iliad*. Diomedes' role in these expeditions, however, is comparatively insignificant, and, indeed, he is scanted in Quintus' poem as a whole. The part he plays in the *Iliad*, the young hero of a unique splendor when Achilles is out of action, is taken in Quintus' poem by Neoptolemus. After Neoptolemus joins the army, sometimes it is hard to remember that we are not reading about Achilles. Although Quintus appears to copy Homer in associating Diomedes with Odysseus, he goes far beyond Homer in emphasizing Aias' close association with Achilles, something which Homer, at most, barely hints at in his portrayal of Achilles' reaction to Aias' speech in the ninth book of the *Iliad*.

Quintus has nothing remotely comparable to Homer's picture of Helen on the walls of Troy in the third book of the *Iliad*, but his account of the reunion of Helen and Menelaus is well managed, in a mood and on a level more like Homer's Odyssean picture of the pair in the fourth book. Quintus' portrait of Thetis is rather different from Homer's, since he not only represents her as full of grief for her son, but also from time to time notes her pride in her son's glory and in her grandson. Quintus' equivalent for Homer's mourning mother is, perhaps, Neoptolemus' mother Deidameia, though her part in the poem is brief.

In many ways, Quintus' most splendid character is Aias, son of Telamon, and it is rather unfortunate that he disappears from the poem in about the middle of it. Apparently he was the character of the Troy Story for whom Quintus had the greatest admiration. Quintus' interest in him and skill in dealing with him appear early in the poem. It was a happy thought to introduce him in the first book, mourning at the grave of Patroclus along with Achilles, thus bringing together near the beginning of the poem the two great Greek princes who are so soon to die. Quintus has also been clever in removing him from the stage. It would not do to have him fight Penthesileia and fail to defeat her; yet he cannot kill her, because it is a "historical fact" that Achilles did. Also, this part of the poem belongs to Achilles in any event. It would be unsatisfactory, also, to have the two greatest Greek heroes fight together against one girl. So Quintus sensibly has Aias share Achilles' laughter at Penthesileia's threats and then contemptuously leave this dove for the single hawk. Quintus has had to pay a price for his admiring portrayal of Aias. From the point of view of his later story, Quintus has been too successful in impressing us with Aias' grandeur, because he has made it hard to understand how Odysseus can possibly have won out over Aias in the matter of Achilles' armor, no matter how the contest was judged.

In dealing with the Trojans, Quintus' story suffers because he has no Hector, as Homer did. His Priam is less interesting than Homer's and seems more like Virgil's colorless Latinus. The death of Hector appears to have broken Priam, so that when he meets Neoptolemus in the burning town Priam merely begs for death. Quintus' treatment of Andromache is satisfactory and he is successful in showing us the effects of the war on numerous nameless Trojans, especially, of course, in his account of the sack of the city. He has been careful to contrast the two Trojan allies who play such similar roles in the first two books, emphasizing the boastful qualities in Penthesileia and the modesty in Memnon.

Although it is Homer who might almost be called the only begetter of Quintus' poem, it is also Homer who provides the obvious comparison. To compare Quintus with Homer is to compare Southey with Milton, and it is only a slight help if we say that to some degree all epic poets suffer by comparison with Homer. Quintus' single greatest inferiority to Homer is that he has no unified plot carefully organized around a central theme like the Wrath of Achilles in the *Iliad* and the Man of Many Devices in the *Odyssey*. Moreover, in Quintus' chronicle poem many of his events are distressingly similar. One after another, for instance, Penthesileia, Memnon, and Eurypylus come to help Troy, have a short period of success, and then die at the hands of a Greek leader. Day after day the two armies meet in battle, their arms gleam, thousands die, and the earth is red with blood.

It is easy, too, to single out particular lapses in otherwise interesting episodes. For example, in the first book, which is one of the best, an evil inspiration caused Quintus to put Penthesileia on a horse, and the horse involves him in a series of unhappy details, including one of his most inappropriate similes.

Quintus' descriptions of shields in Books Five and Six are other illustrations of how reluctant he is to abandon a bad idea. The contrast between Quintus' description of Achilles' shield in Book Five and Homer's description of Achilles' shield in the eighteenth book of the *Iliad* is too great for Quintus' good, and Quintus' repeated assurances that the figures in the designs looked as if they were alive add no life to his account. When in the very next book he adds a similar description of the shield of Eurypylus, he seems almost resolved to show us that he is not willing to let bad enough alone.

A rather different example of incongruity appears in his account of the preliminaries to the sacrifice of Polyxena. He represents the ghost of Achilles as appearing to his sleeping son at night. The ghost gives Neoptolemus varied fatherly advice, sounding more like Polonius than like the brave Achilles whom we knew, and concludes with a special exhortation to gentle kindliness: "Let your mind be gentle to the comrades you love, to your sons, and to your wife, remembering in your heart that the gates of fated doom and the halls of the dead stand close for human kind. The stock of men is like the flowers in the grass, the flowers of spring: some waste away, and some grow. For this reason be kindly." None of this sounds much like Homer's Achilles, but the sentiments are hard to quarrel with. We can hardly believe our eyes, therefore, when in the very next sentence the ghost commands his son to arrange the sacrifice of the girl Polyxena and threatens to stir up terrible storms if the execution of this poor girl is not promptly carried out.

Occasionally we are in a position to compare Quintus with writers other than Homer. Quintus and Virgil, for example, both treat in some detail the role of Sinon in the ruse of the wooden horse, and both give pictures of the sack of Troy. We can also compare one of Quintus' episodes with an extant Greek tragedy. Quintus tells us about the return of Philoctetes to the Greek army, the subject of one of the seven extant plays of Sophocles. It would be hard to devise two treatments of the same story which are more different than these. Sophocles' great interest was clearly in the problem of how the Greeks could possibly induce Philoctetes to rejoin the expedition after they had so heartlessly abandoned him years before, and he elaborates on this theme with his picture of noble youth (Neoptolemus) contrasted with wily maturity (Odysseus), developing these three characters in such a way that only a god from the machine can solve the problem. Quintus, preferring the version in which Diomedes and not Neoptolemus is Odysseus' companion, devotes most of his space to a long description of Philoctetes' squalid condition (also a feature of Sophocles' much longer treatment of the story). He does have Philoctetes reach for his bow in anger when he catches sight of Odysseus and Diomedes. But Quintus obviously cares nothing about the problem which interested Sophocles. After only a short chat, Philoctetes' anger evaporates and he gladly rejoins the formerly hated Greeks.

Every reader of Quintus may be conscious of at least some of his defects, but he also has some genuine merits which deserve mention. While it is true that the sheer number of his battle scenes, for example, can be wearisome, there are times when he rises much above his usual descriptive power. In Book Eleven, when he is describing the attack on the walls of Troy, he has produced some extremely interesting and memorable scenes. Most of Quintus' vivid details, moreover, are connected with kinds of action which Homer did not describe, and therefore were not based on the earlier work. Two of his high points also have the advantage of contrast, since one describes a group action, and the other an individual one. Quintus has been far more successful than usual in his account of Odysseus' brilliant device of the "testudo," or "tortoise," in that he weaves together narrative, description, and simile in pleasant and clarifying variety. The similes are relatively short and thoroughly appropriate: the roof of shields which spears and arrows cannot penetrate is like a tight roof impenetrable by wind or rain; the missiles falling upon the shields are deflected as though from a stubborn cliff, and the men under the shields are no more concerned about the missiles than they would be about drops of rain; the men are crowded together like a dense cloud; the sound of indistinguishable speech coming from under the shields is like the humming from a beehive. Briefer, but also good in its way, is the account of how young Alcimedon mounts a scaling ladder, holding a shield over his head as a protection, reaches the top of the wall, and actually looks over it at the city of Troy itself. But he is seeing the city for the first and last time. Suddenly Aeneas crushes his skull with a stone, and he falls from his lofty position like an arrow from the bowstring.

Quintus has a somewhat un-Homeric interest in depicting the sufferings which the war brings to people in general, combatants and non-combatants alike. Homer is matchless in showing the reactions and miseries of a few individuals, whether an important character like Andromache or some nameless woman in a simile. Quintus, on the other hand, can give us pictures of groups, such as the one in Book Eleven describing how, when some of the Trojans returned from the day's fighting, their wives and children took off their bloody armor and prepared hot baths, doctors hurried to the homes of the wounded, who were surrounded by their weeping wives and children, the wounded groaned in agony, and the luckier soldiers sat down to their supper. There are wounded men in Homer's battles, and he devotes some space, for instance, to telling us how Patroclus looked after the wounded Eurypylus, but in general a wound either kills almost at once or disappears almost at once from the story.

A counterpart to Quintus' picture of the soldiers' return to their families is his moving representation of the busy preparations for the day's fighting in Book Nine. We see the tearful wives bringing the soldiers their equipment, sometimes helped by busy little children. The soldiers are at once saddened by their wives' worry and tears and moved to pride in their children, who give them a further incentive to heroism. Some, too, are assisted by aged fathers, veterans of old wars, who exhort their sons to fight stubbornly, as they help them put on their armor. Homer, of course, is much interested in portraying men putting on their military equipment—indeed the arming scenes are one of his set themes —but he is concerned with showing us the arming of a general like Agamemnon, or Achilles, and has nothing like Quintus' picture of the activities of ordinary Trojan soldiers and their families as they get ready for another day of conflict. Also connected with Quintus' concern for ordinary people, and also un-Homeric, is the frequency with which Quintus reminds us that the coming of night releases men from work.

Quintus was clearly impressed by the merits of the Homeric simile, since he sows them in his poem with a generosity that in places seems excessive. We sometimes have a feeling that he must have proceeded on the principle that if only he puts enough similes into a passage his narrative will be properly impressive and he need not worry about other things. The result is, at times, that these poetical trimmings lose their effectiveness because of their very abundance. But for all that, and in spite of some unfortunate individual lapses, Quintus' similes are often highly successful and add much to the poem. One of his tricks is to employ a simile with two features illustrating two features in the narrative and to organize the simile in such a way that at the beginning one feature of the simile fits one feature of the story, while at the end two other features are paired off. Some of his most ingenious similes are of this type, which we might call "double similes." In Book Three, for instance, the simile comparing the dead Achilles to the dead Tityos begins as though the point of the comparison is to be only the impressive magnitude of the two fallen men. But then a second point of comparison appears: Earth grieves for her fallen son while Leto laughs because her attacker has been killed; so the Greeks grieved for the dead Achilles, while the Trojans rejoiced at his destruction.

At other times, some feature which complicates the simile will have no counterpart in the narrative—just as Homer's similes are often elaborated for their own sake. Again in the third book, the masses of recently killed men lying on the battlefield are compared to the trusses of freshly reaped grain lying in a grainfield; but there is nothing in the narrative equivalent to the pleasure felt by the owner of the field in the simile. And in the ninth book the numberless Greeks falling before Deiphobus are compared to trees being felled by a woodcutter. We are told that the wood-cutter is pleased with his work, but there is no indication of any corresponding pleasure felt by Deiphobus.

Quintus' complications in his similes are not always entirely appropriate. In Book One, for example, the heifer in the simile *eats* some plants and *tramples* others; Penthesileia *kills* some of the enemy and *drives others into flight*. The desire to produce a double reference also brought about what may well be considered Quintus' most atrocious simile, when he is describing the sacrifice of Polyxena near the end of his poem. Polyxena, simultaneously uttering groans and shedding tears, is compared to an olive press simultaneously oozing oil and squeaking as pressure is applied.

Like the *Iliad* and the *Odyssey*, Quintus' poem is a dramatic one in that he makes liberal use of direct speech by his characters. Some of his speeches, too, are notably well done. It is in keeping with Quintus' general tendency to rise above his normal level when dealing with Aias that Tecmessa's speech in Book Five, for instance, is remarkable for the effective way in which Quintus has combined into this one lament a number of motifs which Homer used in different speeches in the *Iliad*: Agamemnon and Diomedes pray that the earth may gape open for them when something disastrous happens; a nameless Greek prays that the black earth may gape for them all if they let the Trojans get possession of Patroclus' armor. Tecmessa says it would have been better if the earth had gaped open for her before she saw Aias' doom. Many other details in her speech are reminiscent of Homeric speechs by Briseis and, especially, by Andromache, notably the picture of the unhappy future of an orphan son. Nestor's speech of consolation to Podalirius at the beginning of Book Seven may be cited as another example of Quintus' skillful use of familiar ideas in a familiar context. Oddly enough, one of his least successful speeches is, perhaps, that in which the great orator Odysseus makes his crucial recommendation about building the wooden horse. His speech sounds more like the preliminary notes for such a speech than the finished product. The extremely brief summary of the plan seems addressed to persons who already know all about it—as, of course, the *readers* of the poem do—and, strangest of all, it does not say a word about the most essential point: the Trojans will, and must, take the horse inside their town.

Another instance, although not in a speech, in which Quintus may have rather absentmindedly let his readers' familiarity with his story influence his telling of it is in his account of the death of Laocoon's sons in Book Twelve. He seems to assume that everybody knows that there were two snakes or dragons who made the attack, and says nothing about their number until the story is over, when he somewhat casually remarks that *both* monsters disappeared underground.

Like most epic poets before and since, Quintus felt it desirable to equip his poem with supernatural machinery. Comparison of his use of this machinery with Homer's is at once inevitable and unfavorable to Quintus. For many readers, Homer's gods are among his most successful creations, and they are surely the finest gods for literary purposes that man has ever invented. Quintus' gods are a dull and solemn lot hemmed in by the irresistible power of Fate.

Quintus is not only less skillful than Homer in his general manipulation of his gods, but is sometimes especially unhappy in his choice of time, place, and method. The saddest illustration is the celestial conversation that interrupts the account of Paris' final hours in Book Ten.

Many readers have felt that Quintus' story of the death of Paris is one of the high points of the poem. There are a few lapses, but in general Quintus has done justice to his material in his portrayal of Oenone, the wronged and abandoned wife, full of love and hate, unable to forgive Paris, but unwilling to survive him. Quintus' treatment of the other women in Paris' life—his melancholy mother, who loved him best of all her sons after Hector, the selfish Helen, pretending grief for Paris, but in her heart concerned only about her own future—also shows more care and more success with the psychology of his characters than Quintus usually displays. In the account of the funeral of Paris, Quintus seems to be under the influence of Alexandrian pastoral and Paris becomes a sort of Daphnis, but the reader may welcome the picture of a different Paris, the kind of person he was long ago, before he had been corrupted by Aphrodite's bribe in the celestial beauty contest.

On the human level, then, Quintus has done unusually well with this episode. Unfortunately, he chose this moment to insert a scene on Olympus. We turn from the miseries of the dying Paris to Hera sitting in her Olympian garden, cheered by the sight of Paris' troubles. Quintus then gives a longish account of Hera's handmaids and Hera's talk with them, and only after this incongruous chat do we return to Paris, who has expired in the interval.

The attempt to combine Homer's conscienceless gods with aspects of Stoic philosophy and various post-Homeric religious views has done little to improve the gods theologically and has made them far less interesting and useful as literary characters. They interfere in the action of the poem with some frequency, but Quintus does not succeed in convincing us that they really are deeply interested in these events. There is no persistent sense of intimate and passionate involvement such as we find in the *Iliad's* Hera, Athena, and Apollo, and no shred of close and amiable friendship between a mortal and one of the great Olympians such as Homer shows us in the relationship between Odysseus and Athena in the *Odyssey*. There is not even anything like Virgil's portrait of Venus and Aeneas.

Two main reasons have determined the choice of prose rather than verse as the medium for this translation: my own lack of the Muses' magic, and a feeling that modern readers would rather have Quintus' story presented in prose than have some not very distinguished Greek verse reproduced in even less distinguished metrical English. I have tried to be clear and faithful to the meaning of the original. I have not intentionally left anything out, except, possibly, a few of Quintus' adjectives and adverbs, and my only deliberate additions have been occasional words and phrases designed to make Quintus more understandable to the modern reader. Most of these additions take the form of names and indications of relationships which may have been clearer to Quintus' original readers than to many of our time. I have, for instance, said in Book Seven that Lycomedes was Neoptolemus' grandfather, although Quintus does not mention that fact. I have not tried to modernize Quintus—by varying the phraseology, for example, where he has repeatedly used the same word in short passages— except where it seemed to me that fidelity to the letter of the original would produce a result less excusable in English than Quintus' usage presumably was in Greek. Probably the most common modification is in the elimination of the compound form of large numbers of adjectives, since this feature of Greek epic style is no longer in fashion. Having decided to do this, now I find myself often doubting the wisdom of the decision.

This version is essentially a translation of the Teubner text of Albert Zimmermann.[1] In a few instances I have preferred a different reading—sometimes that of the manuscripts, sometimes a conjecture—and ordinarily I have not thought it worthwhile to indicate these divergences. The translation was already finished when the first volume of F. Vian's Budé edition reached me.[2] I have been able to introduce a few changes based on his new text of Books One to Four, and I have mentioned one or two others in the notes. Of the commentators (apart from Vian in the first four books), I have found the most useful to be Köchly and De Pauw,[3] although the latter's usefulness is often lessened by his willingness to believe that Quintus was an incompetent bungler capable of saying anything. I have kept my footnotes to a minimum and restricted them mostly to relationships between Quintus and Homer.

Nearly all of the material in F. Vian's two recent monographs on Quintus is of a highly specialized nature and likely to interest only the expert.[4] Vian has prefixed to his *Recherches* a bibliography of 156 editions, translations, and studies of Quintus. Very few of these are likely to interest the ordinary reader. The introduction to the first volume of his new edition now in the course of publication has some thirty-five useful pages on "The Man and His Work," and Vian has prefixed to each of the four books in this volume a short essay which, in addition to giving a careful analysis of the structure of the book, treats in a highly readable way a number of other matters. The edition is also equipped throughout with very numerous learned footnotes on a variety of subjects.

The best literary essay on Quintus is that which Sainte-Beuve appended to his book on Virgil, first published more than a century ago.[5] T. R. Glover included a chapter on Quintus in his *Life and Letters in the Fourth Century*, a book which is unfortunately

---

[1] *Quinti Smyrnaei Posthomericorum Libri XIV* (Leipzig, 1891).

[2] *Quintus de Smyrne: La suite d'Homère*, Tome I, Livres I–IV (Paris, 1963).

[3] *Quinti Smyrnaei Posthomericorum Libri XIV*, recensuit prolegomenis et adnotione critica instruxit Arminius Koechly (Leipzig, 1850); *Quinti Calabri praetermissorum ab Homero Libri XIV* ... J. C. de Pauw (Leiden, 1734).

[4] *Histoire de la tradition manuscrite de Quintus de Smyrne* (Paris, 1959); *Recherches sur les Posthomerica de Quintus de Smyrne* (Paris, 1959).

[5] *Étude sur Virgile, suivie d'une étude sur Quintus de Smyrne* (Paris, 1857).

not easy to come by nowadays.[6] Glover's essay undertakes to give a properly balanced verdict on the qualities of the man he calls "the pale Homer of the fourth century." Many of his points will probably seem just to most readers of Quintus. His brief and admittedly amateurish observations on Quintus' geographical knowledge have been made obsolete by the recent thorough treatment of that subject by Vian in the fourth chapter of his *Recherches*. There have been a number of translations of Quintus into Latin, French, German, and Italian, but the only other English translation known to me is the verse translation by A. S. Way published in the Loeb Classical Library in 1913.[7]

[6] Cambridge, 1901.
[7] Harvard University Press.

BOOK ONE

The Arrival, Deeds, and Death of Penthesileia the Amazon Queen

W HEN GODLIKE HECTOR had been killed by Achilles
Peleusson, and the fire consumed him, and the earth hid his bones,
at that time the Trojans were staying in Priam's town, frightened
of the great might of brave Achilles. Just as cattle refuse to ap-
proach a fierce lion in the woods, but the whole herd draws back
and runs frightened up through the thick scrub; so the Trojans in
their fortress city shrank in terror from the mighty man. They
remembered all those whom he had earlier robbed of their lives, as
he raged by the streams of Idaean Scamander, all those he killed in
flight under the great wall, how he had killed Hector and dragged
him around the city,[1] and how he had slaughtered others, when he
first brought destruction for the Trojans through the restless sea.
These were the things they remembered as they stayed within
their fortress city. A dismal sorrow, too, hovered over them, as
though Troy were already ablaze with cruel fire.

And then from the streams of the broad river Thermodon

---

[1] In Homer, Achilles drags Hector's body from the battlefield to the Greek
camp and for some days thereafter drags the body from time to time around the
tomb of Patroclus. The version followed by Quintus first appears in extant Greek
literature in Euripides' *Andromache* (107–108). It is also followed by Virgil
(*Aeneid* i. 483), and appears to have been the "standard" post-Homeric version.

there came Penthesileia, wearing the beauty of the gods. She was at once eager for cruel war and bent on avoiding loathsome and ugly talk. She was afraid that someone among her own people would attack her with reproaches about her sister Hippolyte, for whom she felt a growing sorrow. (She had killed her with a heavy spear, quite involuntarily, while aiming at a stag.) This was why she had come to the famous land of Troy. Besides, she had this thought in her warlike heart: she might cleanse herself of the hideous defilement of murder and appease with sacrifices the dreadful Furies. These invisible creatures, angry over her sister, had set about following her at once. For they always dog the feet of wrongdoers, and no one who does wrong can escape the goddesses.

With Penthesileia came twelve other Amazons, all splendid and all longing for war and ugly battle. Distinguished though they were, these were her handmaids, and Penthesileia far surpassed them all. Just as when in broad heaven the glorious moon shines out conspicuous among all the stars, when the clear upper air breaks through from the thunderclouds, and the great might of the blustering winds is asleep; so was she conspicuous among all the hurrying Amazons.

These were their names: Clonie, Polemousa, Derinoe, Evandre, Antandre, glorious Bremousa, Hippothoe, dark-eyed Harmothoe, Alcibie, Antibrote, Derimacheia, and Thermodosa, moving proudly with her spear. So many were the Amazons who accompanied and surrounded Penthesileia. Just as the Dawn, her heart exulting in her flashing horses, comes down from indestructible Olympus with the fair-tressed Hours, and her splendid beauty shines out among them all, though they are faultless; so Penthesileia came to the Trojan city, pre-eminent among all the Amazons.

The Trojans hurried round from every side, marveling greatly when they saw tireless Ares' daughter in her tall greaves. She looked like the blessed gods, for about her face there was a beauty at once terrible and splendid. Her smile was charming, and under her brows her lovely eyes sparkled like sunbeams. Modesty brought a blush to her cheeks, and a divine grace clothed her strength. The Trojan people, sad though they had been before, were filled with joy. Just as when country folk, longing for the gods to send rain, see from a hill Iris, the rainbow, rising up out of the broad sea, at the time when their farms, yearning for the rain of Zeus, are now parched, and at last the great sky grows dark, and they see the good sign that wind and rain are close and are glad—though before they had been groaning over their fields—so the sons of Troy naturally rejoiced when they saw within their city terrible Penthesileia, eager for war. For when hope of good comes into a man's mind, it softens painful distress.

For this reason, too, the heart of Priam, who had so many causes for groaning and great sorrow, was cheered a little in his breast. Just as when a man who has suffered much with blinded eyes and longs to see the holy light or to die, either through the work of some fine doctor or because a god has taken the darkness from his eyes, at last sees the light of Dawn, he is not so cheerful as he once was, but nevertheless he is cheered a little after a great evil, though he still suffers from a dreadful pain left in his eyes; so Priam the son of Laomedon looked upon terrible Penthesileia: while he rejoiced a little, for the most part he still sorrowed for his sons who had been killed.

But he took the queen into his palace and was zealous in showing her every honor, just as though she were a daughter come home from far away after twenty years. He had a dinner prepared for her with every sort of food, such as glorious kings eat when they have destroyed nations and feast at great banquets to celebrate their victory. He gave her presents, too, beautiful and precious, and promised many more if she would help the Trojans, who were being cut to pieces. She undertook the task and agreed to do what no mortal had ever hoped: she would kill Achilles, destroy the great army of the Greeks, and throw fire on their ships. Foolish girl, she did not know at all Achilles of the good ashen spear, nor how pre-eminent he was in deadly battle.

When Andromache, Eëtion's noble child, heard Penthesileia, she spoke earnestly like this within her own heart:

"Poor girl, why do you speak such proud words and have   100
such proud thoughts? You do not have the strength to fight with
fearless Peleusson, but he will quickly send death and ruin upon
you. Poor wretch, why are your thoughts so mad? Surely, the
end of death has taken its stand close to you, and the fate of doom.
Hector was far better with the spear than you are, but for all his
might he was defeated and brought great grief to the Trojans, who
all looked upon him as a god in the city. He was a great glory to
me and to his godlike parents, when he was alive. How I wish the
earth had covered me over in the grave before the spear went
through his throat and took his life! As it was, I looked in anguish
upon a pain beyond telling when the swift horses of Achilles
cruelly dragged him about the city. He took from me the husband
of my youth and made me a widow; this is my terrible sorrow for
all my days."

So in her heart Eëtion's daughter of the fair ankles spoke,
remembering her husband.[2] For, truly, great grief increases with
good women, when their husbands are dead.[3]

The sun, whirling through its swift course, sank into Ocean's
deep stream, and the day was done. When the banqueters had
finished their wine and the lovely feast, then the maids prepared a
comfortable bed in Priam's palace for brave Penthesileia. She
went and lay down, and sweet sleep fell upon her, covering her
eyes. Then from the depths of the upper air there came, at the will
of Athena, the force of a guileful dream, so that as she looked upon
it she might become an evil for the Trojans and for herself,

[2] This might be looked upon as a Homeric ornamental epithet, an adjective,
that is, which notes some permanent quality of the noun but which is not always
wholly suited to a given particular context. These melancholy thoughts of the
widow do not comport very well with the reminder that the widow had pretty
legs. Even more incongruous, perhaps, is Quintus' use of the same adjective in
Book Thirteen, 268, where Andromache is longing for death just after her baby
son has been killed and she is herself being led away into slavery. Quintus' adjec-
tive, like "rosy-ankled" applied to the dawn in line 138 below, does not occur in
Homer, although he does have the synonym *kallisphuros*.

[3] This sententious remark is of a sort fairly common in Quintus, and it is
un-Homeric in that Homer usually puts these bits of wisdom into the mouths of
his characters and is not much inclined to present them as his own comments.

through her longing for the confusion of war.[4] This was what the wise Athena Tritogeneia had in mind. And the grim dream stood over Penthesileia, looking like her father, and urged her to fight boldly face to face with swift-footed Achilles. She, when she heard this, was utterly delighted in her heart, because she thought that on that very day she would accomplish a great deed in the dreadful combat. Foolish girl, who put her faith in a miserable dream of the night, which beguiles in their beds the races of toiling men, filling them with cheating words, and which completely deceived her in urging her to the work of war.

But when the early-born one, the rosy-ankled Dawn, came swiftly up, then it was that Penthesileia, her heart full of courage, leapt from her bed and put about her shoulders the decorated armor that the god Ares had given her. First about her silvery legs she put greaves of gold, which fitted her perfectly. Then she put on her dazzling breastplate, and she proudly placed about her shoulders her great sword, all enclosed in a scabbard beautifully fashioned of silver and ivory. She took up her splendid shield, in outline like the moon when over the deep-flowing Ocean stream it rises half full with curving horns; so marvelously it gleamed. On her head she put her helmet, its top covered with golden plumes. So she put about her body the elaborate armor. She looked like a bolt of lightning that the power of tireless Zeus sends to earth from Olympus, showing to men the strength of noisy rain or the steady blast of whistling winds.

Moving quickly to leave the great hall, she took two javelins to hold beneath her shield and in her right hand a double battle-ax. Eris, terrible goddess of strife, had given her this as a great protection in deadly war. Laughing with pleasure at this weapon, she hurried outside the towers and urged the Trojans into battle where men win glory. The princes gathered there were quick to be persuaded, though they had not previously wanted to stand against Achilles, because he utterly defeated everyone.

She, of course, could not restrain her exultation. The stallion

---

[4] Quintus' deceitful dream is clearly modeled after the deceitful dream sent by Zeus to Agamemnon in the second book of the *Iliad*.

she sat upon was beautiful and very fast. Boreas' wife Oreithyia had given him to her as a present some time ago, when she had gone to Thrace. He stood out even among Harpies, who are swift as hurricanes. Seated on this horse, Penthesileia then left the high houses of the city. Dismal Fates were urging her on to go into a conflict at once her first and her last. Round about, many Trojans on unreturning feet followed the brave girl into ruthless battle, in crowds, like sheep after a ram which runs on ahead, as they all, under the shepherd's skill, go along together; so the sturdy Trojans and the high-spirited Amazons, greatly eager in their might, followed after her. She was like Athena when she went to meet the Giants, or like Eris when she darts through an army raising tumult; such was swift Penthesileia among the Trojans.

Then it was that Priam, noble son of rich Laomedon, raised his long-suffering hands to Zeus the son of Cronos and prayed, turning toward the high temple of Idaean Zeus, whose eyes ever look upon Ilios:

"Hear me, O father, and grant that on this day the Greek host fall beneath the hands of Ares' queenly daughter. And then bring her back safely to my house, having respect for your own vast and mighty son Ares and for Penthesileia herself, because she is terribly like the immortal goddesses and in her descent is from your own stock. Show regard also for my heart, since I have suffered many evils in the deaths of my sons whom the Fates snatched especially from me at the Greeks' hands along the battlefront. Keep your regard for us, while a few of us are still left from the glorious blood of Dardanus, while the city is still unravaged, so that we, too, may have respite from dreadful slaughter and from war."

So he spoke in his earnest prayer. And an eagle, with shrill cries and holding in its talons a dove already dying, darted swiftly on his left. Priam's mind within him took fright, and he thought he would never see Penthesileia alive again and returning from war. The Fates were indeed going to bring this about that day, and Priam's broken heart was full of pain.

The Greeks marveled from afar when they saw the onrushing

200

Trojans and Ares' daughter Penthesileia. The Trojans looked like wild beasts that in the mountains bring groans and death to flocks of sheep. She was like a rush of fire that rages in the dry scrub under a strong wind. This is the sort of thing the Greeks were saying as they gathered together:

"Why, who has roused the Trojans, now that Hector is dead? We said they would never again meet us with any eagerness, but now they suddenly rush on full of desire for battle. Someone in their midst is urging them on to the work of war. You might think him a god, so great is the deed he has in mind. We must put into our hearts an insatiate boldness and remember our trained strength. The gods will help us, too, in our fight with the Trojans this day."

So they spoke. Then, putting their shining armor about them, they poured out from the ships, their shoulders clad in might. The armies came together in the bloody conflict like ravenous wild beasts. They held their fine arms close together, spears, breastplates, sturdy shields, and stout helmets, and recklessly struck one another's flesh with the bronze. The Trojan plain grew red.

Then Penthesileia killed Molion and Persinous, Elissus and Antitheus and manly Lernus, Hippalmus, Haemonides, and strong Elasippus. Derinoe killed Laogonus, and Clonie killed Menippus, who earlier had followed Protesilaus from Phylace to fight the powerful Trojans. His death stirred the spirit of Podarces Iphiclesson, because he loved him especially among his comrades. He immediately threw his spear at godlike Clonie, and the strong shaft went down through her belly. Her black blood quickly flowed out around the spear, and all her entrails followed with it. Penthesileia was naturally greatly angered at this, and she struck Podarces on the thick muscle of his right arm and cut through the blood-filled veins. His black blood gushed from the wound he had received, and he darted to the rear, groaning from the severe pain afflicting his spirit. The people of Phylace felt the greatest longing for him as he hurried away. When he had withdrawn a little from the fighting, he died in the arms of his comrades.

Idomeneus killed Bremousa, hitting her on the right breast with his spear and taking her life instantly. She fell like an ash tree, a towering one that woodcutters cut on the mountains. As it falls it produces a dreadful whistling and a thud; so she uttered a wail as she fell. Doom loosened all her joints, and her soul was mingled with the blowing winds.

Meriones killed Evandre and Thermodosa as they rushed at him in the deadly fighting. He drove his spear into the head of one of them, and the other he struck with his sword under the belly. Their life left them forthwith. The mighty son of Oïleus destroyed Derinoe, running his jagged spear through her collarbone. Tydeusson with his terrible sword cut off the heads of both Alcibie and Derimacheia, necks and all right down to their shoulders. They both fell just like heifers that a man quickly deprives of life by hitting their neck tendons with a strong ax; so they, laid low by the hands of Tydeusson, fell on the Trojan plain, and their bodies were far away from their heads. Beside them Sthenelus killed strong Cabeirus, who had come from Sestus, longing to fight the Greeks, but did not return again to his native land. At his death, Paris' heart was stirred to anger, and he shot at Sthenelus. But, much though he wanted to, he did not hit him, because the arrow was driven off to where the pitiless Fates directed it. And so it brought a quick death to bronze-belted Evenor, who had come from Dulichium to fight the Trojans. As he died, Meges, the son of glorious Phyleus, was stirred and quickly jumped into the conflict, like a lion among flocks of sheep. Everyone shrank back from the mighty man, because he killed Itymoneus and Agelaus Hippasusson, who brought their attack upon the Greeks from Miletus. They were commanded by godlike Nastes and high-spirited Amphimachus, whose home was at Mycale and the white peaks of Latmus, the long valleys of Branchus, high-banked Panormus, and the streams of the deep Maeander, which, twisting its waters in many a bend, flows from the Phrygian sheep country to the vineyard land of the Carians. These were the men whom Meges killed in the fighting, along with all the others whom he reached with his dark spear. For Athena Tritogeneia put boldness into his breast, that he might send upon the enemy their day of doom.

Polypoetes, loved of Ares, overwhelmed Dresaeus, whom glorious Neaera bore to wise Theiodamas, sharing his bed under snowy Sipylus. This is the place where the gods turned Niobe to stone. Many a tear of hers still trickles down from the rough cliff on high, and the streams of loud Hermus groan with her, and the lofty peaks of Sipylus, over which always spreads the mist that shepherds hate. The cliff is a great marvel to travelers as they hurry by, because it looks like a woman of many sorrows, who, weeping in wretched grief, pours out the many thousands of her tears. You think it is a perfect likeness when you see it from a distance, but when you come close to it, it is clearly a steep cliff and a spur of Sipylus. Satisfying the deadly anger of the blessed gods, it weeps among the rocks, still like a grieving woman.

One upon another, then, man brought slaughter and cruel fate to man. For dreadful Tumult was moving about in the midst of the armies, and close beside him stood the ruinous doom of Death, and about them moved here and there the dismal Fates, bringing the groans of slaughter. The heart of many a Trojan and many a Greek was undone in the dust that day, and a great shouting arose. Because Penthesileia's strength did not flag at all, but as some lioness in the high mountains darts through a glen deep in the cliffs and leaps upon cattle in her longing for blood, and this greatly cheers her spirit; so then did the warrior girl leap among the Greeks. Their spirits were filled with surprise, and they drew back.

She followed them, just as a wave of the deep-thundering sea follows speeding ships, when a strong wind swells out their white sails, and the headlands roar on every side, as the sea bellows against the long beach; so she kept following and slaughtering the ranks of the Greeks, and, with a heart full of exultation, she threatened them:

"You dogs, how you will pay today for the evil outrage you did Priam. None of you will escape my strength and be a joy to dear parents, sons, and wives, but you will die and lie here a food

300

for birds and beasts; you will find no tomb in the earth. Where is mighty Tydeusson now? Where Achilles? And where Aias? Talk has it that they are your best. But they will not dare to contend with me, for fear I may take their souls from their limbs and dispatch them to the dead."

She spoke and, with proud thoughts, rushed upon the Greeks. Her strength was like the strength of Death, and great was the host she subdued. Sometimes she cut deep with her ax, and sometimes she brandished a sharp javelin. Her nimble horse carried her quiver and pitiless bow, if ever she might need in the bloody turmoil grim missiles and bow. Swift men followed her, brothers and friends of Hector, who had fought his foes hand to hand. Their breasts were full of the breath of mighty war, and with their spears of polished ash they were killing Greeks, who kept falling one after another like swiftly falling leaves or drops of rain. The broad land groaned aloud, wet with blood and packed with corpses. Horses too, pierced with arrows or ashen spears, were neighing for the last time, as they breathed out their strength, while others were biting the dust and writhing. And Trojan horses charging upon them from the rear were trampling them like heaps of grain on a threshing floor where they had fallen with their dead riders.[5]

Many a Trojan was filled with wonder and delight when he saw Penthesileia rushing up through the army like a dark storm which rages on the sea when the sun's might comes together with Capricorn. And in his empty hopes one of them said:

"Friends, how obvious it is that today some one of the immortals has come down from heaven to fight against the Greeks and show kindness to us because of Zeus's bold plan. Zeus is doubtless remembering powerful Priam, who is proud to claim that he is from immortal blood. For I think this is no woman I see before me so brave and wearing such glorious arms, but Athena, or

[5] The text of line 350 is far from certain. I have followed a conjecture of Zimmermann. The readings of the manuscripts seem to mean something like "clutching the dust in grasps." If, with Vian, we adopt this idea, lines 350–52 do not refer to the horses, but to men, and they might be translated, "Some men were writhing on the ground, clutching the dust in their hands, and the Trojan horses, charging upon them from the rear, were trampling them like heaps of grain on a threshing floor where they had fallen among the dead."

mighty Enyo, or Eris, or Leto's famous daughter Artemis. Today I think she will bring the groans of slaughter upon the Greeks and burn with destructive fire their ships in which they once came to Troy, planning many evils for us; bringing woes from war beyond all checking, they came. But never will they return again to Greece and gladden their native land, because a god is helping us."

So a Trojan spoke, his heart running over with joy. Fool, he did not, of course, know that utter ruin was rushing upon himself and the other Trojans, and upon Penthesileia herself. For great-souled Aias and Achilles the city-sacker had not yet heard at all of the noisy turmoil, but both had thrown themselves down at the grave of Patroclus, filled with thoughts of their friend, and one groaned on this side, one on that. Some one of the blessed gods was keeping them from the turmoil, so that many men might meet with a grim death, destroyed by Trojans and by brave Penthesileia.

She was contriving evil for one man after another, and her strength and her courage alike kept growing ever greater.[6] Never did her spear plunge in vain, but it kept tearing the backs of men running away or the chests of those who charged upon her. She was quite drenched in hot blood, but her limbs were light as she rushed on; no weariness overcame her fearless spirit, but might unconquerable possessed her. For grim Fate, not yet rousing Achilles to dreadful battle, was still glorifying her and, standing far from the fighting, felt a deadly exultation because in a little while she was going to destroy the girl at the hands of Achilles. She was hidden in darkness, but, ever unseen, she urged Penthesileia on and led her to evil destruction, glorifying her for the last time. And Penthesileia kept killing, one here, another there.

Just as when in spring a heifer, longing for sweet grass, leaps inside a dewy garden and, since there is no man there, rushes everywhere, ravaging all the plants just now so flourishing, eating some and destroying others with her feet; so, rushing down through the throng the warrior girl killed some of the Greek youths and drove others to flight.

The Trojan women were marveling from afar at Penthesi-

[6] The text from line 383 to 390 is doubtful in a number of places.

leia's military feats. And love of war took hold of Tisiphone, daughter of the cavalryman Antimachus and wife of Meneptolemus. In the vigor of her thoughts, eagerly she made a bold proposal, urging her friends to cruel conflict; boldness roused her strength:

"Put in your breasts stout hearts like our men's, who fight the enemy for our country on behalf of our children and ourselves, never having any respite from misery. We ourselves, too, with brave spirits, should take thought to share the battle. We are not much different from vigorous men. The sort of courage they have, we have too; our eyes and legs are the same, and everything is alike. Light and the flowing air are common to all. Our food is not different. What other thing has god made better for men? Let us not, then, run away from fighting. Why, aren't you looking upon a woman far superior to the men accustomed to close combat? She has nothing here, not her family or her own city, but she fights with spirit for a foreign king. With boldness in her heart and a fearless mind, she cares nothing for the men. While we—troubles lie all around our feet. These women have had dear sons and husbands die fighting for the city; these wail for fathers who are no more; others grieve at the loss of brothers or kinsmen. No woman is without her portion of sorrow and trouble, and we may well expect to look upon the day of our slavery. Let there be, therefore, no further postponement of war for us women in our distress. It is better to die in the fight than later on be led off by foreign men along with our helpless children, when grim necessity is upon us, our city is burning, and our men are no more."

So she spoke, and upon them all there fell a love of loathsome battle. They were planning to go swiftly out before the wall, eager to defend in arms their city and their people, and courage was stirred within them. Just as when, inside a hive, bees hum loudly at the end of winter, when they prepare to go to the meadow and do not like to remain inside, but one summons another to go out; so the Trojan women were busily urging one another to conflict. They put from them their wool and their workbaskets and laid their hands on cruel weapons.

They would have died outside the city along with their men and the mighty Amazons in that fighting, if sensible Theano[7] had not checked them in their haste and won them over with her shrewd words:

"Why this eagerness for toiling in the terrible rout of battle, poor wretches, when you have had no previous experience in fighting, but rush on like fools, ignorantly eager for an intolerable task? Your strength is not equal to that of the Greeks, with their knowledge of fighting. For Amazons, pitiless battle and horsemanship and all tasks done by men are a delight from birth. This is obviously why they have always shown a warlike spirit and feel no need of men, because the work of war greatly strengthens their courage and makes their bodies fearless. This Penthesileia is reported to be the daughter of mighty Ares; so it isn't at all fitting for any woman to compete with her—or, possibly, she is one of the gods come in answer to our prayers. It is, of course, quite true that all human beings are of the same stock, but different persons practice different jobs, and that job is best which a person works at with knowledge in his head. Consequently, we must keep away from the uproar of fighting and work at our weaving within our own homes; our men will take care of the war. We can hope for improvement soon, because we see the Greeks being killed, and the strength of our men is greatly increasing. We have no reason to be afraid of harm, because our pitiless enemies are not surrounding the city at all, and there is no painful need for women as well to join in the fighting."

So she spoke, and they were won over by her, old though she was, and watched the battle from a distance. Penthesileia was still destroying hosts, and the Greeks around her were terrified. They had no way of escaping wretched death, but were being killed like bleating goats under the savage jaws of a leopard. It was no longer a desire for battle that possessed the men, but a desire for flight. They were rushing in various directions, some of them with their armor, others throwing their armor from their shoulders to the

[7] In the *Iliad*, Theano, priestess of Athena, offers a robe to the goddess and prays that she will pity Troy and destroy Diomedes (vi. 297–310).

ground. And horses went running without their drivers. Joy of battle belonged to the attackers; from the dying came many a groan. They had no strength in their afflictions, but short-lived were they all whom she came upon, along the chill edge of battle. Just as when a howling gale presses hard upon tall trees all abloom with flowers and pulls some up by the roots and throws them to the ground and breaks others from their base, and the shattered trees are thrown one upon another; so the great army of Greeks was laid in the dust by the will of the Fates and the spear of Penthesileia.

But when the very ships were going to be set afire by the hands of the Trojans, then it was, doubtless, that steadfast Aias heard the wailing and said to Achilles:

"Achilles, a vast shouting assails my ears, as though a great battle were in progress. Let's go, for fear the Trojans may destroy the Greeks beside their ships and burn up the ships before we get there; that would be a sad disgrace to us both. Men descended from great Zeus ought not to shame the holy stock of their fathers, who themselves, some time ago, along with valiant Heracles, utterly destroyed with their spears Laomedon's Troy, a splendid city. This is what I think will be done now by our hands, since the strength grows great in us both." 500

The bold might of Achilles was persuaded by what he said, because his ears heard the melancholy clamor. They both rushed for their bright arms, put them on, and took their stand to meet the crowd. Their beautiful weapons clanged loudly, and their spirits were raging like Ares'; so great was the might that shielded Athena Atrytone gave to them both as they pressed on.[8]

The Greeks were glad when they saw the pair of mighty men. They looked like the two sons of great Aloeus who once upon a time thought to put upon broad Olympus high mountains, steep Ossa and lofty Pelion, so that in their eagerness they might actually reach heaven. Such were the two descendants of Aeacus,

---

[8] Aias does not share any battle exploits with Achilles in the *Iliad*, but it is clear from Achilles' attitude in the Embassy scene (ix.) that Aias is a man for whom Achilles feels special respect.

Aias and Achilles, as they stood to face the ruinous battle, a great joy to the Greeks in their longing, as they both pressed forward to destroy the army of the enemy. Many were the men whom they subdued with their invincible spears. Just as when a pair of destructive lions find fat sheep in the scrub far from their fond shepherds and rush to kill them and then drink all the black blood and fill their great bellies with the inner flesh; so did these two destroy a vast army of men.

Then Aias killed Deïochus and warlike Hyllus, Eurynomus, a war lover, and glorious Enyeus. Achilles killed Antandre and Polemousa and Antibrote, with them spirited Hippothoe and Harmothoe besides. He advanced upon the whole army with great-hearted Telamonson. Beneath their hands the crowded, sturdy ranks were thrown down easily and quickly, just as a thick forest falls to fire in the narrow valleys of a mountain when the wind rages.

When Penthesileia, the skillful warrior, noticed them rushing like wild beasts through the dreadful battle, she started toward them both. Just as in a thicket a grim leopard with destruction in her heart lashes her tail terribly and rushes out to meet oncoming hunters, and they, equipped with fighting gear, await her charge, confident of their spears; so the warrior men lifted their spears and awaited Penthesileia. Their bronze armor was noisy about them as they moved.

Brave Penthesileia first threw a long spear. It landed on Achilles' shield, but broke and was deflected as though from a rock; such were the immortal gifts of skillful Hephaestus.[9] With her hands, she aimed another swift javelin at Aias, and she threatened them both:

"Although just now the spear leapt from my hands to no purpose, I think with this one I shall soon destroy the strength and spirit of you both, who boast of being the mighty ones among the Greeks. Then the misery of war will be lighter for the Trojan

---

[9] The manufacture of this divine armor is related by Homer in the eighteenth book of the *Iliad*, the shield being described in great detail.

horsemen. But please come closer up through the turmoil, so that you may see how much strength rises in Amazons' hearts. My stock, too, is warlike, and no mortal man sired me, but Ares himself, who can never have his fill of the shouts of battle. This is why my might is far better than men's."

So she spoke, but her proud talk made them laugh.[10] Quickly her spear point drove at Aias' solid silver greave. But it did not penetrate inside, for all its eagerness to reach his handsome flesh. For the cruel point had not been fated to mix with that man's blood in the battles of enemies. Aias disregarded the Amazon and leapt into a crowd of Trojans. He left Penthesileia to Peleusson alone, since he knew in his heart how easy a task she would be for Achilles, strong though she was. It would be like a dove against a hawk.

She gave a deep groan at having thrown her spear without result, and the son of Peleus spoke to her insultingly:

"Woman, how proud you were of your empty words, when you came against us filled with desire for battle. We are easily the best of the heroes upon the earth, and we are proud of our descent from the stock of loud-thundering Zeus. Even swift Hector was afraid of us, though he caught sight of us only from a distance rushing into cruel battle. My spear point killed him, for all his might. You are completely out of your mind in being so bold and threatening us with destruction today. Your own last day will quickly come. No, not even your father Ares himself will save you from me now, but you will die an evil death, just like a young deer that meets a destructive lion in the mountains. Haven't you heard by now about the number of men who fell under my hands by the streams of Xanthus?[11] Or, though you heard, have the blessed gods taken away your wits and senses, so that cruel Fates may gape wide for you?"

With these words, he swooped upon her, brandishing in his

[10] A line of the text may well be lost here.

[11] A reference to the "fight at the river" described by Homer in the twenty-first book of the *Iliad*. The death of Hector is described in the twenty-second book.

powerful hand the long, murderous spear that Chiron made.[12] Quickly he stabbed brave Penthesileia above the right breast. The dark blood flowed swiftly out, and the strength in her limbs was broken at once. The great battle-ax fell from her hand, night veiled her eyes, and anguish sank into her heart. But even so she revived and looked at her enemy, now about to drag her down 600 from her swift horse. She wondered to herself whether she should draw her great sword in her hand and await the onset of Achilles rushing at her, or speedily leap down from her fast horse and entreat the glorious man, offering him at once abundant bronze and gold, which warm the hearts of mortals within them, no matter how bold a man may be. Somehow with these she might persuade the deadly strength of Achilles, or he might let her return home, out of regard for the youth that they shared—and she longed to escape.

These were the thoughts she had; but the gods arranged it otherwise. For the son of Peleus rushed upon her filled with rage and quickly pierced the body of the girl and the wind-swift horse alike.[13] Just as a man hurrying with his dinner pierces meats on a spit over a hot fire, or as a hunter in the mountains throws a cruel javelin and cuts through the mid-belly of a deer, and the strong point, flying right through, is fixed in the base of a tall oak or pine; so Peleusson with his raging spear cut quite through Penthesileia and her beautiful horse. Still comely, she fell quickly to the ground and rolled in the dust and destruction. Nothing shameful disgraced her beautiful body, but she was stretched out face down, still quivering about the long spear and resting against her swift horse. Just like a fir tree broken by the force of the cold north wind, one which earth nourishes by a spring, a great adornment for herself, the tallest, perhaps, in the long glens and the forest; so did marvelously beautiful Penthesileia fall from her swift horse, and her strength was shattered.

[12] In the *Iliad*, Homer mentions that Chiron had given to Achilles' father this spear of Pelian ash (xvi. 143-44). No one else in the Greek army at Troy was able to wield it.

[13] Possibly we should follow Vian in keeping the manuscript reading and translate, "As she moved quickly toward him, Achilles was filled with rage . . ."

The Trojans, when they saw her cut down in the fight, at once rushed in terror toward the city, their spirits grieving with a sorrow beyond telling. Just as when on the wide ocean sailors who have lost their ship in a heavy wind escape from death—a few of them—after many sufferings in the dreary sea, and at last land appears close by and even a city, and, although their bodies are completely worn out by their cruel troubles, they rush from the sea full of sorrow for the ship and their comrades whom the wave has driven under the dreadful darkness; so the Trojans escaped from the war to their city, all wailing for the daughter of invincible Ares and the soldiers who had died in the savage fighting.

Peleus' son was laughing over her and loudly boastful:

"Lie now in the dust and feed the dogs and birds, you wretched girl. Who tricked you into coming against me? I have no doubt you thought you would go home from battle with splendid gifts from old Priam for the Greeks you had killed. The gods did not carry out this idea of yours, because we are far the best of heroes, a great light to the Greeks, a disaster to the Trojans and to you. Unlucky you were, because dark Fates and your own mind roused you to leave women's work and go to war, which frightens even men."

With these words, Peleus' son pulled his ashen spear from the swift horse and dread Penthesileia; both of them, killed by a single spear, were in their death throes. Then he took from her head the helmet gleaming like the rays of the sun or the radiance of Zeus. Though she had fallen in the dust and blood, her face shone out under her lovely brows beautiful even in death. The Greeks who thronged around marveled when they saw her, for she was like the blessed gods. She lay on the ground in her armor like strong Artemis asleep, Zeus's child, when her limbs grow weary as she hunts swift lions in the mountains. Aphrodite of the fine crown, wife of mighty Ares, personally made Penthesileia attractive even among the dead, so that noble Peleus' son too might feel some pain. Many men prayed that they might return home and sleep by wives like her. Achilles could not stop the pain in his heart because he had killed her and had not brought her as a glorious wife to Phthia,

41

land of good horses, for in size and beauty she was faultless and like the immortal goddesses.

Sorrow fell upon Ares' heart, and his spirit was grieved for his daughter. Quickly he leapt from Olympus like a terrible, loud-roaring thunderbolt that Zeus sends forth. It darts from his tireless hand either upon the boundless sea or upon the earth, all blazing, and great Olympus is shaken by it; so Ares darted in his armor through the outspread air, sad at heart, when he heard of his child's horrible fate. When he was in the broad heaven, the Winds, swift daughters of Boreas, had told him of the girl's horrible death. When he heard of it, he set foot like a storm wind on the Idaean hills and made the long glens move under him, the deep-cut canyons, the rivers, and all the endless foothills of Ida.

He would have given the Myrmidons a day full of groaning, if Zeus himself had not from Olympus frightened him with terrible lightnings and horrid thunderbolts, which before his feet flew thick through the air, blazing dreadfully. Ares, when he saw them, recognized the loud call of his thundering father, and he stayed his rush toward war's turmoil. Just as when a huge rock is broken off from a sheer cliff by wild winds and rain from Zeus, rain or thunderbolt, and the glens re-echo as it rolls wildly down, and with a steady whistling it rushes on with many a jump until it reaches level ground, and then it comes to a quick stop, for all its desire to go on; so Ares, Zeus's mighty son, with unwilling spirit stopped his eager onset. (All the Olympians alike yield to the ruler of the blessed ones, because he is far the greatest of them, and his might is beyond telling.) But Ares was deeply troubled, and sometimes his swift-moving mind would urge him to return to heaven, in fear of the terrible rebuke of a very angry Zeus, and sometimes it urged him to disregard his father and mix his indestructible hands in Achilles' blood. Finally, however, his heart remembered how many of Zeus's sons, too, had been destroyed in wars without even Zeus himself helping them as they perished.[14]

700

[14] Homer, in a most impressive scene, portrays Zeus considering the possibility of saving his son Sarpedon from death at the hands of Patroclus and deciding to let him die as he was fated to do (xvi. 431–61).

For this reason he left the Greeks. He was certainly destined to be struck with the painful thunderbolt and lie with the Titans if he had any plans at variance with the thought of immortal Zeus.

Then the soldier sons of the sturdy Greeks, rushing everywhere, quickly stripped the bloody armor from the dead. But the son of Peleus felt deep sorrow as he looked at the girl's lovely strength in the dust. Strong pains were eating his heart on this account, as great as he had felt before when his comrade Patroclus had been killed.

Thersites stood before him and vigorously reviled him with evil speech:[15]

"Achilles, grim of mind, what heavenly power has beguiled the spirit in your breast because of a destructive Amazon? She was eager to plan many troubles for us, but the heart within you is woman-mad, and you are as concerned for her as for a sensible wedded wife whom you courted with presents in your desire to marry her. It would have been better if she had hit you first with a spear in the fighting, because your heart takes such excessive pleasure in women. Your destructive mind feels no interest at all in a glorious deed of valor, when you catch sight of a woman. Poor wretch, where are your strength and your intelligence? Where the might of a noble king? Don't you have any realization of how much pain has come to the Trojans because they were woman-mad? There is no other pleasure more ruinous to mortals than sexual desire, which makes even a wise man a fool. Glory is won by work. The fame of victory and the works of war are a soldier's delights. The beds of women are a coward's pleasure."

[15] Thersites appears in a similar role in the second book of the *Iliad* (211–77). Although in that scene his invective is directed at Agamemnon, we are told in passing that he was in the habit of reviling Achilles and Odysseus, who especially hated him. At the end of the scene, he is given a severe beating by Odysseus. Contrary to his usual practice, Homer gives a longish description of Thersites' appearance and says he was the ugliest man who came to Troy. In Homer, as in Quintus, "public opinion" is hostile to Thersites. There was an ancient tradition that Thersites was Homer's guardian, who had embezzled the estate Homer should have inherited. In revenge, Homer put him into the *Iliad*. There is no reason to suspect that this story is anything but the creation of someone's imagination.

At these reviling words, quick-tempered Achilles felt a great anger in his heart and at once struck Thersites on the jaw and ear with his mighty hand. All Thersites' teeth poured out together on the ground, he fell on his face, and blood gushed in floods out of his mouth. Quickly the feeble spirit fled from the body of the worthless man. The Greek soldiers were, of course, delighted, because he was absolutely insulting to them with his evil abuse, being a man given to scurrility and a disgrace to the Greeks. This is what many of the Greek soldiers said:

"It isn't good for an inferior man to insult kings openly or secretly, because terrible anger follows. There is Themis, and a shameless tongue is punished by Ate, who always makes grief grow upon grief for human beings."

So many a Greek spoke. But quick-tempered Peleusson, angry at heart, spoke to Thersites like this:

"Lie there in the dust, forgetful of your follies. A bad man ought not to match himself with his betters, as you did before when you deeply stirred Odysseus' patient heart by babbling your endless insults. But Peleusson did not, you see, turn out to be like him. I took your life away and did not this time just hit you with a heavy hand. A pitiless fate enfolded you, and you lost your life by your own feebleness. Now leave the Greeks, and speak your abusive words among the dead."

So spoke the fearless son of bold Peleus. Diomedes was the only man among the Greeks who was angry at Achilles when Thersites fell. This was because Thersites was a relative of his. Diomedes was famous Tydeus' mighty son; Thersites was the son of godlike Agrius. Agrius was the brother of glorious Oeneus, while Oeneus gave the Greeks a soldier son in Tydeus, and Diomedes was his sturdy son.[16] This was why he was angry when Thersites was killed. And he would have lifted his hands against Peleusson if the finest Greeks had not checked him, earnestly appealing to him as a group—just as they were also doing to Peleus-

[16] Agrius is said by Homer to have been the brother of Oeneus, but Homer does not connect either him or Diomedes with Thersites.

son. For the best men the Greeks had were ready now to fight with swords, since an evil anger was urging them on. But they listened to their friends' advice.

Seized with pity for splendid Penthesileia—and themselves, too, struck with admiration—the royal Atreussons gave her body to the Trojans to carry along with her armor to the city of famous Ilus, when they learned that Priam had sent a message. Priam had in his mind the plan to put the brave girl, her armor, and her horse as well into the great tomb of rich Laomedon. He had a funeral pyre heaped up for her in front of the city, lofty and broad. On this he had them place the girl with all the many possessions that it is right to burn in the fire with a wealthy queen who has been killed. The swift strength of Hephaestus, destructive fire, devoured her. The people standing around, some on this side, some on that, quickly quenched the fire with fragrant wine. They collected the bones, poured sweet oil lavishly over them, and put them into a hollow chest. And about them they threw on top the rich fat of a cow that had been pre-eminent among the herds pasturing on the hills of Ida. The Trojans uttered shrill laments for her as for a loved daughter, full of pain as they buried her by their strong wall at a projecting tower, putting her beside the bones of Laomedon as an honor for Ares and for Penthesileia herself. Along with her they buried all the other Amazons who had accompanied her into battle and had been killed by the Greeks. For the Atreussons did not begrudge them a tomb and much lamenting, but allowed the courageous Trojans to take them away from the battlefield along with the men who had been killed. We no longer feel anger at the dead, but enemies receive our pity when they have lost their lives and are no more.

800

The Greeks, on their side, gave to the fire the bodies of many heroes who had died along with their enemies and been killed by the hands of the Trojans up through the mouth of the battle. Great was their sorrow for their dead, but, beyond all the others, they mourned for brave Podarces. In battle he had been the equal of his fine brother Protesilaus. (Noble Protesilaus had been killed long ago now by Hector.)[17] Podarces had been hit by Penthesi-leia's spear and his death overwhelmed the Greeks with dismal sorrow. For this reason, they buried the mass of the dead apart from him, and about him alone they built with much toil a conspicuous funeral mound, because his heart was bold.

After they had buried separately the wretched body of worthless Thersites, they came to the beautiful ships, glorifying greatly in their hearts Aeacus' grandson Achilles. And when the bright day had gone down into the ocean stream, and wonderful night was spread over the earth, then in the quarters of rich Agamemnon Peleusson banqueted, and with him the other princes enjoyed themselves at the feast until the glorious dawn came.

[17] Homer mentions the death of Protesilaus in the Catalogue of Ships (*Iliad* ii. 699–702). He was the first of the Greeks to be killed at Troy, being struck as he jumped off his ship. In Homer, he is killed by "a Dardanian man." In the post-Homeric tradition, his death is regularly attributed to Hector.

✻ ✻ ✻

The Arrival, Deeds, and Death of Memnon

Wᴀᴇɴ ᴛʜᴇ ʙʀɪɢʜᴛ ʟɪɢʜᴛ of the unresting sun came up over the peaks of the echoing mountains, the vigorous sons of the Greeks were gay in their quarters, greatly exulting over tireless Achilles. The Trojans, however, were sad in their city. They sat about their walls and kept watch, because the fear possessed all of them that the powerful man might perhaps leap over their great wall, kill them, and burn up everything with fire. In their grief, the old man, Thymoetes, spoke among them:[1]

"My friends, for my part, I am no longer able to figure out in my mind how there will be any protection against the distresses of war, now that Hector is fallen. He used to meet the enemy in close combat and was formerly the Trojans' great strength. Yet not even he escaped Fate, but he was subdued at the hands of Achilles. I think even a god who meets that man in battle is destroyed. What a queen it was that he subdued in the turmoil, just the one whom the other Greeks feared, brave Penthesileia. And she was indeed

---

[1] Thymoetes is only a name in Homer, one of the group of old men sitting on the Trojan wall with Priam when Helen comes walking toward them (*Iliad* iii. 146).

terrible. For my part, when I saw her, I thought one of the blessed ones had come here from heaven to show us favor. I see now that I was wrong. But come, let us consider what may be better for us, to continue to fight perhaps against our loathsome enemies, or to flee now from a dying city. For we shall no longer be able to oppose the Greeks, now that pitiless Achilles is fighting in the war."

So he spoke. Priam, son of Laomedon, answered him:

"My friend, you other Trojans, and their powerful allies, let us not, because of some fear, withdraw from our country, nor continue to fight the enemy at a distance from the city, but fight from the towers and wall, until strong-spirited Memnon comes, bringing the countless tribes of his peoples who live in Ethiopia, land of the black man. I really think that by now he is close to our land, since not at all recently I sent him a message in the great distress of my heart. He gladly promised that he would come to Troy and do everything I asked. I am confident he is close. Come, endure for a little longer, because it is far better to die bravely in battle than to run away and live in disgrace among foreigners."

So the old man spoke. But fighting was no longer pleasing to sensible Polydamas, and he made a well-meant proposal:

"If Memnon really did make a clear agreement to force terrible destruction away from us, I have nothing whatever against waiting in the city for the splendid man. In my heart, however, I am afraid that when he and his companions come he will be defeated and will become a disaster for many others on our side as well. Because a terrible strength has arisen among the Greeks. I urge that we neither run far away from our city and suffer the many disgraces resulting from our wretched helplessness as we make our way to a foreign land, nor continue to stay here and be killed in fighting the Greeks. Even now, although we have been slow about it, it would still be better to give back to the Greeks Helen and her possessions. Restore all that she brought from Sparta and offer twice as much besides on behalf of the city and ourselves, while hostile peoples have not divided up our property, and destructive fire has not obliterated our town. Now is the time for your minds to listen to me. I think no one else has devised a better plan among the Trojans. I wish Hector had listened to my suggestion before, when I was trying to keep him inside the city."[2]

So spoke the sturdy Polydamas. The Trojans roundabout were approving him in their hearts as they listened. They did not, however, say a word openly, because they were all afraid of their king and respectful of him—and of Helen too, although it was because of her that they were dying. Polydamas' good qualities did not keep Paris from vigorously reviling him to his face:

"Polydamas, you are a coward and a weakling, and in your breast, instead of a brave heart, are fear and flight. You proudly claim to be our best in council, but your ideas are the worst in Troy. I suggest that you keep away from battle yourself and stay sitting in your home. The others will arm themselves around me all through the town until we find a satisfactory cure for this desperate war. Men's glory and deeds do not grow great apart from work and cruel war; it is children and women who find great pleasure in running away. Your spirit is like theirs. I for my part have no confidence in you as a fighter. You are sapping the courage and strength of everyone."

So his bitter insults went. Polydamas spoke back in anger and was not afraid to shout at him in his presence. A man is loathsome and reckless and witless who is friendly and fawning before your face but broods over other thoughts in his mind and expresses a secret anger when you are not there. Polydamas, therefore, bitterly reviled the glorious lord quite openly:

"You are the most destructive of all the men upon the earth. Your rashness brought troubles upon us. Your mind was prepared to venture upon a vast war, and you will continue with it until you see your native land and your people destroyed. I hope no such

2 Polydamas urged caution on Hector twice in the *Iliad* and both times to no purpose. In xii. 211-29, he interprets an omen unfavorably and urges Hector not to break through the Greek wall. More notably, and more important for the story of the *Iliad*, he is impressed by the reappearance of Achilles in book xviii and urges Hector to withdraw inside Troy (254-83). Hector angrily rejects his advice, and Hector's recollection of this later, when the Trojans have been disastrously defeated, is one of the reasons which move Hector to fight Achilles instead of withdrawing inside Troy (xxii. 100-107).

rashness ever takes possession of me, but that I will always have a steady caution to keep my home safe and strong."

So spoke Polydamas, but Paris did not answer him at all. He remembered all the troubles he had brought upon the Trojans, and he thought of all he was still to bring them because his heart was on fire with love. He preferred to die rather than be separated from divine Helen, for whose sake the youth of Troy, high on the towers, kept watch from the lofty city, awaiting the Greeks and Achilles, descendant of Aeacus.

100   It was not long after this that martial Memnon came to help them. Memnon was lord over the dark Ethiopians, and the host he brought seemed infinite. The Trojans were delighted to see him in their city. Just as when sailors after a destructive storm, thoroughly exhausted by now, see the gleaming stars of the Great Bear revolving in the clear sky; so the people thronging around Memnon rejoiced, and above them all Priam Laomedonson. His heart was full of the hope that the Ethiopian soldiers would destroy the ships with fire, since their king was gigantic, they were numerous themselves, and they were all enthusiastic for war. In consequence, he could not have his fill of honoring Memnon, the Dawn's son, with fine gifts and lavish festivity.

They conversed together at their feasting and banqueting. Priam told of the Greek princes and all the sorrows he had suffered. Memnon told of the deathless life of his father and his mother the Dawn, the streams of boundless Tethys, the holy wave of deep-flowing Oceanus, the limits of the tireless earth, and the risings of the sun.[3] He told, too, of all his journey from Oceanus

[3] Memnon is not mentioned in the *Iliad* and receives only passing reference in the *Odyssey*: Odysseus, talking with the ghost of Achilles in the world of the dead, mentions that Eurypylus was the most handsome man he had seen "after glorious Memnon." Memnon's father Tithonus is mentioned once in each poem, neither time being connected with Memnon. In the *Iliad* he appears in a Trojan genealogy as brother of Priam (xx. 237). In the *Odyssey*, "the Dawn rose from her bed from the side of splendid Tithonus" (v. 1). Homer says nothing about the story which was later famous: Tithonus was given immortality, but not immortal youth. He grew steadily older and more wizened, until he was finally metamorphosed into a cicada.

up to Priam's city and the crags of Ida; in particular, how he killed with his mighty hands a great army of troublesome Solymi who had tried to stop his advance and thereby brought upon themselves ruin and certain death. These things he spoke of, and how he saw a thousand tribes of men. Priam's heart rejoiced as he listened, and he expressed his high regard in these words:

"Memnon, the gods have given me this sight, your army and you yourself in my palace. I hope they continue to fulfill my wishes, so that I may see the Greeks dying, all of them at once, under your spears. Why, you are in every way wonderfully like the tireless blessed ones, more so than any other earthly hero. So I think you will fling upon them death and all its groans. Come, for the present, delight your heart at my feasts today. Then you will go to battle as is proper."

Saying this, he lifted in his hands a huge cup, and in friendly fashion he pledged Memnon with the massive goblet of gold. The wise, lame Hephaestus, when he married Aphrodite, had given this masterpiece to powerful Zeus.[4] Zeus gave it as a present to his son, godlike Dardanus; he passed it to his son Erichthonius, and Erichthonius left it to proud Tros; he left it with his other possessions to Ilus, and he gave it to Laomedon. Laomedon handed it on to Priam, who was to give it to his son.[5] But this the gods did not bring to fulfillment. Memnon, as he handled that gorgeous goblet, marveled at it in his heart and said this in answer:

"A feast is no place for great boasts or for making promises, but for feasting at one's ease in the halls and acting to suit the occasion. Whether or not I am still brave and strong, you will learn in battle, where a man's worth is seen. For the present, let us

[4] Quintus told us earlier in Book One that Aphrodite was married to Ares. In Homer's *Iliad*, Hephaestus is married to Charis ("Grace." xviii. 383), but the *Odyssey* relates how he caught his wife Aphrodite in bed with Ares (viii. 267–366). Anyone interested in reconciling these data can, if he chooses, assume that after the discovery of the adultery Ares married Aphrodite and Hephaestus married Grace.

[5] This family heirloom is handled by Quintus in the same way as Homer handles Agamemnon's hereditary scepter in *Iliad* ii. 100–107, both treasures being described as the work of Hephaestus and originally designed for Zeus himself.

think of rest and not go on drinking all night long. Unlimited wine and wretched lack of sleep are a handicap for a man who is in a hurry to fight."

So he spoke, and the old man was seized with admiration and said to him:

"Do just as you like about the feasting. Suit yourself. I shall not force you against your will. One should not try to hold back a man who wants to leave a feast or speed from the hall one who wants to stay. That's the way people ought to act, you know."

So he spoke, and Memnon rose from the table and went to his bed—for the last time. Along with him, all the other banqueters went to take their rest, and sweet sleep came to them quickly.

But in the halls of Zeus, the god of lightning, the immortals were feasting. And among them father Zeus from his deep knowledge was telling of the deeds of war's ill-sounding tumult:

"Know, all you gods, the heavy trouble that is hastening on in the war tomorrow. You will see the might of very many horses in both armies destroyed beside their chariots, and you will see men dying. Each one of you, no matter how great his concern for them, must stand firm and not come about my knees with supplications. For the Fates are pitiless even for us."

So he spoke among the gods, who knew this well themselves, to insure that even a god who was distressed would turn away from the war and not come in vain to indestructible Olympus begging his help for a son or a favorite. And when they heard the words of loud-thundering Cronosson, their hearts bore up and they did not say a word against their king, for they were extremely afraid of him. Instead, they went sorrowfully to where each had his home and bed. And, immortals though they were, the gentle blessing of sleep was drawn over their eyelids.

When over the tops of the tall mountains and up the broad heaven the morning star hurried, who rouses to their work the harvesters, however sweet their sleep, then his last sleep released the warlike son of light-bringing Erigeneia, the Dawn. He, with strength growing in his heart, was already eager to fight the enemy, but the Dawn moved up the broad heaven against her will.

Then the Trojans speedily put on their war gear, and the Ethiopians did the same, as did all the allied peoples who had gathered about mighty Priam. They rushed at full speed out before the wall, like black clouds such as Zeus collects when the air grows dark in a rising storm. The whole plain was soon filled, as they poured over it like grain-devouring locusts, which fly like a cloud or a great rainstorm over the broad plains of the earth, terrible bringers of miserable famine to men; so they came in their numbers and strength. The roads were packed with the rushing crowds, and dust rose from under their feet.   200

The Greeks over on their side marveled when they saw them rushing on. At once they put the bronze about their bodies, confident of Peleusson's strength. He moved in their midst like the mighty Titans, exulting in his horses and his chariot. His armor shone all over like lightning. Just as from the ends of the earthenfolding ocean the brilliant sun comes into the heaven, bringing light to men, and the earth and the air laugh all around; so this day the son of Peleus moved quickly among the Greeks. So too among the Trojans went martial Memnon, just like raging Ares, and the soldiers followed him eagerly, rushing on beside the king.

Soon the long ranks of both Greeks and Trojans were at war's work, and conspicuous among them were the Ethiopians. The armies fell upon each other with a crash like waves of the sea when winds are rising from every quarter in the winter season. They killed one another, hurling their spears of polished ash, and groans of men and the clang of metal blazed out among them. Just as thundering rivers roar loudly as they pour into the sea, when there is a furious rainstorm from Zeus, and the clouds, whetted by each other, rumble incessantly, and the blast of flame darts out; so the great earth rumbled under the feet of these fighting armies. Through the divine air swept a terrible shouting, for they were shouting dreadfully on both sides.

Then Peleusson killed Thalius and noble Mentes, both famous men, and struck many another. As when a furious subterranean hurricane assails buildings, and immediately everything pours down upon the ground from its foundations, for the deep earth is severely shaken; so they fell down in the dust at the swift doom from Peleusson's spear.[6] For his heart was filled full with rage.

In the same way, on the other side, the Dawn's brave son was slaughtering Greeks like an evil doom which brings evil, miserable ruin upon peoples. First he killed Pheron, hitting him in the chest with his grim spear, and then he killed glorious Ereuthus. Both of these men had been enthusiastic for war and miserable battle. They lived at Thryon by the stream of the Alpheus and under Nestor had come to Ilion's sacred town. When he had killed them, Memnon set out after Nestor, Neleus' son, eager to kill him. But godlike Antilochus came in front of his father and hurled his long spear. Antilochus missed Memnon, however, who barely avoided it, but killed his dear comrade Aethops Pyrrasusson. Angered by his death, Memnon leapt at Antilochus as a high-spirited lion leaps upon a boar, which itself knows how to fight both men and beasts, and its attack is deadly beyond telling; so Memnon rushed swiftly at Antilochus. But Antilochus hit him with a great stone. Memnon's life was not lost, though, because his strong helmet kept off painful death. But the heart in his breast was terribly stirred when he was hit, and his helmet rang with the blow. He was in more of a rage at Antilochus than ever, and his great strength seethed within him. And so he hit Nestor's son, able fighter though he was, above the breast and drove his great spear into his heart, where death comes quickly for mortals.

The death of Antilochus brought grief to the Greeks, to all of them, but especially sorrow came to Nestor's heart, when his son was killed before his eyes. No greater grief, surely, comes to men than when sons die with their father looking on. And so, even though made with a stubborn heart, he was grieved when his son was destroyed by an evil doom. He called at once to Thrasymedes, who was some way off:

"Up, my glorious Thrasymedes, and help me chase the killer of your brother and my son far from the poor body or fall beside it ourselves and take our fill of groans and grief. If you have any

---

[6] Some textual details here are doubtful. The notion that earthquakes were caused by subterranean winds enjoyed a long popularity.

fear in your heart, you are no son of mine and are not of the stock of Periclymenus, who ventured to go to meet even Heracles face to face.[7] Come, to our work, because necessity often gives great strength to even worthless fighters."

So he spoke, and Thrasymedes' spirit was crushed by a terrible sorrow as he heard him. He was quickly joined by Phereus, whom pain had also seized at his lord's death, and they started to go up through the bloody turmoil of battle straight for mighty Memnon. Just as when a pair of hunters along the wooded folds of a high mountain, full of enthusiasm over the hunt, rush at a boar or a bear, longing to kill it, and the animal rushes at them both with eager spirit and defends itself against the men's strength; so at that time Memnon was full of proud thoughts as they came close to him.

They could not kill him with their long ashen spears, but the points were deflected from his flesh. The Dawn, I fancy, turned them aside. The spears did not fall useless on the ground, but stout-hearted Phereus, with quick eagerness, killed Polymnius, son of Meges, and Laomedon fell to Nestor's sturdy son, angry because of his brother whom Memnon had killed in the fighting. Memnon now, beside the body, was undoing with tireless hands the armor of solid bronze, paying no attention to the power of Thrasymedes or brave Phereus, because he was so much their superior. They stopped their eager advance, just like a pair of jackals afraid of a great lion bestriding a stag.

Nestor, looking on from close at hand, was sadly grieved and ordered other companions to join in the attack on Memnon. He also started to participate in the fight himself from his chariot. Longing for his dead son was drawing him into a conflict beyond his strength. He would himself have soon fallen beside his dear son and been counted among the dead, if stouthearted Memnon had not said to him as he rushed against him, feeling respect in his heart for the man who was as old as his father: 300

---

[7] Periclymenus is mentioned in the *Odyssey* (along with Nestor) as one of the sons of Chloris and Neleus (xi. 286). Nestor himself says in the *Iliad* that all of Neleus' sons except himself were killed by Heracles (xi. 690–93).

"Sir, it is not right for me to fight against you who are an older man, and my mind is aware of this. I certainly thought you were a young fighting man, as you went against your enemies, and my bold heart expected you to be a task worthy of my hand and spear. Now withdraw far away from the turmoil and loathsome slaughter, draw back, or I may have to hit you without wanting to, and you may fall beside your son because you fought with a far better man. Why, men will say that you are a fool; it is not right to attack a man better than yourself."

So he spoke, and the old man said in reply:

"Memnon, what you say is, I am sure, all worthless as the wind. No one will say that that man is foolish who fights with the enemy for his son's sake and in the battle tries to drive away from the body the pitiless man who killed his son. Oh! I wish my strength were still unimpaired; then you would know my spear. As it is, you make the most tremendous boasts, because a young man's spirit is bold and his mind is less stable. So, with your proud thoughts, you talk nonsense. If you had come against me when I was young, your friends would have had no joy of you, for all your strength. As it is, I am burdened by terrible old age, like some lion which a dog chases boldly from a farmyard filled with sheep, and the lion, however much he wants to, does not defend himself, for he no longer has sound teeth or strength, and his sturdy heart has been wrecked by time. So the strength no longer rises in my breast as it did before. But just the same, I am better than many men still, and my hands yield to few."

With these words, he drew back a little and left his son lying in the dust, because he no longer had in his bent limbs anything of the vigor he had before. He was weighed down by the many sufferings of old age. So likewise Thrasymedes of the good ashen spear ran away, and stout-hearted Phereus, and all the other comrades. They were afraid, because a truly deadly man was coming against them.

Just as from great mountains a deep, swirling river rushes on, foaming and with a loud roar, when Zeus stretches a gloomy day over mankind, raising a great storm, and there is the sound of thunder everywhere, and lightning, as multitudes of huge clouds come together, and the hollow fields are flooded by the noisy rushing rain, and the long ravines in all the mountains re-echo terribly; so Memnon chased the Greeks to the shores of the Hellespont and killed them as he followed. Many lost their lives in the dust and blood at the hands of the Ethiopians. The earth was defiled with the gore of the dying Greeks. Memnon's heart was filled with joy as he kept up his steady pursuit of the enemy ranks. The Trojan earth around him was packed with corpses, and still he did not abandon the rout. He hoped to be a light of safety to the Trojans; ruin for the Greeks. But grim Fate was beguiling him, standing close and urging him into the fighting.

About him his strong attendants were fighting: Alcyoneus, Nychius and brave Asiades, the warrior Meneclus, Alexippus, Clydon, and others as well, eager participants in the pursuit, men who were themselves strong in battle and full of confidence in their king. It was then that Nestor killed Meneclus as he charged upon the Greeks, and stout-hearted Memnon, angry because of his comrade, killed a large company. Just as when a hunter in the mountains presses hard upon swift deer within the circle of dark nets, a herd gathered into this last trick of the hunt by the will of men, and the dogs are glad and bark continuously, and the hunter eagerly deals grim death with his javelin to the swiftest does; so Memnon killed a large host. His comrades rejoiced about him, but the Greeks ran away from the famous man. Just as when from a steep mountain a huge rock falls off which tireless Zeus on high thrusts from a crag by hitting it with a cruel thunderbolt, and, as it bursts into the thick scrub and the long valleys, the glens re-echo, and if sheep are pasturing anywhere in the forest below it as it rolls on, or cattle, or anything else, they are afraid and try to avoid its terrible and pitiless rush; so the Greeks were afraid of the heavy spear of onrushing Memnon.

It was then that Nestor came close to strong Achilles and, full of grief for his son, said:

"Achilles, great bulwark of the powerful Greeks, my dear son is dead, Memnon has my dead boy's armor, and I am afraid he may become spoil for the dogs. Quick, protect him. That man is indeed a friend who thinks of a comrade who has been killed and grieves for him when he is gone."

So he spoke, and sorrow fell upon Achilles' heart as he heard him. And when he noticed Memnon through the fierce tumult killing Greeks in crowds with his spear, he quickly abandoned all the Trojans whom his hands had killed among the other ranks and, eager for battle and angry because of Antilochus and the others who had been killed, went straight for Memnon. That glorious man took up in his hands a stone which men had set to mark the boundary of a fine wheat field and threw it upon the shield of tireless Peleusson. But he did not fear the great stone at all, but quickly came close to Memnon, brandishing his long spear before him. (He was on foot, having left his horses behind him in the fighting.) He struck Memnon's right shoulder above his shield. But Memnon, hit though he was, fought on with fearless spirit. He hit Achilles' arm with his great spear and drew blood. This brought the hero an empty joy, and he immediately spoke arrogantly to Achilles:

"Now I think you will have your fill of evil doom and die, destroyed by my hands. You will not escape from battle any more. Wretch, why were you recklessly killing Trojans, boasting that you were far the best man in the world and that your mother was a deathless Nereid? At last the day of doom has come for you, because I am of divine stock, the Dawn's mighty son, and the lilylike Hesperides raised me far away by the stream of Ocean. This is another reason why I do not shun conflict with you that admits no quarter: I know how much superior my divine mother is to a Nereid, whose son you boast yourself to be. My mother shines out for the blessed ones and for human kind. Through her all things are done within everlasting Olympus, the fine and famous things that are profitable to men. While your mother sits in the barren hiding places of the sea, living like the sea monsters and going proudly among the fish, useless and invisible. I have no regard for her, and I do not even feel she is like the deathless goddesses of heaven."

So he spoke. And bold Achilles rebuked him:

"Memnon, why has your malfunctioning mind roused you to come into battle against me and match yourself with me? I am your superior in strength, lineage, and ability, since I won as my lot distinguished blood from proud Zeus and powerful Nereus. The Nereids of the sea are his daughters, and the gods on Olympus honor them. And of them all they especially honor Thetis of the famous devices. The reason is, I think, that she received Dionysus in her halls when he was frightened by the destructive power of Lycurgus, and because she received in her home Hephaestus, the shrewd worker in bronze, when he fell from Olympus, and because she released from bonds Zeus himself, lord of the bright lightning.[8] It is because they remember these things that the all-seeing heavenly ones honor my mother Thetis on holy Olympus. You will know she is a goddess too, when the spear of bronze thrown by my strength pierces your liver. Angry for Patroclus, I took vengeance on Hector; angry for Antilochus, I will take vengeance on you. The man whose comrade you killed is no weakling. But why do we stand here like foolish children, talking of our parents' deeds and our own? It is time for fighting and time for strength."

With these words, he took his long sword in his hands, and Memnon did the same. Quickly they rushed together and, in the eagerness of their hearts, struck repeated blows on each other's shields, which Hephaestus had made with his immortal skill. They clashed together again and again, their helmets pressed upon each other, and the plumes touched. Zeus's mind was filled with love for them both, and he put vigor into both and made them untiring

[8] All three of these services to the gods rendered by Thetis are mentioned by Homer in the *Iliad*. Glaucus, explaining to Diomedes that he will not fight him if he is a god, summarizes the story of how Lycurgus chased Dionysus' nurses, beating them with an ox-goad, and how the frightened Dionysus leapt into the sea and was taken care of by Thetis (vi. 130–37). Achilles, trying to get his mother to ask Zeus to help the Trojans, reminds her how often he heard her tell at home how she had rescued Zeus when the other Olympians wanted to tie him up (i. 396–406). Hephaestus himself tells how he "fell far away," when his mother Hera wanted to get rid of him because he was lame, how Thetis and Eurynome took care of him, and how he hid with them for nine years, manufacturing beautiful jewelry (xviii. 394–405).

and larger, not at all like men, but like gods. Eris, too, took delight in them both. Longing to drive the point at once into the flesh, they would often direct their force between shield and plumed helmet and then again a little above a greave or below the elaborate breastplates fitted to their mighty bodies. Both of them were full of eagerness, and the immortal armor rang on their shoulders.

As the Trojans and the Ethiopians continued their fight with the brave Greeks, the shouting reached high into the glorious air, and the dust rose from under their feet all the way to the wide heaven, because very great things were being done. Just like a mist on the mountains, when rain is coming on, and the noisy channels fill with rushing water, and every ravine roars loudly, and all the shepherds become immediately afraid of the torrents and the mist dear to deadly wolves and all other beasts that the huge forest supports; so under their feet the annoying dust flew. It shadowed over the sky and quite hid the noble light of the sun. Cruel hardship was overpowering the armies in the dust and the terrible conflict. Then one of the blessed gods suddenly pushed the dust away from the battlefield. Deadly Dooms on each side kept urging the swift ranks on to fight vigorously in the grim battle. Ares did not stop his savage slaughter, and the ground everywhere roundabout was stained with flowing blood. Black Destruction was enjoying it. The great plain where horses had pastured became packed with dead, all the expanse that Simois and Xanthus enclose with their streams, as they flow down from Ida into the holy Hellespont.

When now the great struggle of the fighting heroes had been sufficiently prolonged, and their straining strength was equal, then the Olympians were looking on from afar with pleasure in their hearts, some at tireless Peleusson and some at the glorious son of Tithonus and the Dawn. The broad heaven resounded on high, the sea roared, and the dark earth roundabout shook beneath the feet of the pair. All the daughters of haughty Nereus trembled beside Thetis and were terribly afraid for mighty Achilles. The Dawn too, mounted on her chariot in the sky, was fearful for her dear son. Beside her the daughters of Helios marveled, standing in

500

the great circle that Zeus gave to the unwearying sun for his splendid annual course, whereby all things live and decline as time moves unceasingly day by day and the years go round.

Pitiless fighting would now have fallen upon the blessed ones, except that, at the suggestion of Zeus, the loud thunderer, two Dooms suddenly took their stand, one by each hero. The dark one went to Memnon's heart, a bright one to brave Achilles. And the immortals raised a great shout at the sight, and immediately a dismal grief took hold of some, while others felt a fine and glorious delight. The heroes, though, fought steadily on in the bloody conflict and did not notice at all the Dooms that had come to them; their courage and great strength were directed at each other. You would say that tireless Giants were fighting in savage battle that day, or mighty Titans. It was a great contest of strength between them, whether they rushed together with swords or impetuously threw huge stones. Neither of them drew back when hit, neither felt any fear, but, clad in their might, they stood like unwearying headlands. Both could boast they were of great Zeus's stock, and this, of course, was why Enyo, goddess of war, made their conflict equal as they contended for a long time in that duel. She made it equal, too, for their fearless comrades, who with their lords fought with steady enthusiasm, until the spearpoints of the weary fighters were bent back on enemy shields. Men on both sides were being struck, and no one was left unwounded. From all limbs alike blood and sweat flowed to the ground as their struggle went steadily on. The earth had become covered with corpses, as the heaven is with clouds when the sun moves into Capricorn, and the sailor greatly fears the sea. Along with the charging soldiers, neighing horses trampled upon the dead, countless as the leaves in a grove at the beginning of winter after the abundance of autumn.

But these glorious sons of gods fought on amid the corpses and the blood and did not stop their wrath at each other. Then Eris held upright the grim scales of war, and they were no longer level, but Peleusson struck glorious Memnon at the base of the chest, the black sword went straight through him, and his precious life was quickly spent. He fell down into the black blood, and his armor rang loud. The earth resounded under him, and the comrades around him were terrified. Achilles' Myrmidons stripped him of his armor, the Trojans fled, and Achilles set out in swift pursuit like a great storm.

The Dawn, with a groan, covered herself in clouds, and the earth grew dark. All the breezes together, at their mother's bidding, rushed along one path to the plain of Priam and enfolded the dead Memnon. Softly and speedily they took up the Dawn's son and bore him through the grey air. Their hearts were sad for their fallen brother, and the air about them groaned. All the drops of blood that fell from his limbs to the ground have become a marvel to men yet to be. For the gods gathered them from everywhere into one place and made a noisy river, which all the men who live under the ridges of Ida call the Paphlagoneios. The river flows blood-red over the dry land, when the dismal day comes on which Memnon died. An unpleasant, inescapable smell comes from the water. You would think that from the deadly wound the rotting juices still gave off their hideous vapors. Well, this is what the will of the gods later brought about. The swift breezes were flying on, carrying the Dawn's mighty son a little above the earth and veiled in murky darkness.

Nor were the Ethiopians driven far away from their dead lord, because a god led them too, giving them in their longing the sort of speed they were to have after a short time, when they moved quickly through the air. So they followed the winds, grieving for their king. Just as when a hunter has been killed in the woods by the fierce jaws of a boar or a lion, and his troubled comrades lift his body and carry it sorrowfully away, and after them the dogs, longing for their master, follow whimpering because of the hunt's sad end; so they left the pitiless fighting and, groaning loudly and veiled in a magical mist, followed the swift winds.

The Trojans and the Greeks were seized with amazement when the Ethiopians all disappeared along with their king, and for a long time they were speechless. But the tireless winds, with heavy groans, set the corpse of Memnon, who fought his enemies hand to hand, down beside the deep streams of the river Aesepus. A handsome grove of the fair-tressed Nymphs is there, which, later, the daughters of Aesepus put around the tall memorial, thickly shaded by trees of every sort. The goddesses wailed there long, glorifying the son of early-born Dawn of the beautiful throne.

Then the light of the sun sank, and Dawn came down from heaven wailing for her dear son. About her were the twelve fair-tressed girls who have charge of the steep paths of ever-revolving Hyperion, of night and Dawn, and everything that comes into being from Zeus's plan. They move here and there about his home and unbreakable gates, bringing round the year heavy with its fruits, as the seasons move in their circle: cold winter, flowery spring, lovely summer, and autumn with its abundant vintage. These twelve came down, then, from the lofty sky, in infinite grief for Memnon. With them the Pleiades mourned, the tall mountains re-echoed, and the stream of Aesepus. A lament unceasing arose. Among them the Dawn, in her great misery, threw herself about her son and raised a loud lament: 600

"My dear child, you are dead and have brought your mother painful sorrow. Now that you have been killed, I will not endure shining for the immortals in heaven, but will go down into the dreadful depths of the regions beneath the earth, where your soul flits separated from your dead body, where chaos and ugly darkness are spread everywhere.[9] In this way some grief may come to the heart of Zeus, too. I am myself no less honorable than a Nereid or Zeus. I survey all things; I bring all things to fulfillment —to no purpose, since Zeus cared nothing for my light. So I am for the dark. Let him bring Thetis to Olympus out of the sea to shine for gods and men. After heaven the melancholy darkness is my pleasure. I would not cast my light upon your murderer's body."

[9] Vian may well be right in arguing for the interpretation proposed by J. T. Struve in 1860: this line does not refer to the underworld, but to Dawn's plans for the earth and Olympus. We might translate, therefore, "I will go down into the dreadful depths of the regions beneath the earth, where your soul flits separated from your dead body, while chaos and ugly darkness spread themselves everywhere in the universe."

As she said this, the tears streamed down from her divine face like an ever-flowing river, and the black earth about the corpse grew wet. Ambrosial Night shared her dear daughter's grief, and the heaven hid all its stars in mist and cloud, showing favor to the Dawn. The Trojans inside their city were sad at heart for Memnon and longed for king and comrades alike. Even the Greeks felt no great joy. They were bivouacked in the plain among the men who had been killed, and, while they glorified Achilles of the good ashen spear, they were naturally weeping for Antilochus; so their joy was mixed with sadness.

All night long the sorrowing Dawn groaned terribly. The darkness enfolded her, and she gave no thought to rising; she hated great Olympus. Close to her, her swift horses gave many a groan, pawing the unfamiliar earth, looking at their sad queen, and full of longing to return. Zeus was angry and set up a steady thundering, and all the earth roundabout began to shake. Then fear took hold of immortal Dawn.

Then the dark-skinned Ethiopians sadly gave swift burial to Memnon. In their great grief, the ox-eyed Dawn turned them into birds around the grave of her mighty son and gave them the power to fly in the air. Even today countless races of mortals call them Memnons. They still dart to the tomb of their king, grieve for him, and pour dust down over his grave.[10] They raise a great noise of battle against each other there, to do honor to Memnon. And he, in the halls of Hades, or perhaps among the blessed ones in the earth's Elysian field, laughs, and immortal Dawn's heart is cheered as she watches. They toil at this fighting until, grown weary, one group kills the other in the conflict or both of them meet with doom as they fight around their lord. These are the things the swift birds do at the command of light-bringing Dawn.

Then the immortal Dawn leapt into heaven along with the fruitful Hours. They brought her against her will to Zeus's floor, persuading her with all the words that tame deep sorrow, even though she was still grieving. She did not, though, forget her

---

[10] Vian gives good reasons for keeping the manuscripts' *sêmatos*, "grave," in preference to Zimmermann's conjecture *sômatos*, "body." (*Recherches*, 29.)

course, because she was too much afraid of Zeus's unending rebuke. (Everything depends on him, all that the streams of Ocean contain within them, and the earth, and the seat of the blazing stars.) The Pleiades went before her, but she herself opened the heavenly gates and scattered the darkness.

❋ ❋ ❋

BOOK THREE

The Death and Funeral of Achilles

W HEN THE LIGHT of fair-throned Dawn came, then the soldiers of Pylos, groaning loudly for their lord, brought the body of Antilochus to the ships. They buried him by the shores of the Hellespont, and great was their grief.[1] The sturdy Greeks groaned around them; sorrow with no softening held them, and they were showing their regard for Nestor. His spirit, however, was not completely crushed. It is characteristic of a sensible man to endure sorrow in his heart with courage and not be entirely numb with grief.

The death of his comrade Antilochus filled Peleusson with anger, and he was terrible to look upon as he armed himself against the Trojans. They too, fearful though they were of Achilles and his fine ashen spear, poured out of their walls. They were full of enthusiasm, because the Fates put boldness into their hearts. Truly, many of them, under the hands of brave Achilles, were going to descend to Hades' halls, from which there is no return. And Achilles himself was likewise going to die by Priam's city.

Quickly, then, they came together from both sides into one

---

[1] Homer refers to Antilochus' burial in the last book of the *Odyssey*, noting that his bones were laid apart from those of Achilles and Patroclus (76–79).

place, the many tribes of Trojans and the steadfast Greeks, both eager for war now that the battle had begun. Among them, Peleusson destroyed a great host of the enemy. Everywhere the life-giving earth was wet with blood, and the streams of Xanthus and Simois were choked with corpses. Achilles pursued the Trojans and kept on killing them right up to the city, because terror possessed the people. He would have killed them all; he would have pulled the gates from their hinges and thrust them to the ground, or he would have dashed against them and shattered their bars and made a way for the Greeks into Priam's city and sacked the rich town, except that Phoebus' pitiless heart was filled with great anger when he saw the vast throngs of heroes being killed. He came down quickly from Olympus like a wild beast. He had his quiver on his shoulders and his arrows whose wounds are beyond cure. He stood opposite Achilles, and his bowcase and his bow made a great noise about him. Raging fire blazed from his eyes, and the earth stirred beneath his feet. Hideously the great god shrieked. He wanted to terrify Achilles by a god's enormous voice, turn him from the war, and save the Trojans from death:

"Draw back, Peleusson, far from the Trojans. It is not right for you to send evil dooms upon the enemy any longer. Some one of the immortals from Olympus may crush you."

So he spoke. But Achilles felt no fear at all of the god's immortal voice. By now the pitiless Fates were hovering about him. This was why he paid no heed to the god, but cried out loudly at him:

"Phoebus, why, in your defense of the proud Trojans, do you urge me to fight with gods, even when I do not want to? Before now, too, you tricked me and turned me away from the battle—the first time you saved Hector, to whom the Trojans used to make their earnest prayers in the city.[2] Draw far back and go to the home of the other gods, or I may strike you, immortal though you are."

---

[2] In the twentieth book of the *Iliad*, Homer describes an encounter between Hector and Achilles which leads to nothing because Apollo snatches Hector away (419–54).

With these words, he abandoned the god and went against the Trojans. They were still in steady flight before the city, and he continued his chase. Phoebus, with anger in his heart, spoke this way to himself:

"The man is mad. But not even Zeus himself will give him any protection now, nor will anyone else, when he is in such a frenzy and is opposing gods."

So he spoke and hid himself in clouds. Clothing himself in mist, he shot a loathsome arrow, and the swift missile struck Achilles on the ankle. Immediately pains sank in under his heart. He fell like a tower which the force of a typhoon swirling underground shatters over the land as the earth is deeply shaken; so the fine frame of Achilles fell to earth. Looking about him, he gave a loud and savage cry:

"Who now has secretly fired a terrible arrow at me? Let him dare to come against me openly, that his black blood and all his guts may be poured out about my spear, and he may come to grim Hades. For I know that no hero upon the earth will be able to master me with his spear if he comes close to me, not even if he have an utterly fearless heart in his breast—not if he have a completely fearless heart and should be made of bronze. Weaklings are always ambushing their betters. Let him, therefore, come against me, even if he is proud to say that he is a god angry at the Greeks. I really suspect in my heart that it is Apollo covered in sinister darkness. So my dear mother told me once: under his missiles I should perish miserably at the Scaean Gates. This was no idle tale."[3]

He spoke and with harsh hands pulled the hateful arrow from the wound that was beyond all cure. The blood rushed out of the

---

[3] There are numerous references in the *Iliad* to the imminent death of Achilles, and they tend to become more explicit as the poem progresses. At first, there is only the indication that Achilles will die young if he stays at Troy. By the eighteenth book, Thetis has told him that he is doomed to die immediately after Hector (95-96). In book xxi, Achilles, thinking he is about to be destroyed by the river Xanthus, complains that his mother told him he would die by the missiles of Apollo under the Trojan walls (275-78), and in the next book the dying Hector tells Achilles that Paris and Apollo will kill him at the Scaean Gates (xxii. 358-60).

suffering man, and doom was overpowering his heart. In his vexation, he threw the arrow away, and the winds quickly came, of course, snatched it up, and gave it to Apollo, who was on his way to the holy floor of Zeus. It is not fitting that an immortal arrow which comes from an immortal should perish. Apollo took it and quickly reached high Olympus and the gathering of the other gods, in the place where especially they assemble all together and watch the battle of men. Some of them were eager to grant the Trojans their prayers, some the Greeks, and, divided in their plans, they used to watch the men killing and dying in the turmoil of battle. As soon as Zeus's wise wife noticed Apollo, she railed at him with stinging words:

"Phoebus, why have you committed this outrage this day, forgetting that marriage which we immortals personally arranged for godlike Peleus? You sang in the midst of the feasters, telling   100 how Thetis of the silver feet left the great gulf of the sea and was taken to wife by Peleus. Crowds came all together as you played your lyre, wild beasts, and birds, mountain peaks with their tall crags, rivers, and all the deep shadowy forests. You forgot this, and you did a cruel deed and killed a glorious man. When you were pouring libations of nectar with the other gods, you prayed that he be born as a son to Peleus and Thetis, but you forgot your prayer—and all to show favor to the people of powerful Laomedon. You tended cows for him, and, although he was mortal and you immortal, he brought you trouble.[4] And you, in your foolish heart, show favor to the Trojans, forgetting all you suffered. You cruel god, you have no realization in your wretched wits either who is a troublemaker and deserves to suffer or who is honored by the immortals. For Achilles has certainly been kind to us, and he was of our stock.

"Well, I am confident that the war will be no easier for the Trojans, now that Achilles has fallen, because his son will come

[4] In *Iliad* xxi. 441–56, Poseidon reminds Apollo of the time when the two of them worked for Laomedon. Poseidon built a wall around his city, and Apollo looked after his cows. At the end of their year of service, Laomedon refused them the stipulated pay and drove them off, threatening to tie them up, cut off their ears, and sell them abroad.

immediately from Scyros to help the Greeks in the harsh conflict. His strength is like his father's, and he will bring evil to many enemies. You weren't really concerned for the Trojans, were you? You begrudged Achilles his heroic quality, since he was the best of men. Poor fool, how can you now look Thetis in the face among the immortals, when she comes to Zeus's house? She used to honor you before, and she looked on you as a dear son."

Hera spoke, in her grief vigorously reviling mighty Zeus's son. He did not say a word in reply, because he stood in awe of his tireless father's wife. He did not have the strength to look her in the face either, but he sat with downcast eyes, apart from the gods who are forever. All the immortals on Olympus who were protecting the Greeks were violently angry with him, but all those who wanted to grant the Trojans' prayers honored him and laughed in their hearts, concealing it from Hera. For all the heavenly ones stand in awe of her when she is angry.

Peleusson had not yet forgotten his courage, for the dark blood was still hot in his invincible limbs, and he longed to fight. No Trojan, of course, dared to come close to him, wounded though he was, but they stood at a distance, just as country people stand in the scrub marveling at a lion which a hunter has hit, and the lion, although its heart is pierced with the javelin, does not at all forget its courage, but rolls its savage eye and roars terribly with its grim jaws; so anger and a dreadful wound kept Peleusson's spirit fully keyed up.[5] But the arrow of the god was overwhelming him. Nevertheless, he darted up and leapt among the enemy, brandishing his mighty spear. He killed glorious Orythaon, Hector's brave comrade, hitting him on the temple. The helmet did not check the spear for the eager warrior, but the long spear sped through it and, penetrating the bone, reached the forces of the brain and so destroyed his lusty life. Then Peleusson destroyed Hipponous, thrusting his spear down through his forehead to the roots of his eye. The eyeball fell out onto the ground, and his soul

---

[5] Homer has many lions in his similes, but no lion in Homer's works ever roars, a fact which has led some persons to conclude that he had no firsthand knowledge of them.

flew down to Hades' house. Next he pierced the jaw of Alcathous and cut off all his tongue. Alcathous fell to the level ground, breathing out his life, and the spear point was visible, sticking out through his ear. These the glorious man killed as they rushed against him, and he took the life from many others as they were running away, for the blood was still hot in his heart.

But when his limbs were growing cold, and his spirit was ebbing away, he stopped and leaned on his ashen spear. They in their terror were all running from him, and he called out to them like this:

"You cowards, Trojans and Dardanians, not even when I am dead will you escape my merciless spear, but all of you together will pay my avenging Furies for this hideous destruction."

So he spoke, and they were terrified as they heard him. Just as in the mountains fawns are frightened at the sound of a roaring lion, timorous creatures running away from the great beast; so the hosts of the Trojan horsemen and their foreign allies were frightened by Achilles' last shout, imagining him to be still unwounded. But he, his bold heart and mighty limbs weighed down by doom, fell among the corpses like a lofty mountain. The earth rang under him, and his armor gave a loud crash as noble Peleusson fell. The hearts of his enemies, however, were still vastly afraid as they looked upon him. Just as sheep are afraid of a savage beast that has been killed by young men, when they see the shot animal in the fold, and do not care to go close to it, but shudder at the dead body as though it were alive; so the Trojans feared Achilles even though he was no more.

But even so, Paris was vigorously urging the people on with his words. His heart was happy, because he was quite sure the Greeks would give up the terrible fighting with Achilles fallen. For he had been the Greeks' strength:

"My friends, if you are really my steadfast defenders, let us today either be defeated by the Greeks or win safety and drag to Troy with Hector's horses the fallen Peleusson. Now that my brother is dead, these horses carry me into battle, sadly and longing for their lord. If somehow with them we could drag away the dead Achilles, we should give great glory to the horses and also to Hector himself—if there is among the men in Hades' house either intelligence or justice—for Achilles did harm to the Trojans. Great 200 will be the laughter in the hearts of the Trojan women too, as they stand around him in the town, like grim leopardesses made angry for their young or lionesses standing around a worn-out man who was an expert at difficult hunting; so the Trojan women will rush in crowds about the corpse of dead Achilles, infinitely angry, some wrathful for fathers, some for husbands, some for children, and some for valued relatives. And most of all my father will rejoice, and all the old men whom age keeps within the town against their will, if we drag this body to the town and set it out as food for the soaring birds of the air."

So he spoke, and they quickly surrounded the body of brave Achilles, men who had been afraid of him before, Glaucus, Aeneas, and stout-hearted Agenor, and others, too, who were skilled in destructive pursuit, eager to drag him to Ilion's holy city. But Aias, who was like the gods, was not heedless; he quickly bestrode the body and with his long spear pushed them all away from it. They did not, though, give up the attack. They surrounded Aias and fought on, constantly darting at him one after another, like long-nebbed bees which fly in swarms about their hive, fighting off a man, and he, paying no attention to their attacks, cuts out the honey-colored combs, and they are distressed by the rushing smoke and by the man, but even so dart at him, and he does not pay the slightest attention; so Aias paid no attention to them as they rushed at him. The first man he killed was Agelaus Maeonson, hitting him above the breast, and next he killed glorious Thestor. He killed Ocythous, Agestratus, and Aganippus, Zorus, Nissus, and famous Erymas, who came from Lycia under the command of heroic Glaucus and lived at steep Melanippion, Athena's holy place, opposite Massicytus near the Chelidonian height. Sailors at sea are amazed and greatly frightened at this place, when they round these very rugged crags. At his death, Glaucus, famous son of Hippolochus, was struck to the heart with chill sorrow, for he was his comrade. Quickly he stabbed with his spear Aias' shield, made of many oxhides, but did not drive it through into his handsome flesh.[6] The oxhides protected him as did the cuirass he wore fitted to his tireless frame under his shield. Glaucus, however, did not give up the deadly fight. He longed to kill Aias, grandson of Aeacus, and boastfully made great threats in his folly:

"Aias, they say that you are far the best of the Greeks, who have the same vast regard for you as for brave Achilles. He is dead, and I think that you this day will yourself die with him."

So he spoke, hurling out idle talk; he had no realization of how much better a man he was using his spear against. With a dark look, brave Aias said to him:

"You poor wretch, don't you realize at all how much better Hector was than you in battle? But he kept away from my power and spear; he had sense as well as brawn. Your thoughts are surely turned toward the darkness, since you dare to come into battle against one far superior to you. You can't boast that your family are hereditary friends of mine, and you won't turn me from battle with beguiling gifts as you did Tydeus' sturdy son Diomedes.[7] You got away from his might, but I won't let you escape alive from battle now. Do your hopes rest with the others on the battlefield, who along with you dart about the body of noble Achilles like feeble flies? Well, I'll attack them, too, and give them death and dark dooms."

With these words he turned upon the Trojans like a lion upon hunting dogs in the long, wooded valleys. Quickly he destroyed many men who were eager to win their prayer, Trojan and Lycian alike. The hosts around him were afraid, like fish in the sea when a terrible whale comes after them or a great sea-fed dolphin; so the Trojans were frightened by strong Telamonson as he kept rushing at them in the fight. Even so, however, they fought on, and around

[6] For Homer, the shield of Aias was unique. Often called "like a tower," it was made by "Tychius, far the best of leather workers." Tychius manufactured it out of seven oxhides and an eighth layer of bronze (*Iliad* vii. 219–23).

[7] Aias is referring to the incident described by Homer in the sixth book of the *Iliad* (120–236). Diomedes and Glaucus meet on the battlefield, but before they come to blows they hold a conversation from which it transpires that their ancestors were friends. On this account, they agree to avoid each other in the fighting thereafter, shake hands, and exchange armor.

Achilles' body thousands were killed in the dust on every side, like boars around a lion. The conflict that arose among them was deadly.

Then stout-hearted Aias killed Hippolochus' brave son Glaucus, and he fell back upon Achilles. Just as on the mountains a shrub falls about a solid oak; so he, struck by the spear, fell dead upon Peleusson. Aeneas, Anchises' strong son, fought vigorously for him and with brave comrades dragged his body to the Trojan lines and had it carried to Ilion's sacred city by his comrades, whose hearts were filled with sorrow. Aeneas himself fought on around Achilles. But the warrior Aias struck him with a spear above the muscle of his right arm. Aeneas rushed quickly away from the deadly battle and was soon inside the town. Skilled doctors went to work on him. They cleaned the blood from the wound and did all the other things which cure the severe pains of wounded men.

Aias was fighting continuously, killing one man here, another there, like bolts of lightning. His spirit was in great distress, and the heart within him grieved for the cousin Achilles he had lost. Close beside him the noble son of brave Laertes fought against the enemy, and the hosts fled in terror from him. He killed Pisander's swift and warlike son Maenalus, who lived in the famous land of Abydus. Then he killed glorious Atymnius, whom the fair-haired nymph Pegasis bore once to sturdy Emathion beside the stream of the river Grenicus. Beside him he killed Oresbius, Proteus' son, who lived under the folds of lofty Ida. His famous mother, Panacea, did not receive him home again, but he fell before Odysseus' hands. Many another man's life he took with his eager spear, killing anyone who came near the body. But Alcon, son of the nimble fighter Megacles, hit him with a spear by the right knee, and the dark blood gushed out around his bright greave. Odysseus, careless of his wound, quickly became an evil to the man who had wounded him. In spite of his eagerness for battle, Odysseus struck him with a spear through his shield and with the great strength of his powerful hand thrust him to the ground on his back. The armor of the wounded man clanged about him in the dust, and the

300

cuirass on his body grew wet with bloody gore. Odysseus pulled the fatal spear from his flesh and from his shield, and the spirit followed the spear point from his limbs, and his divine life left him. Odysseus, wounded though he was, rushed upon Alcon's comrades and did not leave the noisy battle.

So, too, all the other Greeks as well fought zealously in the melee around great Achilles, and they quickly killed many a soldier with the polished spears in their hands. Just as the winds pour to the ground the swiftly falling leaves when they swoop fiercely upon the wooded groves at the beginning of the year when autumns die; so the steadfast Greeks struck them with their spears. They all, and especially brave Aias, were concerned for the dead Achilles. For this reason Aias naturally kept slaughtering Trojans like an evil Doom. But then Paris drew his bow at him. Aias, though, noticed him at once and hit him on the head with a rock. The destructive rock shattered his double-crested helmet, and night seized him. He fell down in the dust, and his arrows did not help him in his desires, but were poured out everywhere in the dust. The quiver lay stretched out empty beside them, and the bow flew from his hands. His friends, however, seized him and with Hector's horses carried him to the Trojan town, still breathing a little and groaning terribly. They did not leave their lord's weapons either, but fetched them also from the plain and brought them for their king. Aias, in great annoyance, shouted out loudly at him:

"You dog! Today you have slipped out from under the heavy weight of death. But soon your last day will come, either at the hands of some other Greek or my own. At the moment my mind has other concerns: how I may save from the terrible slaughter the body of Achilles for the Greeks."

With these words, he hurled evil dooms upon the enemy who were still fighting around the body of Peleusson. And they grew afraid when they saw many men dying beneath his powerful hands and stood their ground no longer. Like worthless vultures which an eagle, supreme of birds, frightens away when in the mountains they are devouring sheep that have been killed by wolves; so brave Aias scattered them this way and that with swift stones, his sword, and his might. They were full of fear and fled the battle in a body, like starlings which a hawk swoops at and kills, and they, in crowded flocks, rush one upon another, avoiding the great disaster; so they fled from the battle to Priam's city, pitifully clothed in disgraceful panic. They were thoroughly frightened at the attack of great Aias, pursuing them with his hands all spattered with human blood. He would have killed all of them one after another, except that the gates were open wide, and they poured into the city, short of breath because fear had struck their hearts. He penned them in the city as a shepherd pens his bright sheep.

Then he returned to the plain, and his feet did not touch the ground; he walked on armor, blood, and dead men. Over a vast area, all the way from the city of broad squares clear to the Hellespont there lay stretched far and wide a mass of men killed in action, all those whom Doom sent from the gods had taken. Just as when a thick stand of ripe grain falls to the reapers, and the many trusses lie there heavy with ears of grain, and the heart of the man who owns this fine land rejoices as he watches the work; so they, brought low all around by an evil destruction, lay on their faces, forgetful of cruel war.

The noble Greeks did not strip any armor from the Trojans cut down in the dust and blood until they had given to the funeral pyre Peleus' son, who had been such a help to them in battle, as he rushed along in his wild strength. For this reason, the kings fought about his great body and rescued it from the battlefield. They carried it and put it down among the huts in front of the swift ships. Then they gathered all together around it and groaned, with sorrow in their hearts. He had been the strength of the Greeks, and now, forgetful of spears, he lay among the huts by the shores of the thundering Hellespont. So insolent Tityos fell, when he attacked Leto on her way to Pytho, and Apollo, filled with anger, quickly subdued him with his swift arrows, powerful though he was. And Tityos lay in frightful gore, extended over many an acre of the wide earth, who was his mother. She groaned for her fallen son, who was hateful to the blessed gods, but queenly Leto laughed. Just so Achilles fell in the land of the enemy, bringing joy to the Trojans, but incessant sorrow to the mourning army of   400 the Greeks. And the depths of the sea were roaring roundabout.[8]

All their hearts were broken within them, and they foresaw death in battle at Trojan hands. Then, when by the ships they remembered the dear parents whom they had left at home, and their newly wedded wives, who doubtless were wasting away in sorrow on their lonely beds, waiting with their little children for the husbands they loved—when they thought of all this, they groaned all the more, and a longing for lament fell upon their hearts. They cried without stopping, poured out, face down on the deep sand around Peleusson. They pulled their hair from their heads by the roots and defiled their faces with floods of sand. Just as after a battle there is a wailing of persons who have been crowded into a fortress, when the eager enemy are burning a great city and killing people in vast numbers and plundering everywhere; such was the cry of the Greeks by the ships, because their savior, the son of Peleus, lay in his greatness by the ships, killed by weapons divinely made. He looked like Ares when Athena, the terrible goddess with the powerful father, struck him down on the Trojan plain with a painful rock.[9]

The Myrmidons mourned on ceaselessly for Achilles, crowding about the body of their noble lord, a gentle man, who had been like a comrade to them all. He was not arrogant to men or malevolent, but in all matters he had been renowned for good sense as well as strength.

Among the foremost, Aias, groaning loudly, cried out in longing not only for a comrade but for a cousin as well. Struck by a god he had been, not hit by any of the mortals who live on the broad earth. With aching heart, Aias grieved for him then, sometimes going to the quarters of dead Peleusson, sometimes falling in

[8] The text is dubious here, and it may well be that we should assume, with Köchly, that something has been lost before this line.

[9] Another Homeric reference. In the twenty-first book of the *Iliad*, Homer reports a short battle between two groups of gods. The only really serious conflict is that between Athena and Ares. Ares directs a spear at Athena, but Athena hits him in the neck with a huge rock and knocks him to the ground. When Aphrodite comes to help him, Athena knocks her down beside him (391–425).

his great bulk by the sands of the sea. He spoke such melancholy words as these:

"Achilles, great bulwark of the powerful Greeks, you died in Troy, far from the broad plains of Phthia, struck from some unexpected quarter by a hateful arrow. This is the weapon that weakling men use in battle. No man who is confident that he can handle a great shield, arrange his helmet about his temples well and skillfully for war, wield a spear in his hands, and split the bronze about an enemy's breast—no man like that darts away and fights with arrows from a distance. If the man who hit you had come straight at you, then he would not have escaped unwounded from your spear's attack. But Zeus was somehow, I suppose, planning to wreck all this, and is making worthless what our efforts have accomplished. Now he will probably grant the Trojans victory over the Greeks, since he has taken so great a bulwark from us. How the old man Peleus in his halls will be moved, when he comes upon this great sorrow in joyless old age! The very report, perhaps, will destroy his life. Better so, really, to forget his misery at once. But if the bad news about his son does not kill him, a wretched old age indeed will assail him in his grievous troubles, as he eats his heart out in anguish by his fire—Peleus, who was pre-eminently dear to the blessed ones. But the gods do not grant everything to wretched mortals."

So Aias in his sorrow lamented Peleusson. The old man Phoenix, too, wailed loudly, holding in his arms the noble frame of brave Achilles. With deep anguish in his wise old heart, he cried out in his grief:

"My dear child, you are gone, and you have left me a pain I shall never escape. I wish the heaped-up earth had covered me, before I saw your cruel doom. No disaster worse than this has ever come to my heart, not even when I left my native land and my kindly parents and went as a exile through Greece to Peleus.[10]

[10] It is somewhat odd that, in a passage so heavily indebted to parts of a long speech by Phoenix to Achilles in the ninth book of the *Iliad* (434-95), Phoenix should speak here in this way of his parents. According to the *Iliad*, he ran away from home after a most bitter quarrel with his father, followed by his father's curses, which condemned him to childlessness.

He took me in, gave me presents, and made me lord of the Dolopians. And carrying you in his arms around his hall, he put you in my lap and gave me careful orders to look after the baby as if it were my own dear son. I did as he said. And you, happy in my arms, would often say 'Da Da,' still babbling indistinctly. Many a time, too, in your childishness you wet my chest and shirt. I gave many a laugh as I held you in my arms, because my heart was sure that I was rearing one who would look after me during my life-time and protect me in my old age. For a little while, everything went as I hoped, but now you have gone out of sight into the dark. An anguish of grief holds my heart; hideous sorrow afflicts me. I wish it would kill me as I mourn for you, before noble Peleus learns of this. There will be no end to his wailing, I think, when the news about you reaches him. The pain for you will be most pitiable for us, your father and me. Now that you are dead, we in our great sorrow will hurry to go down into the earth before our time. And this would be far better than to live on without you to help us."

So the old man spoke, cherishing in his heart an endless sor-row. Agamemnon Atreusson wept and lamented beside him. His heart within him was ablaze with pain, and he cried aloud:

"You are gone, Peleusson, far the best of the Greeks. You are gone, and you have left our vast army without defense. With you dead, we shall surely be easier for our enemies. You brought much joy to the Trojans in your fall. They were afraid of you before, the way bright sheep fear a lion. But now they will fight en-thusiastically beside our swift ships. Father Zeus, clearly you beguile mortals with lying words. You promised me that I should sack Priam's city, but now you do not fulfill your promise. You have completely cheated my heart. I don't expect to reach my goal in the war, now that Achilles is dead." 500

So spoke Agamemnon, with deep pain in his heart. The sol-diers around brave Peleusson cried out from their very souls. As they uttered their laments around him, the ships re-echoed, and a vast noise went up through the everlasting upper air. Just as when long waves raised by the power of a strong wind rush terribly from the deep ocean to the shore, as the sea crashes constantly all along the coast, and the huge headlands roar along with the breakers; such was the terrible groaning that rose about the body, as the Greeks endlessly lamented fearless Peleusson.

They would probably have continued their wailing until dark night came, if Nestor, the son of Neleus, had not spoken to Atreusson. Nestor's heart, of course, was still full of its vast grief, as he brooded over his son, amiable Antilochus.

"Marshal of the Greeks, supreme commander Agamemnon, let us now give up at once this noisy lamenting for this day. Hereafter no one will prevent the Greeks from thoroughly satisfying their grief by lamentation for many days. But we must now wash the terrible gore from brave Achilles and lay him on his bed. It is not right to shame the dead with long neglect."

These were the suggestions of Neleus' very sensible son. Agamemnon hastened to order his companions to put cauldrons of cold water on the fire at once, heat them, bathe the body, and put on it the beautiful clothing dyed with the purple dye of the sea that Achilles' mother had given to her dear son when he set out for Troy. Speedily they obeyed their lord. When they had done all these tasks carefully and properly, they put the fallen Peleusson on his bed.

Wise Athena Tritogeneia felt pity as she saw him, and she sprinkled ambrosia down over his head. They say that this preserves for a long time the flesh of those overpowered by doom. She made him look fresh and like one who still had the breath of life. She gave the brow of the corpse a terrible frown, such as was on his fierce face when he was angry because of the slaughter of his friend Patroclus. She made his body larger and more handsome to look at. Amazement seized the Greeks as they crowded round and saw Peleusson in every way like a living man. His great form, lying upon his bed, was exactly like one who was asleep.

Then the wretched captive women took their stand around him. He had himself once taken these girls as booty when he captured holy Lemnos and the high fortress of the Cilicians, Eëtion's

Thebe.[11] They now lamented him, tearing their beautiful flesh; they beat their breasts with both hands and groaned from their souls for gracious Peleusson. He had shown them honor, even though they were from the enemy. Of them all, especially sad at heart was Briseis, concubine of the good soldier Achilles. She moved back and forth about the body, tearing her beautiful flesh with both hands, and she cried aloud. Bloody welts rose on her soft breast as she beat it; you would think that red blood had been poured upon milk. Even though she was wretched in her misery, her beauty had a lovely gleam, and grace was all about her. This was what she said, along with pitiful groans:

"Alas, my sufferings are terrible beyond those of all the others. No other sorrow has come upon me—not for my brothers, nor for my country with its broad dancing places—so great as this that your death has brought. You were holy day to me, the light of the sun, life's sweetness, hope of good, and mighty protection against sorrow, far better than all beauty or even my parents.[12] All alone you were everything to me, slave though I was. You took away my slavish tasks and made me your wife. But now some other Greek will take me in his ships to fertile Sparta or to thirsty Argos. Serving him, I shall endure evil miseries, deprived of you and utterly wretched. How I wish the heaped up earth had covered me before I looked upon your death."

So she bewailed the dead Peleusson with the unhappy slave-women and the grieving Greeks, mourning both her lord and her husband. Her sad tears never stopped, but flowed from her eyes to the ground, just as if dark water were flowing from a rocky spring when much ice and snow have spread over it in a rugged place,

[11] Very possibly we should follow Vian in reading *Lesbos* instead of Lemnos. Agamemnon remarks in *Iliad* ix. 128-30 that Achilles captured Lesbos, and Quintus himself tells us in the next book (277) that Achilles had captive women taken from that island.

[12] Though Briseis mentions her parents and her brothers, she says nothing of her husband. In Homer (*Iliad* xix. 291-300), Briseis says that Achilles killed her husband and her three brothers in the sack of her city. Possibly Quintus, like many modern readers, preferred to think that Briseis had not been previously married when she became Achilles' concubine.

and then the frost is melted by the southeast wind and the rays of the sun alike.

It was then that all the daughters of Nereus, who live in the depths of the sea, heard the stir of lamentation. A sad pain fell on all their hearts. They groaned piteously, and the Hellespont resounded in answer. They covered their bodies in dark robes and moved quickly all together through the swell of the gray sea to the place where the Greek army was. The sea separated for them as they went on. They moved with a noise like that of swift-flying cranes who foresee a hard winter. The creatures of the sea groaned dismally about the grieving goddesses. They soon reached their destination, and their laments were loud for their sister's stout-hearted son. The Muses, too, quickly left Helicon and, with unforgettable pain in their hearts, came to do honor to Nereus' bright-eyed daughter Thetis. Zeus took away the Greeks' fear and inspired them with boldness, so that they would not be terrified when they saw this splendid company of goddesses appearing openly in their camp.[13] All the goddesses alike, immortal though they were, mourned about the body of Achilles, and the shores of the Hellespont resounded. All the earth around Achilles' body grew wet with their tears, so great was their grief. As the soldiers mourned around them, all the armor was stained with tears, as were the huts and the ships, for great grief was there. Peleusson's mother embraced her son, kissed him on the lips, and tearfully spoke like this:

"Let Dawn of the rosy robe be glad up in the sky; let broad-flowing Axius put aside his anger because of Asteropaeus and be glad in his heart; let Priam's race be glad.[14] But I will go to Olympus and throw myself at the feet of immortal Zeus. I will groan loudly, because against my will he gave me to be mastered by a mortal man, a man whom pitiless old age has quickly taken. The Fates are close to him, bringing the end of death. But my care is

[13] Homer, too, felt the need of some intervention to keep the Greeks from running in terror before this vast company of goddesses. He says that the aged Nestor reassured the frightened soldiers (*Odyssey* xxiv. 47-56).

[14] The *Iliad* relates how Achilles killed Asteropaeus, grandson of the river Axius (xxi. 139-204).

not so much for him as for Achilles. Zeus promised me in Peleus' halls that he would make my son mighty, since the marriage bed was so distasteful to me. I turned myself first into blowing wind, then to water, then I was like a bird or the rush of fire.[15] The mortal man could not master me on the marriage bed. I took on the appearance of everything that earth and heaven enclose within them, until the Olympian promised me that he would make my son outstandingly glorious and warlike. Well, he really did this, I suppose, because Achilles was the finest of men. But he gave him a short life and brought me pain. So I will go to heaven; I will go into Zeus's house and wail for my dear son. I will remind Zeus in my pain of all I did for him and for his sons when they were in serious trouble.[16] This will stir his heart."

So spoke the sea goddess Thetis in her sad lament. Then the Muse Calliope, whose heart was full of sense, said to her:

"Check your wailing, goddess Thetis, and do not in your frenzy for your son be angry with the ruler of gods and men. Zeus, the loud-thundering lord, has himself lost sons too, destroyed by an evil doom. And my son Orpheus died, though I am myself immortal. Every forest would follow his music, every jagged cliff, and the streams of rivers, the blasts of great whistling winds, and the birds swooping on swift wings. But I endured my great grief, because it does not at all befit a god to have a spirit that aches with wretched griefs and pain. And so, full of sorrow though you are, give up this lament for your fine son. Through my will and that of the other Muses, singers will sing among men forever about his glory and his strength. Do not subject your spirit to dark grief, wailing like weak women. Don't you see that deadly Fate whom none can restrain encompasses all human beings who dwell on the earth? She cares nothing even for gods; she alone has won power

[15] This great aversion to marriage, common in later accounts of Thetis' marriage to Peleus, is not dealt with by Homer, though she does say to Hephaestus that she was most unwilling to marry a *man* (*Iliad* xviii. 429–34), and some readers, ancient and modern, have interpreted this as showing that Homer was aware of the kind of story Quintus tells here.

[16] Quintus is referring to Thetis' help given to Dionysus and Hephaestus on the occasions mentioned above, Book Two, 438–42. See note eight in Book Two.

vast as this. She will, moreover, sack the city of wealthy Priam now, when she has destroyed whatever Greeks and Trojans she wants. No one of the gods will hold her back."

These were the sensible ideas that Calliope expressed. Then the sun went quickly into the streams of Ocean, and in the great sky dark night arose, which helps even sorrowing mortals. There on the sands, the Greeks lay down in crowds around the body, weighed down by their great disaster. But sleep did not take hold of the goddess Thetis; she sat close by her son, along with the deathless Nereids. All around her the Muses, taking turns, earnestly tried to induce her to forget the grief in her sad heart.

When Dawn came through the sky, she was laughing aloud, and she brought a most brilliant light to Priam and all the other Trojans. But the Greeks, in their enormous grief, went on wailing for Achilles and did so for many days. The long shores of the sea groaned roundabout, and great Nereus moaned, doing honor to his daughter, the Nereid Thetis. All the other gods of the sea joined in the lament for the dead Achilles. Then the Greeks gave the body of mighty Peleusson to the fire. They heaped up huge timbers which they brought from Mt. Ida, all of them working alike. The Atreussons had urged them on and sent them to get vast amounts of wood, so that the body of dead Achilles might be burned quickly. They heaped around the pyre quantities of armor taken from men he had killed. They also slaughtered many handsome Trojans and threw them upon the pyre together with neighing horses and strong bulls. Sheep, too, they threw on and pigs heavy with fat. Wailing slave women brought quantities of woven stuffs from chests and threw them all on top of the pyre, and they heaped up gold and electrum upon them.[17] The Myrmidons cut their hair and with it covered the body of their lord. The sorrowing Briseis herself cut the locks of her hair beside the body and

[17] The Greek word means either "electrum," an alloy of gold and silver, or "amber," and it is often difficult to decide which is meant in a given case. Since it appears in this passage along with gold, I have treated it as the metal, but the choice is only arbitrary. The same word is used in the account of the funeral of Aias near the end of Book Five (625), and the description of it there clearly identifies it as amber; so it may well be that Quintus meant amber here, too.

gave them as a last gift to her lord. Then they poured out many jars of ointment and put around the pyre other jars of honey and of sweet wine, whose delicious juice had the bouquet of nectar. They threw on many other fragrant things that men admire, all the sweet-scented things the earth bears and the glorious sea.

When they had got the pyre completely ready, the foot soldiers, along with the cavalry, moved quickly about the sad pyre under arms. Zeus from somewhere on Olympus poured down over the body of Achilles drops of ambrosia, and, showing honor to Thetis, he sent Hermes to Aeolus to summon the holy strength 700 of strong winds. Achilles' body would this day surely burn. Hermes went speedily, and Aeolus obeyed him. He at once called the cruel north wind Boreas and the blustering blast of Zephyrus and sent them rushing in a swift storm to Troy. They dashed away at once and swooped over the sea in a mighty current. Sea and earth alike were noisy about them as they rushed on, and up above all the clouds were driven in wild confusion through the vast sky. In accordance with Zeus's plans, they rushed quickly all together upon the funeral pyre of Achilles, killed in battle, and a blast of fierce flame arose. There arose, too, the incessant lament of the Myrmidons. The winds, although they blew with strong, rushing gusts, worked all day and all night about the body before their united blast consumed it. A huge smoke went up into the glorious air; the enormous pile of wood groaned as it was all mastered by the fire and turned to black ashes. When the stubborn winds had finished their great task, they rushed with the clouds back to their several caverns.

The destructive fire burned the Myrmidon's massive lord last of all, after the horses and young men who had been slaughtered around the corpse and after all the treasures that the weeping Greeks had put around the vast body. When it was consumed, then the Myrmidons quenched the funeral pyre with wine. The bones of Achilles were perfectly apparent, because they were not like the other bones, but like a stubborn giant's. Then, too, no other bones were mixed with them, because the cattle, the horses, the Trojan youths, mixed up with the other creatures who had been

85

killed, lay around the body, but a little apart. Achilles, conquered by the blast of the fire, lay all alone in their midst. His sorrowing comrades gathered all his bones into a strong, capacious chest. It was made of silver and all decorated with gleaming gold. The daughters of Nereus honored Achilles greatly by drenching the bones in ambrosia and ointments. They put in the fat of oxen for their burial and covered them all with warm honey. His mother provided for him a huge jar which Dionysus had once given her as a present, splendid work of skilled Hephaestus.[18] Into this they put the bones of noble Achilles. The Greeks constructed over them a tomb and an enormous monument on the highest headland beside the depths of the Hellespont. Loudly they wailed for the Myrmidons' brave king.

The immortal horses of fearless Achilles did not remain tearless beside the ships either, but they too mourned for their king who had been killed.[19] The grief they felt was so great that they did not care to mingle any more with wretched men or with horses. They wanted to go far from unhappy men, over the streams of Ocean and the caverns of Tethys to the land where, long ago, glorious Podarge bore both these horses, swift as the wind, after union with blustering Zephyrus. And they would soon have done all that their hearts were planning, except that the gods' purpose held them back until Achilles' nimble son came from Scyros. They were actually themselves waiting for him to come to the army, because holy Chaos' daughters, the Fates, had spun for them at their birth this destiny: immortal though they were, they must first serve Poseidon, then bold Peleus and tireless Achilles, and fourth after these, noble Neoptolemus. Later, at Zeus's orders, they were to carry Neoptolemus into the Elysian plain to the land of the blessed. For this reason, even though their spirits

18 Though Quintus makes clear that the funerary urn was of metal by saying that Hephaestus made it, he does not specify the material. Homer speaks of this splendid work of art once in each poem (*Iliad* xxiii. 91–92; *Odyssey* xxiv. 73–75) and says it was of gold.

19 These immortal horses of Achilles appear a number of times in the *Iliad*, and on one occasion, one of them, Xanthus, is temporarily given the power of speech and prophesies to Achilles that he has not long to live. Somewhat similar to their grief here is their grief at the death of Patroclus (*Iliad* xvii. 426–40).

were struck with loathsome pain, they waited for their lord by the ships, sad at heart for the one they had lost, but longing to see the new one.

And then, leaving the mighty swell of the thundering sea, Poseidon, god of earthquakes, came to the shore. Invisible to the men, he took his stand beside the divine daughters of Nereus. And he spoke to Thetis, still grieving for Achilles:

"Check now your endless lament for your son. He will not associate with the dead, but with the gods, just like noble Dionysus and powerful Heracles. No dreadful doom, no Hades, will keep him forever under the darkness, but he will speedily come to the sunlight of Zeus.[20] I personally will give him a present, an island fit for gods in the Euxine Sea, where your son will be a god forever. And all around the tribes of neighboring peoples will greatly glorify him with splendid sacrifices and will give him the same honors they give to me. Do you stop your wailing at once and do not harry your spirit with sorrow."

When he had said this, he went away to the sea, like a breeze. His words encouraged Thetis, and the spirit in her breast had a little respite. The god did as he promised for her. The sad Greeks went away, each to the ship that had brought him from Greece; the Pierian Muses returned to Helicon, and Nereus' daughters sank into the sea, groaning for gracious Peleusson.

[20] The *Odyssey* gives us a picture full of pathos depicting Achilles in the world of the dead. He declares that he would rather work as a laborer for a poor man on earth than be a king in the land of the dead (xi. 488ff.). Quintus' more cheerful version is common in post-Homeric writers.

✱ ✱ ✱

BOOK FOUR

The Funeral Games of Achilles

T HE TROJANS had their misery, too. They did not leave un-
wept brave Hippolochus' mighty son Glaucus, but they put the
glorious man upon a funeral pyre in front of the Dardanian Gate.
Apollo himself, however, very speedily lifted him out of the blaz-
ing fire and gave him to the swift winds to carry to the land of
Lycia. They quickly carried him away to a lovely place under the
glens of Telandrus, and they placed above him an unbreakable
stone. The nymphs caused the sacred water of a never-failing
river to gush out around it. The races of men to this day call it
"the fair-flowing Glaucus." The immortals did this, I think, as a
prize of honor for the king of the Lycians.

The Greeks continued to lament Achilles by their swift ships.
A dismal grief and sorrow oppressed them all. They longed for
him as though he were their own son, and there was not a dry-
eyed man in the whole wide camp. The Trojans, on the other
hand, felt a steady pleasure as they saw the Greeks in misery and
Achilles destroyed by the fire. This is the sort of boastful talk that
went among them:

"Now from Olympus Zeus Cronosson has given to us all an

unexpected pleasure. We longed to see Achilles fallen at Troy. I think with him gone the glorious Trojan people will have a breathing space without deadly bloodshed and murderous battle. His pestilential spear was always raging in his hands and always spattered with hideous gore. No man of us who went against him ever saw the dawn again. But now that Achilles has been cut down, I think the sturdy Greek youths will run away in their beautiful ships. How I wish that mighty Hector had been left to us until he destroyed all the Greeks together at their huts."

This was the sort of talk that came from Trojans whose hearts were overflowing with joy. But there were other sensible men who talked like this:

"You think that the Greeks' deadly army will soon take to their ships and fly home over the misty sea. But they will certainly not be afraid—full of longing for battle, rather. They still have other strong and sturdy men, Diomedes Tydeusson, Aias, and the powerful sons of Atreus. Even though Achilles is dead, I am still afraid of them. How I wish that Apollo of the silver bow would kill them. On that day a breathing space from war and ugly doom might come in answer to our prayers."

So the talk went. In heaven all the gods who were helpers of the powerful Greeks were groaning, and they were so dispirited that they covered their heads in vast clouds. But the gods of the other faction were delighted, boasting that they had given to the Trojans the goal on which their hearts were set. It was then that glorious Hera spoke to Cronosson:

"Father Zeus, lord of the bright lightning, why are you helping the Trojans? You have forgotten the fair-haired girl whom you gave once to godlike Peleus in the glens of Pelion as the wife of his heart's desire. You personally arranged for them a marriage fit for gods, and all of us immortals were at the wedding feast that day, and we gave them many splendid gifts. You have forgotten this and devised great sorrow for Greece."

So she spoke, but unwearying Zeus did not give her any answer. He sat there, sad at heart and full of thought. The Greeks were soon to sack Priam's city, and he was planning to give them dreadful trouble in savage war and on the roaring sea. He was now thinking over in this way these things he did later.

Then Dawn arrived at Ocean's deep stream, and a vast darkness came over the black earth, when mortals have a little breathing space from work. Sad though they were, the Greeks were taking their dinner at the ships. For it is not possible to thrust troublesome hunger away from the eager belly, when once it comes. Our nimble limbs grow quickly heavy, and there is no help except to satisfy the pangs in the belly. So they ate their dinner, in spite of their grief for Achilles. A terrible need was strongly impelling them all. When they had eaten, sweet sleep came upon them, taking the pain from their limbs and restoring their strength.

When the constellations of the Bears held their heads toward the East, awaiting the swift light of the sun, and Dawn arose, then the army of the vigorous Greeks arose, plotting slaughter and the fate of annihilation for the Trojans. Just as the great Icarian Sea moves, or a tall field of ripe grain, whenever a great blast of cloud-gathering Zephyrus comes; so the army moved on the shores of the Hellespont. It was then that Diomedes, the son of Tydeus, spoke to the eager troops:

"My friends, if we are really persistent fighters, let us now all the more give battle to our loathsome enemies. We cannot let them grow bold because Achilles is no more. Come, with our armor, our chariots, and our horses, let us advance upon the town. The work of war, we know, will give us glory."

So he spoke among the Greeks, and sturdy Aias answered him:

"Tydeusson, your words are good and far from idle, when you urge the Greeks to fight the brave Trojans. The Greeks themselves are eager, too, and like hand-to-hand fighting, and the Trojans are able in battle. We must, however, stay at the ships until divine Thetis comes from the sea. Her heart is set on holding splendid contests in connection with her son's funeral. She told me so yesterday, when she was going into the depths of the sea, taking me apart from the other Greeks. I think she is close by and hurrying toward us. As for the Trojans, even though the son of Peleus is dead, they will not grow very bold, as long as you and I and noble Atreusson himself are still alive."

So Telamon's noble son spoke and did not realize at all that   100 destiny was preparing for him after the contests a harsh and evil fate. Tydeus' son then said again:

"If Thetis is really coming today to provide splendid prizes for her son's funeral games, you and I must stay by the ships, and both of us must hold back the others too. It is certainly right to obey the blessed gods. And, in any event, we should be making plans ourselves to give satisfactory honor to Achilles, even apart from the immortals' desire."

So spoke the sturdy heart of brave Tydeusson. Then Peleus' wife came from the sea, like a morning breeze. She came at once into the crowd of Greeks, where they eagerly awaited her. Some were going to compete in the huge contest, others were going to cheer their minds and hearts by watching the contestants. Thetis, wearing a dark veil, brought the prizes and set them down among the assembled men and urged the Greeks to begin the contests at once. They obeyed the goddess.

The first to stand up among them was Nestor, son of Neleus. He had no desire to participate in the exhausting sports of boxing or wrestling. Dismal old age had subdued his limbs and all his joints. But his spirit was still unimpaired in his breast and so was his mind. No other Greek would compete with him, when there was any verbal contest at a meeting. When it was a matter of talk, even Odysseus, the famous son of Laertes, yielded to him in the meeting, as did great Agamemnon of the fine ashen spear, who was the most kingly of all the Greeks. Nestor, consequently, was the one who in their midst sang the praises of the gracious daughter of Nereus—how, among all the goddesses of the sea, she stood out for intelligence and beauty.[1] Thetis was delighted as she listened. He

[1] It is not altogether clear whether this speech of Nestor is meant to be part of the contests, thus giving these funeral games a "cultural" event absent from the funeral games of Patroclus described in book xxiii of Homer's *Iliad*, or a preliminary funeral oration which no one imagines will be contested by any rival orator. Probably the latter.

told of Peleus' lovely wedding, which the blessed immortals joined in arranging on the heights of Pelion; how they ate their immortal dinner at the banquets, when the swift Hours brought divine food in their immortal hands and heaped it beside them in baskets of gold; how laughing Themis busily set up the silver tables; how Hephaestus lit a fresh fire; how the Nymphs mixed ambrosia in golden goblets; how the Graces turned to lovely dance and the Muses to song; how all the hills rejoiced, and the rivers, and the wild beasts; how the infinite air was cheered, along with the splendid cave of Chiron and the gods themselves.

All these things Neleus' able son related to the eager Greeks, and they were delighted as they listened. He told, too, in the midst of the gathering, of noble Achilles' imperishable deeds, and the great army shouted with pleasure. Wonderfully, and in appropriate style, he glorified the famous man. He began by telling how he sacked twelve cities of men in attacks by sea and eleven cities spread over a wide area on land; how he cut down Telephus and strong, famous Eëtion on the plains of Thebe;[2] how he killed with his spear Poseidon's son Cycnus, godlike Polydorus, handsome Troilus, and noble Asteropaeus; how he made the streams of Xanthus grow red with gushing blood and covered the whole noisy river with countless corpses, when he took away Lycaon's life beside the roaring river; how he killed Hector and Penthesileia and the divine son of the Dawn with the beautiful throne.[3] These were the things he told to the Greeks, who knew them well themselves. He spoke also of how huge Achilles was; how no one had the strength to compete with him, either in the young men's contests, when they held foot races, or in chariot racing, or in hand-to-hand fighting; how he was far the handsomest of the Greeks,

---

[2] In a military context, the verb used regularly means "kill," and Achilles did kill Eëtion. He did not, however, kill Telephus, but only wounded him, as Quintus himself soon reminds us (175-77).

[3] Some of these exploits are related by Homer in his *Iliad*: Polydorus xx. 407-18; Lycaon, xxi. 34-135; Asteropaeus, xxi. 139-204; Hector, book xxii. Andromache reminds Hector how Achilles killed her father Eëtion (vi. 414-20), and Priam refers to the fact that Troilus is dead (xxiv. 257). Neither Telephus nor Cycnus appears in Homer, but they are familiar figures in the post-Homeric Troy Story.

and how infinite his strength was in the swift rush of war. Finally he prayed to the gods that he would see another such man when Achilles' son came from wave-swept Scyros.

The Greeks, of course, shouted their approval of all he said, and silver-footed Thetis did too. She gave him the swift horses that Telephus had once presented to Achilles of the good ashen spear by the streams of the Caicus river. (Telephus had been suffering from a nasty wound that Achilles had given him in battle, driving his heavy spear right through into his thigh, and then Achilles had cured Telephus with the spear with which he had hit him.) Nestor Neleusson gave the horses to his comrades, and they took them to the ships, loudly singing the praises of their godlike king.

Thetis then put in the midst of the gathering ten cows, the prize for the foot race, and each one had a fine suckling calf with it. Tireless Peleusson, brave and strong and full of confidence in his great spear, had once driven them from Mt. Ida in a raid.[4]

Two men arose to compete for them, burning with desire for victory: first, Teucer Telamonson, and then Aias—the Aias who was pre-eminent among the Locrian archers. Quickly they girded their clothes about their loins, carefully hiding their sex organs, as is proper, out of respect for powerful Peleus' wife and all the other Nereids of the sea who had come along with her to see the Greeks in contests of strength. Atreusson, who was lord of all the Greeks, showed them the goal of the fast course, and lovely Eris urged them on. They darted swiftly from the starting point like hawks, and the race was closely contested. The Greeks, watching on each side, cheered on their favorites. When the eager runners were approaching the goal, then the immortals, I fancy, entangled the **200** powerful limbs of Teucer. For a god or some mischievous spirit threw him painfully against a shoot of a deep-rooted tamarisk. Crashing into this, he fell to the ground. The tip of his left foot was bent painfully backwards, and the veins stood out, swollen, on each side. The Greeks at the contest gave a shout, and Aias darted

---

[4] These are probably the cows mentioned twice in the *Iliad* in connection with an encounter on Mt. Ida between Achilles and Aeneas (xx. 89–92; 187–90).

happily past him. His Locrian followers ran up together, and all their hearts felt a quick delight. They drove the cows off to be fed near the place where the ships were assembled. The limping Teucer was quickly led away by his bustling companions. Doctors speedily removed the blood from his foot and put on top of shredded linen an abundance of wool that they had soaked in oils. Then they carefully tied a bandage round it and relieved the terrible pains.

Over on the other side, two other stout-hearted men had quickly turned their thoughts to strenuous wrestling: Diomedes, the son of the horse-tamer Tydeus, and powerful Aias. They came into the center, and wonder held the Greeks when they saw them, because they were both like blessed gods. They threw themselves upon each other like ravenous wild beasts that fight in the mountains over a stag. The strength of the two is equal, neither is in the slightest inferior to the other, and they are both deadly; so equal was the great strength of the two men. But at last Aias seized Tydeusson in his sturdy arms, doing his best to break his ribs. But Diomedes, combining skill with strength, bent down a little and, thrusting his shoulder under Aias' arm muscles, suddenly lifted up Telamon's mighty son. Then, moving his thigh the other way to disentangle it from Aias' foot, he threw the powerful man to the ground and sat on top of him.[5] The spectators raised a shout.

Aias was very angry. He got up again, his bold heart set on a second bout, with no holds barred. He quickly covered his terrible hands with dust and in a great rage shouted for Tydeusson to come into the ring. Diomedes was not a bit afraid, and rushed to meet him. The dust rose in clouds from under their feet. They rushed together as fearlessly as bulls which come into one place in the mountains, trying out their bold strength and kicking up the dust. The peaks around them echo their bellowing and, full of uncontrollable eagerness, they bring their tireless heads and great

[5] The details, and even the text, of this wrestling bout are uncertain. I basically follow the interpretation of Köchly. A somewhat different text and interpretation are given by Vian.

strength together, putting forth all their effort against each other for a long time. They pant furiously from the exertion of their fierce fighting, and floods of foam pour from their mouths to the ground; so Aias and Diomedes were fighting with all the might of their powerful arms. Their backs and their sturdy necks cracked under the noisy blows of their hands, just like trees in the mountains striking their vigorous branches together. Many a time Tydeusson got his powerful hands under the strong thighs of great Aias, but he was never able to push him over backwards, he stood so firmly on his feet. And Aias, charging down upon him from above, shook him by the shoulders and tried to press him to the earth. Then again they tried other attacks with their hands. The soldiers who watched them raised great shouts, some on this side cheering famous Tydeusson, others on that side cheering powerful Aias. Then Aias, when he had shaken sturdy Tydeusson this way and that by the shoulders, got his hands under his belly and suddenly, with his great strength, threw him down on the ground like a stone. The Trojan earth roared loudly as Tydeusson fell, and the soldiers shouted. But even so, Diomedes leapt up, eager to fight huge Aias a third time. But Nestor stood between them and said to them both:

"Enough, my glorious sons, enough of strenuous wrestling. We all know how far the best of all the Greeks you are, now that Achilles is dead."

So he spoke, and they stopped their effort. With their hands they wiped off the sweat that was streaming down from their faces, and then they kissed each other and ended their competition in friendship. The queenly goddess, divine Thetis, gave them four captive women. The powerful and fearless heroes themselves marveled as they looked at them, because in intelligence and accomplishments they were the best of all the captive women, except for fair-haired Briseis. Achilles had taken them once as booty out of Lesbos, and they had brought his heart much pleasure. One of them had been in charge of his meals and food, another had poured the pleasant wine at his dinners, another had poured water over the diners' hands after a meal, and the fourth always removed the tables when a meal was over. Strong Tydeusson and powerful Aias divided the prize and sent the women to their beautiful ships.

The first man to stand up for the boxing contest was strong Idomeneus. He was skilled in all contests, and so no one came to oppose him. They all readily yielded to him out of awe, because he was an older man.[6] Thetis put in the ring for him the chariot and fast horses that great strong Patroclus had a short time before driven away from the Trojans after he had killed glorious Sarpedon. Idomeneus gave them to an attendant to take to the ships, while he stayed on himself at the splendid games. Then Phoenix spoke among the sturdy Greeks:

"This time the gods have given Idomeneus a fine prize without his doing anything for it. He did not work with the strength of his hands and shoulders. He did not need to spill any blood; they honored an older man. But, you young men, you must arrange another contest. Direct against each other your hands skilled in boxing and warm the heart of Peleusson."

300   So he spoke, and as they listened they looked at one another. They would all have remained quiet and refused the contest, if Nestor, the son of glorious Neleus, had not rebuked them:

"My friends, it is not proper for men skilled in war to shun the pleasures of boxing. Young men enjoy boxing, and it brings fame as well as weariness. I certainly wish I had in my limbs the strength I had when I joined my cousin Acastus in holding the funeral games of his father, godlike Pelias. As that time when I competed in boxing against glorious Polydeuces, the match was a draw, and I got a prize equal to his. In wrestling, even Ancaeus, who was stronger than all the others, marveled at me and feared me, and he did not dare to compete with me, because once before among the heroic Epeians I beat him, good though he was. He covered his back with dust when he fell near the funeral mound of dead Amarynceus, and many men around him marveled at my

---

[6] Idomeneus is described in the *Iliad* as "half-grey" (xiii. 361), and he does not participate in any of the contests at the funeral games of Patroclus. It seems odd that Quintus, though noting that he is rather old, should have chosen him as the entrant in the boxing match.

strength and power.[7] So he was no longer willing to lift his hands against me, strong though he was, and I got the prize without dirtying my hands. But now old age and its troubles are upon me, and so I have asked you, who are fitted for it, to try for prizes with the strength of your hands. It is a distinction for a young man to carry off a prize from a contest."

At these words of old Nestor, a bold man stood up, Epeius, son of daring and godlike Panopeus. (Later he fashioned the horse that brought evil to Priam's town.) Although he was not at all able in hideous war, when a battle was raging, no one ventured to compete with him in boxing.[8] And on this occasion, glorious Epeius would have carried the splendid prize to the Greek ships without sweating for it, except that the son of glorious Theseus came up to him, the spearman Acamas, his heart full of great and growing strength. He had around his nimble hands the dry leather thongs which Agelaus Evenorson had cunningly put round his palms, urging on the prince. In the same way, the comrades of Panopeus-son were encouraging the lord Epeius. He stood in the ring like a lion, and had on his hands the dry thongs from the hide of an ox killed in its prime. The men on either side were giving great shouts, urging the powerful men to use their strength to cover their tireless hands with blood. They stood in the narrow ring, full of eagerness themselves. They both tested their arms to see if they were nimble as before and had not grown heavy from battle.

Suddenly they raised their hands against each other. Watching each other carefully and walking on tiptoe, they kept moving slowly about, for some time avoiding each other's great strength. Then they clashed like racing clouds, which rush upon each other, driven by the blasts of the winds, and emit lightning, so that the wide sky is thrown into confusion as the clouds rub against each other, and a deep roar comes from the winds; so their jaws resounded under the blows of the dry leather thongs. Blood

[7] Nestor boasts of this victory over Ancaeus (and many other victories) in a speech to Achilles at the funeral games of Patroclus (*Iliad* xxiii. 635).

[8] Epeius defeats Euryalus in the boxing match at Patroclus' funeral games (*Iliad* xxiii. 664–99). His making of the wooden horse is mentioned in the *Odyssey* (viii. 493; xi. 523).

streamed down, and a bloody sweat from their foreheads made their fresh young faces red. But they fought on with enthusiastic persistence. Epeius did not pause, but kept pressing Acamas with all his raging strength. But Theseus' son was so skillful in the contest that he often caused Epeius to drive his mighty hands into the empty air, and then, cunningly getting through both his hands, he leapt upon him, struck his brow, and reached the bone. Blood flowed down from Epeius' eye. But even so, Epeius caught Acamas with his heavy hand, hitting him on the temple, and knocked him to the ground. But he jumped up at once, leapt upon his mighty opponent, and hit him on the head. As he was drawing back, Epeius bent aside a little and, with his left, hit him on the forehead and then jumped at him and drove his right at his nose. Acamas, though, was using his hands in defense with every sort of skill.

They wanted to fight on with each other for the pleasure of victory, but the Greeks stopped the bout. Their attendants quickly took the bloody thongs from their sturdy hands, and they had a little time to catch their breath after their effort, wiping their faces with porous sponges. Their dear companions then brought them face to face, urging them to forget their grim anger at once and become friends. They listened to their comrades' persuasions. Sensible men always have gentle minds. They kissed each other, and their hearts forgot their fierce combat.

Thetis, wearing her dark veil, quickly satisfied their desires with two silver mixing bowls. Euneus, Jason's powerful son, had given them to godlike Achilles on the island of Lemnos as the purchase price for sturdy Lycaon. Hephaestus had made them as a present for glorious Dionysus, when he brought to Olympus his splendid wife Ariadne, Minos' famous daughter, whom Theseus had once involuntarily left behind on the island of Dia. Noble Dionysus gave them full of nectar as a present to his son Thoas, and Thoas gave them with much treasure to Hypsipyle. She left them to her glorious son Euneus, and he gave them to Achilles as Lycaon's ransom. The son of famous Theseus took one of these bowls, and able Epeius sent the other with delight to his ships.

Podalirius properly and quickly healed all the wounds their blows had produced. First of all, he personally sucked out the blood, then he stitched the wounds together with his skillful hands and put upon them those drugs that his father had given him long ago.   400 With them, even men's incurable wounds are speedily healed in one day from deadly evil. So the wounds that these men had around their faces and under the thick hair of their heads were completely healed at once, and the pains were assuaged.

For the archery contest, Teucer and Aias, Oïleus' son, stood up—those who had previously competed in the foot race. Agamemnon of the good ashen spear set far off from them a helmet with a horsehair crest and said:

"The man who cuts off the hair with the sharp bronze will be by far the best."

Aias was quick to shoot his arrow first. It hit the helmet, and the bronze rang sharply. Then Teucer, with spirit most intent, shot his arrow. The sharp missile quickly cut away the horsehair crest. The people, when they saw it, gave a loud shout and praised him greatly, because the hurt his swift foot had received in the race still pained him, but it did him no harm as he directed the swift missile. Peleus' wife gave him the beautiful armor of godlike Troilus. He was the finest by far of Hecabe's unmarried sons in holy Troy, but she got no good from so splendid a son, because fearless Achilles' spear and strength together robbed him of his life. Just as when in a dewy, flourishing field that grows luxuriantly, close to an irrigation ditch, someone with a freshly sharpened scythe cuts off a stalk of grain or a poppy before it ripens and does not allow it to reach its sweet goal and come to another sowing, but reaps it when it is empty and has no seed for men yet to come, when it might have grown in the dewy spring; so Peleusson killed Priam's son who looked like the gods, still beardless, still with no knowledge of a bride, still youthful as a child. Fate brought him to destructive war when his joyous youth was just beginning, the time when men are bold, and their courage is full-grown.[9]

---

[9] The space and loving care that Quintus devotes to Troilus are a kind of anticipation of the day when Troilus (only a name in Homer) will become one

Next, many men tried to hurl from their nimble hands a very large and heavy piece of metal, but it was so massive that no Greek was able to throw it. The firm fighter Aias alone threw it from his mighty hand, just as if it were a piece of dry forest oak in the warm season of summer, when all vegetation in the land is dried up. Everybody was amazed when the bronze flew from his hands, a weight so vast that two men had to work hard to lift it in their hands. Long ago strong Antaeus used to throw it easily from his hands, when he was testing his strength, before he was subdued by the powerful hands of Heracles. Noble Heracles took it with much other booty and kept it as a prize won by his tireless hands. Later he gave it to brave Telamon when he joined with him in sacking the famous, well-fortified city of Troy. Telamon gave it to his son Aias, and he brought it in the fast-sailing ships to Troy, so that it might remind him of his father, as he zealously fought against the powerful Trojans, and might also give him a task when he was testing his strength. This was the weight Aias threw a long way from his sturdy hand. Then Nereus' daughter Thetis gave him the splendid armor of godlike Memnon. The Greeks looked upon it with much wonder, because every piece was unusually large. The glorious man laughed aloud as he received it. He was the only man who could put it about his huge body and have it fit his massive frame. He took, too, the great weight of metal, that he might enjoy it when he wanted to exercise his vast strength.

Many men stood up to compete in the broad jump. Agapenor of the good ashen spear leapt far beyond the marks of the others, and the people raised a shout for the man who had jumped so far. Divine Thetis gave him the beautiful armor of great Cycnus. He had robbed many of their lives after killing Protesilaus, and he was the first prince whom the son of Peleus killed. His death had filled the Trojans with sorrow.

In the javelin throw, Euryalus far surpassed his competitors. The people shouted aloud, for they did not think his throw would

---

of the leading characters in the medieval Troy Story. There was a tradition in antiquity that after killing Troilus Achilles cut his head off. Some have found an allusion to this in Quintus' simile of the grain or poppy cut with the scythe.

be surpassed even with a feathered arrow. And so brave Achilles' mother gave him a capacious bowl to carry away. It was made of silver, and Achilles had got it once as booty, when he struck down Mynes with his spear in the sack of the rich city of Lyrnessus.

Stouthearted Aias was eager for the difficult work of fighting with hands and feet alike, and so he stood up and called the best of the heroes into the arena. They looked with wonder on the strength of the powerful man, and no one dared to come against him. A terrible dread broke the manly courage of them all, and their hearts were afraid that he would strike someone with his tireless hands and by his blows immediately crush the man's face and bring him great pain. Finally, they all nodded toward bold Euryalus, knowing that he was an expert boxer. But he, frightened of brave Aias, stood among them and spoke like this:

"My friends, I'll stand my ground against any other Greek you want, when he comes against me, but I'm afraid of great Aias. He is far superior. He'll destroy my life, if he gets angry while attacking me, and I don't expect to get safe to the ships from the hands of that tireless man."

They laughed at him when he said this, and brave Aias' sturdy spirit was greatly pleased. He lifted up the two talents of bright silver that Thetis gave to him for winning the contest without any effort. As she looked at Aias, however, Thetis was reminded of her dear son, and sadness fell upon her heart.

Next, those whose hearts were interested in chariot racing 500 leapt up speedily at the challenge of this contest: Menelaus first, and bold Eurypylus, Eumelus, Thoas, and godlike Polypoetes. They threw the straps around their horses and hitched them to the chariots, all pressing on for the glorious victory. Mounted in their chariots, they quickly went together along a sandy place into the plain. Then they all took their stand at the starting post and at once grasped the reins in their sturdy hands. The horses, held close to the chariots, were restless, waiting for one to jump forward. They kept their feet in useless motion, pricked up their ears, and made their frontlets wet with froth. Suddenly the drivers lashed their vigorous, light-footed horses. They leapt away immediately like rushing Harpies, much annoyed at their harness straps. They drew the chariots so swiftly that they kept bouncing up from the ground. No wheel tracks or signs of hoof prints were visible on the ground, the horses ran so fast. A great cloud of dust from the plain rose to the sky, like smoke, or a mist which the force of Notus or Zephyrus pours around the crags in the mountains, when a storm is coming on and the mountains are wet with rain. Eumelus' horses leapt far in front, and those of godlike Thoas followed. As the chariots flew through the wide plain one man cheered for one, another for another. [A number of lines (Vian has shown that they were almost certainly forty-eight) containing the description of the race are missing at this point. When the narrative resumes, someone is praising Menelaus' horses and speaking of the chariot race between Pelops and Oenomaus. It becomes clear a few lines later that Thoas and Eurypylus were thrown from their chariots during the race.] "... from glorious Elis. It was truly a great thing that Pelops did in defeating the swift chariot of malevolent Oenomaus, who in those days used to destroy without mercy the young men who wanted to marry his daughter Hippodameia, an intelligent girl. But Pelops, interested though he was in racing, had no such swift-footed horses as these. His were, I know, far less speedy, because these are like the winds."

This was what he said in giving great glory to the strength of these horses and to Menelaus Atreusson himself. And Menelaus was delighted. Attendants quickly took from the harness his panting horses, and all the others who had competed in the chariot race unhitched their fast teams personally. Podalirius soon healed all the wounds that godlike Thoas and brave Eurypylus had suffered when they fell from their cars and were badly torn. Atreusson felt a steady joy at his victory. Fair-haired Thetis gave him a beautiful golden goblet, an important possession of godlike Eëtion, before Achilles sacked the famous city of Thebe.

Now in another part of the field other men were getting their race horses ready and directing them to the racecourse. They took in their hands oxhide whips and leapt up and sat on their horses. The horses, frothing at the mouth, were champing the bits in their jaws and noisily pounding their feet on the earth, eager to be off. The race immediately became a tense one, as they dashed speedily from the starting post, full of zest for the competition. They were like the blasts of strong-blowing Boreas or blustering Notus when it stirs up the broad sea with tempest and noisy gales at the time when the malign constellation called the Altar rises and brings grief and tears to sailors; so they swept along on speedy feet, raising a vast dust in the plain. The several riders called out orders to their horses, while raining blows of the whip with one hand and with the other constantly shaking the noisy bridle about the horses' jaws. The horses sped on. A mighty shout rose through the crowd, as they flew through the level plain.

The fast horse from Argos, ridden by Sthenelus, would soon have won an easy victory if he had not repeatedly pulled off the course and gone into the plain. Sthenelus, son of Capaneus, was a good rider, but he did not have the strength in his hands to force him back, since the horse was still a novice at racing. He was certainly not from bad stock, but came from the divine race of swift Arion, which a Harpy bore to loud-roaring Zephyrus as far the best of all horses. Arion used to race with his swift feet against the storm blasts of his own father Zephyrus. Adrastus had him as a gift from the blessed gods, and from this Arion came Sthenelus' horse. Diomedes, the son of Tydeus, had given it as a present to his comrade Sthenelus at holy Troy. Sthenelus, having complete confidence in the horse's speed, brought the fast racer to the games and entered him in the horse race, thinking that among the princes he would himself win great glory for his horsemanship. But his efforts in the funeral games of Achilles did not cheer his heart. He stayed in second place, and Atreusson skillfully rode past him, for all his speed. The people glorified Agamemnon, Sthenelus' horse, and bold Sthenelus himself because he had come in second, even though his horse had often swerved off the course in his frenzy of strength and speed. Then Thetis gave to laughing Atreusson the silver breastplate of Polydorus, descended from gods, and she gave to Sthenelus the stout bronze helmet of Asteropaeus, two spears, and a durable belt.

Thetis gave presents also to the other horsemen and to all those who, that day, had come to compete around Achilles' grave. Odysseus, son of wise Laertes, was pained at heart by all this. He longed to have his strength back, but was kept from the contests of the powerful by the severe wound that vigorous Alcon had given him as he was fighting around the body of mighty Achilles.

✱✱✱

BOOK FIVE

The Defeat, Madness, and Suicide of Aias

WHEN THE OTHER CONTESTS were finished, then it was that the goddess Thetis set in their midst the immortal armor of heroic Achilles. There was a bright gleam everywhere from all the decorations that strong Hephaestus had put on the shield of brave Achilles.[1]

First of all, the heaven and the sky had been skillfully fashioned on this work of art made by a god, and the sea was put there along with the land. The winds were on it, and the clouds, the moon, and the sun, all in their separate places here and there, and he fashioned all the constellations that move around in the revolving heaven. Underneath them, too, was spread the vast sky, in which long-beaked birds flew. You would say they were living birds rushing along with the winds. Tethys and the deep flow of Oceanus had been placed around the edge. From them poured out the streams of the noisy rivers, winding their circling courses here and there through the land.

[1] Homer tells in his *Iliad* how Thetis came to Hephaestus' home on Olympus and asked him to make new armor for Achilles, and he then describes in detail the designs on the shield (xviii. 369–613). The shield described by Quintus has altogether different designs. Quintus' decision to change the designs and to devote a hundred lines to describing them may seem to some readers to be among his less happy inspirations.

On high mountains around the shield, terrible lions and impudent jackals had been skillfully fashioned. There were dangerous bears and leopards, too, and along with them powerful boars, noisily whetting their savage clattering tusks in their fierce jaws. Behind these animals on the shield there were hunters directing their strong hounds, while others were busily throwing stones and swift javelins at the animals, just as if it were real.

Also on it, of course, were destructive battles and grim conflicts. Men and swift horses, all mixed together, were being killed, and an entire plain on the durable shield looked as though it were drenched in blood. Phobos (Terror) and Deimos (Dread) were on it, along with the war goddess, cruel Enyo, all their limbs spattered with hideous blood. Deadly Eris, goddess of strife, was there and the stubborn Furies; Eris was urging men to come into uncontrolled conflict, and the Furies were breathing out a blast of fatal fire. Pitiless Dooms were darting about, and among them ranged strong and dismal Death. Around him were placed shrieking Combats, and from all of their limbs blood and sweat were streaming to the ground.

The ruthless Gorgons were on it, too, and about them, in the locks of their hair, terrible snakes had been fashioned, their tongues darting dreadfully. These decorations were a vast marvel and produced great fear in men, because they were like living creatures in motion.

These, then, were all the marvels of war that he fashioned. Separate from them were the works of beautiful peace. Countless races of long-suffering human beings were shown living in fine cities, and Justice was watching everything. The various persons were turning their hands to their various tasks. The fields around were heavy with crops, and the black earth was in flourishing condition.

There was also fashioned on this work of art made by a god the very steep rugged mountain of holy Virtue. She herself stood upon it, her feet set on top of a palm tree. She was very tall, reaching up to heaven. Around her everywhere trails, interrupted by numerous crags, kept men away from the noble path, because many drew back, frightened by the steep approaches, and only a few, with much sweat, were moving up the sacred way.

There were reapers on the shield, moving up along a broad swath and working rapidly with freshly sharpened sickles. Under their hands, the harvest of ripe grain was being completed. Many others followed them to bind the sheaves. A great deal of work was being done. Oxen were on it, too, their necks always under yokes. Some were drawing wagons heavy with sheaves of grain in full ear, while others were plowing the fields. The earth grew black behind them, and men followed them, carrying ox-goads that they moved from hand to hand. A vast amount of work was apparent.

Flutes and lyres could be seen, and feasts, and beside the feet of young men stood groups of dancing women, who moved vigorously, just as though alive. Close by the dancing and the gay feasting, Aphrodite of the beautiful crown was coming up out of the sea, her hair still covered with foam. Desire, smiling his lovely smile, was hovering near her, and with him were the fair-haired Graces.

On it, too, were the daughters of high-spirited Nereus, bringing their sister Thetis up out of the broad sea to her wedding with brave Peleus. All the immortals were feasting on the tall height of Pelion, surrounded by well-watered, flourishing meadows covered with the innumerable flowers of the grass, and by groves and springs of beautiful, limpid water.

Ships in distress were being swept over the sea, some of them drifting fast, others moving on a straight course. The violent, rising waves were growing bigger. Frightened sailors here and there were terrified by the swooping storms; just as though they were real they were drawing in the white sails to escape from death. Others were sitting at the oars pulling hard, and around the ships that were being vigorously driven by the oars the black sea grew white.

Poseidon the earth-shaker, exulting in all this, was represented among the sea creatures. Horses fast as the winds were carrying him swiftly above the sea, driven by the lash of his golden whip, just as if they were real. The sea was leveled around them as they rushed on, and there was flat, calm water before them. Gathered about their lord on both sides, crowds of dolphins fawned upon their king with vast delight, and, made of silver though they were, they looked as if they were swimming along the dark swell of the sea.

A thousand other wonders had been put upon this shield, so full of art by the immortal hands of wise Hephaestus. Set like a garland around them all was the deep stream of Oceanus. It ran along the outside on the rim, and within it the whole shield had been set and all the decorations attached.

Thetis set down beside the shield the great, heavy helmet. Zeus had been fashioned on it, standing in heaven and looking like one who was very angry. The immortals were hard at work around him, toiling along with Zeus against the rebel Titans. They were already surrounded by the mighty fire, and thunderbolts were pouring steadily from heaven like snowflakes, because Zeus's strength was roused beyond telling. The Titans, though like creatures on fire, were still breathing. Thetis stood against the helmet the beautiful hollow breastplate, unbreakable and massive, large enough to hold Peleusson.

Hephaestus had also made huge greaves. They were so heavy that only Achilles found them light. Close beside them, Achilles' invincible sword was shedding its brilliant gleam all around. It was fitted with a baldric of gold and a scabbard of silver, and the ivory hilt that was attached to it shone conspicuously even among these divine arms. Stretched alongside these on the ground was the heavy spear of Pelian ash, looking like tall fir trees and still redolent of the blood and gore of Hector.

Then Thetis, wearing her dark veil and sorrowing for Achilles, made this divine speech among the Greeks:

"Now you have finished all the contests in the funeral games that, in my great grief, I arranged for my dead son. Next I want that man to come forward who saved his body and is the best of the Greeks. I will give him these splendid immortal arms to wear. They brought great pleasure even to the blessed deathless gods."

So she spoke, and two men jumped up ready to argue for them: the son of Laertes, and Aias, son of godlike Telamon, who towered above all the Greeks, conspicuous as a star in the gleaming heaven—Hesperus, the evening star, which shines most brilliantly among all the stars. This is the way Aias looked, as he took his stand beside the arms of Peleusson. He asked for Idomeneus as judge and the son of Neleus and wise Agamemnon, for he believed they had accurate knowledge of the work he had done in glorious battle. Odysseus also had complete confidence in them, because among the Greeks they were sensible and incorruptible. Idomeneus and the glorious son of Atreus were both eager to act as judges, but Nestor took them apart from the others and spoke to them:

"My friends, the carefree heavenly ones are certainly bringing to us today a huge and uncontrollable disaster: great Aias and brilliant Odysseus are rushing headlong into an irrepressible and troublesome conflict. Whichever of them heaven permits to get what he prays for will rejoice in his heart, but the other one will cherish a great sorrow, blaming all the Greeks, but us far beyond all the others. He will not take his stand among us in battle as before, either. No matter which of them this grim anger seizes, there will be enormous sorrow for the Greeks, because among all the heroes these two are pre-eminent, the one in battle, the other in counsel. I suggest to you that you listen to me; I'm a great deal older than you, not just a little, and, besides my advanced years, I'm a sensible man. I've been through a lot, good and painful both. In making plans, a well-informed old man is always better than a younger one, because of his vast knowledge. I suggest, therefore, that we allow the intelligent Trojans to decide this dispute between godlike Aias and war-loving Odysseus. Let them say which one the enemy is most afraid of, and which one saved the body of Peleusson from deadly battle. We have many Trojan captives in fresh subjection. They will give a fair judgment between them. They have no reason to favor anybody, because they loathe all Greeks equally, remembering their ruin."

When Nestor had finished speaking, Agamemnon of the good ashen spear said to him:

"Sir, how true it is that there is no other Greek among us, either young or old, shrewder than you, who now say that whichever of these men the gods cause to lose the victory will be recklessly angry at the Greeks. And our best men are in competition for the arms. The heart within me is eager to do this—to turn the decision over to our captives. Anyone who finds fault with them will plan deadly deeds against the Trojan soldiers and will not direct his anger against us."

So he spoke, and they, in complete agreement, publicly refused to undertake the painful decision. On their refusal, distinguished Trojans, captives though they were, took their seats among them to decide what was right in this soldiers' quarrel.[2] Then Aias, deeply annoyed, spoke out among them:

"Odysseus, so feared for your intelligence, why has a god tricked your mind into thinking you are my equal in stubborn strength? Do you really claim that you kept the terrible crowd away from Achilles, when he lay in the dust, and the Trojans stood around him? I sent a painful death upon them, while you were cowering out of sight. And no wonder, because your mother bore you as a coward and a weakling, as much inferior to me as any dog is to a roaring lion. The heart in your breast is not courageous; your whole concern is trickery and wicked deeds. Or have you forgotten this—that you tried to avoid going against Troy's sacred city with the mustering Greeks?[3] You were cowering down, and the Atreussons had to lead you much against your will. I wish you had never come. It was because of your sugges-

[2] Among those whom Odysseus sees in his visit to the world of the dead in the *Odyssey*, Aias is one of the most memorable figures. The other ghosts converse freely with Odysseus, but Aias' ghost stands apart, "angry because of the victory which I won when we competed by the ships for the arms of Achilles" (xi. 543–46). Odysseus pleads for a reconciliation, but Aias moves off without even answering. In Homer as in Quintus, the decision was given by Trojans, although Homer says "Trojans and Pallas Athena."

[3] Homer has no mention of this effort to dodge the draft. The common later story was that when a group of princes came to get Odysseus to join the expedition against Troy, they found him plowing the sands by the sea and sowing salt. Palamedes went to Odysseus' house, got the baby Telemachus, and placed him a short distance ahead of the plowing team, confident that Odysseus was really sane and Telemachus really safe. So it proved, and Odysseus joined in the war—but he never forgave Palamedes.

tions that we left Philoctetes, famous son of Poeas, on holy
Lemnos, filling the air with his groans.[4] And he wasn't the only
man for whom you contrived terrible outrage. You also brought
destruction on godlike Palamedes, your superior in strength and
in intelligent planning.[5] And now on this occasion you dare to
come against me, not remembering what I did for you, and with   200
no respect at all in your heart for one who is far better than you
are. I was the one who saved you once in battle, when you were
frightened by the enemy's tumult. During the fight you had been
isolated, the others had abandoned you in the confusion of the
enemy, and you were running away yourself. I wish now that
Zeus in the sky had personally frightened my bold spirit in that
battle, so that the Trojans with their two-edged swords could have
cut you to bits and scattered the pieces as a feast for their dogs.
You wouldn't then be eager to oppose me, relying on your tricks.

"You scoundrel, why, when you boast that you are better
than others in strength, do you keep your ships in the center of
our line? Why didn't you have the courage to draw them up on
the outside as I do? You were afraid. And you didn't keep the
terrible fire from our ships, either. I stood against fire and Hector
both, with fearless spirit. Hector always retreated before me in
battle, but you were always terribly afraid of him. I wish some-
body had set this contest for us in battle, when the conflict arose
around fallen Achilles, and you saw me carrying the beautiful
armor and brave Achilles as well to the huts, away from the enemy
and the horrible tumult. As it is, you're grasping at great deeds
because of your confidence in your ability with words. You don't
have the strength to get into the stubborn armor of brave Achilles
or to handle his great spear. They are all of a size to fit me, and it's
right for me to wear this splendid armor; I won't shame the god's
beautiful gifts. But why do we both stand here quarreling with
evil words for the fine armor of noble Achilles, to determine which

[4] Philoctetes will begin to become important in Quintus' story in the second
half of Book Nine.
[5] A character who is not mentioned in either Homeric poem. Later stories
do not agree about the manner of his death, but there is general agreement that he
was killed treacherously and that Odysseus was responsible.

of us is the better man in destructive battle? Silver-footed Thetis set this contest before us as a soldiers' contest of strength, not of cruel words. Words are what men need in assemblies. I know how much more noble, how much better, I am than you; my stock is the same as that of great Achilles."

So Aias spoke. The son of Laertes, using his wily arts, reproached him with cutting and malicious words:

"You babbler, Aias, tell me, why are you talking so long to no purpose? You said I was worthless and annoying and feeble. I am proud to say that I am far better than you in plans and talk, and these are the things that multiply men's strength. By using skill, quarrymen in the mountains easily cut out a sheer rock that is unbreakable; with their skill, sailors cross the great roaring sea when waves are high; with their arts, huntsmen subdue powerful lions, leopards, boars, and other kinds of wild animals; spirited oxen are brought under the yoke by the will of men. It's with his mind that man accomplishes everything. Always, in every kind of work and planning, a man with wide knowledge is better than a thoughtless one. This is why, out of all the army, Diomedes, the brave son of Tydeus, selected me and my good sense to help him get right up to the Trojan guards; it was a great deed that we did together.[6] And I was the one who brought the famous son of sturdy Peleus himself to help the Atreussons.[7] If the Greeks ever need another hero, he won't come because of the strength of your hands, nor because of the plans of the other Greeks, but I alone of the Greeks will bring him, persuading him with my soothing words to join in the battle of men. Speech has great power among men when it is used intelligently. A man's strength is useless and his size comes to nothing if they are not accompanied by a shrewd intelligence. To me, however, the gods gave strength and intelligence as well, and made me a great help to the Greeks.

[6] A reference to the nocturnal scouting expedition described in the tenth book of the *Iliad*.

[7] Odysseus wisely does not dwell on the details of this affair (not mentioned by Homer), because it puts the dead hero in a bad light. Thetis, eager to keep her son from going to war, arranged for him to live, disguised as a girl, on the island of Scyros in the palace of the king. The ruse was uncovered by Odysseus.

"Moreover, you did not, as you say, save me as I was running from battle. I didn't run, but I stood my ground as all the Trojans rushed upon me. They streamed at me in their eager strength, and with the might of my hands I took the lives of many. What you say is not true. You did not protect me in the fighting, but you stood there looking out for yourself, making sure that no one hit you with a spear as you were running out of the battle.

"As for the ships, I did not draw mine up in the center because I had any fear of the enemy's power, but so that I could constantly make plans for the war along with the Atreussons. It is true that you stationed your ships out on the edge. But I inflicted terrible wounds on myself and then went into the Trojan citadel to find out all the plans they were making for the grim war.[8]

"I was not afraid of Hector's spear, but when in the confidence of his manhood he challenged us all, I was one of the first to jump up, eager to fight him.[9] And just now I killed far more of the enemy than you did beside Achilles' body, and I saved the dead man along with his armor. I'm not afraid of your spear either, but I am still encompassed by the pains from the severe wound that I received because of this armor and dead Achilles. Finally, Achilles and I share the distinction of Zeus's blood."

So he spoke, and mighty Aias answered him:

"Odysseus, you trickster, you're the most annoying man in the world. I didn't notice you at work in that fighting, nor did any other Greek, when the Trojans were trying to drag away Achilles' body. I was the one who, with spear and strength, made their legs grow slack in the conflict. I kept attacking them, and put them to flight. They were terribly frightened; they were like geese or cranes attacked by a eagle, when they are feeding in a field by the

---

[8] When Odysseus' son Telemachus is a guest of Helen and Menelaus in Sparta ten years after the war, Helen tells Telemachus how his father disfigured himself with blows and came into Troy disguised as a beggar. He was recognized by Helen alone (*Odyssey* iv. 244–64).

[9] Hector's challenge and the Greek reaction are related in the seventh book of the *Iliad* (54–205). As Homer tells it, none of the Greek princes was eager to fight Hector. In the list he gives of those who finally volunteered, Odysseus is named last. Aias is chosen by lot to represent the Greeks and is doing rather better than Hector when the duel is broken off because it is getting dark.

banks of a river. That's the way the Trojans cowered down before
300 my spear and swift sword and avoided doom by going inside of
Troy. If you actually were feeling strong at that time, you were
not fighting the enemy anywhere near me. You were off at a dis-
tance somewhere, fighting with other ranks, not around the body
of godlike Achilles, where the really hot fighting was."

So he spoke. But Odysseus had a cunning reply:

"Aias, I don't think I'm your inferior in either intelligence or
strength, although you are very distinguished. In intelligence I am
vastly your superior among the Greeks; in strength, there may be
room for argument, or I may actually be more illustrious. And I
fancy the Trojans know this, too. They're terrified of me, even if
they see me at a distance. You yourself, too, have a clear knowl-
edge of my physical strength, since I gave you hard work in the
difficult wrestling match, when Peleusson held the famous games
at the funeral of dead Patroclus."[10]

So spoke the famous son of godlike Laertes. Then the sons of
Troy gave their decision on the grim quarrel of the heroes: victory
and the immortal arms they awarded with complete unanimity to
the able fighter Odysseus. His heart was vastly pleased. But the
army gave a groan. Mighty Aias stood stock-still, overwhelmed
with sudden and terrible bewilderment. All his blood seethed
within him, harsh bile gushed out, and his bowels were con-
founded with his liver. A horrible ache came to his heart, and a
sharp pain, darting through the roots of his brain, enveloped its
membranes. His mind was in confusion, his eyes were fixed on the
ground, and he stood like a man who could not move. His com-
panions, sorrowing around him, led him to the shapely ships,
earnestly encouraging him. Much against his will, his feet went
this way for the last time, and Doom followed close behind him.

When the Greeks had gone to the ships and the vast sea, ready
for their dinner and for sleep, then it was that Thetis went down
into the great sea, and the other Nereids went with her. Many sea

---

[10] *Iliad* xxiii. 700–39. Achilles declares the match a draw, although the
description appears to give Odysseus the edge. His superiority, however, seems at
least in part due to low cunning.

creatures that the salt swell breeds swam about them. The Nereids were very angry at Prometheus the planner, remembering it was at his suggestion that Zeus had given Thetis in marriage to Peleus, even though she objected. Cymothoe, in great annoyance, spoke among them:

"Well, it is clear now that the scoundrel deserved the sufferings he had in chains of adamant, when the great eagle, going down into his belly, tore his liver as it grew!"

So spoke Cymothoe to the dark-haired goddesses of the sea. Then the sun swiftly disappeared, the fields were covered in shadows, night rushed upon the earth, and the stars were spread over the sky. The Greeks were sleeping by their long-prowed ships, overpowered by divine sleep and by the sweet wine which sailors used to bring over the surging sea from the Crete of glorious Idomeneus.

Aias, however, wrathful at the Greeks, of course did not think of pleasant food in his hut, nor did sleep enfold him. In his rage he put on his armor, took his sharp sword, and brooded over unspeakable deeds: should he set fire to the ships and destroy all the Greeks, or quickly kill guileful Odysseus alone, cutting him to bits with his grim sword? These were the plans he was pondering, and he soon would have carried them all out, if Athena had not thrown upon him an ungovernable madness. She felt concern in her mind for long-suffering Odysseus, remembering the sacrifices that he regularly made to her. For this reason, she turned the might of great Telamonson away from the Greeks.

Aias moved like a tempest, heavy with terrible and loathsome squalls, which brings a portent of chill terror to sailors, when the Pleiads, cowering down before famous Orion, sink into the streams of tireless Ocean. The air is thrown into confusion, and the sea rages in a storm; like that Aias rushed wherever his legs carried him. He ran around everywhere, like a reckless wild animal that runs through the bends of a deep ravine, foaming at the jaws and planning many pains for the dogs or the hunters who dragged its young out of their cave and destroyed them. The animal runs about roaring, in the hope that it may still see its dear young in the thickets, and if anyone meets it when it is in this frenzied state, it is a sad day in his life; so Aias was raging unmercifully, and his black heart was boiling. Just as a cauldron rages steadily at a hearthfire, boiling furiously from the heat of a blazing fire, when many a log burns all around its surface, serving the plans of a workman eager to remove the bristles from a fine fat pig; so the great spirit in Aias' breast was seething. He raged like the vast open sea, or a hurricane, or the rushing might of tireless fire, when the force of a great wind rages steadily in the mountains and a huge forest falls, blazing on every side with fire; so Aias, his stout heart pierced with pain, raged in anguish. Froth streamed from his mouth, he noisily gnashed his teeth, and his armor rang on his shoulders. All those who saw him trembled at his cry, although it was of only one man.

Then Dawn of the golden reins came from Ocean, and Sleep went up the broad heaven like a breeze. He met Hera, just arriving at Olympus from holy Tethys, where she had gone the previous day. She took hold of him and kissed him. She could find no fault with her son-in-law, ever since he had put Zeus to sleep in a bed on the peaks of Ida when he was angry with the Greeks.[11] Then Hera went quickly to Zeus's home, Sleep hurried to Pasitheë's bed, and the races of men awoke.

Aias was stalking about like tireless Orion, with a baleful madness still in his heart. He leapt among the sheep, like a bold lion whose savage heart has been overpowered by harsh hunger. It throws the sheep down in the dust here and there one upon another, just as the power of mighty Boreas makes the leaves pour down, when summer is over and winter is coming on; so Aias, in his frenzy of distress, leapt upon the sheep, thinking he was hurling evil dooms upon the Greeks.

Then Menelaus, standing close to Agamemnon and concealing his words from the other Greeks, spoke to his brother like this: "Today will surely soon be a day of doom for everyone, since

11 This meeting seems to have no point except to remind the reader of the fine account in the fourteenth book of the *Iliad* relating how Hera, with the help of Sleep, seduced her husband so as to draw his attention away from the battlefield and make it possible for Poseidon to give further help to the hard-pressed Greeks.

great Aias is raging mad. He will soon set fire to the ships, and he will kill us all in our quarters, because he is so angry over the arms. I wish that Thetis had never set a contest for them and that Laertes' son had not with witless spirit ventured to compete against a much better man. As it is, we have been ruinously foolish, and some evil power tricked us. For, with Achilles dead, the only bulwark in war still left to us was Aias with his fine strength. But the gods will destroy him, too, and bring evil upon us, so that we may all meet our doom and disappear."

When he said this, Agamemnon of the good ashen spear replied to him:

"Do not, Menelaus, for all the great pain in your heart, be angry at Odysseus, the shrewd king of the Cephallenians, but at the gods. They are planning doom for us. Odysseus is not responsible. He has often been of great use to us and brought much grief to our enemies."

So they were talking in their grief for the Greeks. But the shepherds over by the streams of Xanthus were cowering under the tamarisks, trying to avoid serious hurt. Just as when hares cower among the thick scrub in fear of a swift eagle, and he utters shrill cries as he flies this way and that, close to them, stretching out his wings; so they, here and there, ran in terror from powerful Aias. At last he stopped beside a ram he had killed, and, with a burst of deadly laughter, he spoke to it like this:

"Lie then in the dust, food for dogs and birds. Not even Achilles' glorious armor saved you, for which you foolishly competed with a much better man. Lie there, you dog. The wife of your youth will raise no lament over you. She and your son will not embrace you in unrestrained sorrow, nor will your parents. You will not satisfy their desire to have you with them as a fine help in their old age. You have fallen far from your native land, and the birds and the dogs will devour you."

So he spoke and thought that guileful Odysseus lay covered with blood among the creatures he had killed. It was then that Tritonian Athena scattered from his mind and eyes grim death-breathing Madness. She went swiftly to the steep streams of Styx where the Furies live, who always send evil sorrows upon over-proud mortals.

Aias, when he saw the sheep in their death struggles on the ground, was utterly astounded. He suspected it was a trick played by the blessed gods. All the strength in his limbs was broken, and his warlike spirit was struck with pains. In his misery he had no power to move forward or backward, but he stood like a peak which in the mountains stands far the highest of all. When his spirit recovered, he gave a terrible groan and spoke sad words like these:

"Why, why am I so hated by the immortals? They damaged my mind and inflicted on me an evil madness that made me kill the sheep which I do not feel are responsible at all for my passion. How I wish my hands had got vengeance on Odysseus and his trouble-making heart. He is a man full of mischief, and he has overwhelmed me with ruin. I wish he might suffer in his heart all the pains that the Furies devise for troublemakers. I wish, too, that they would give deadly conflicts to the other Greeks and sorrows to make them weep—and to Atreusson Agamemnon himself. I pray he will not come easily home to the house he longs to reach. But why, with all my bravery, do I associate with those I loathe? No deadly Greek army for me, and no life grown intolerable. The brave man no longer wins the prize, but the inferior man is honored and better liked. Odysseus is honored among the Greeks, and they have completely forgotten me and all that I did and suffered for the Greek army."

With these words, the brave son of sturdy Telamon thrust through his neck the sword he had received from Hector, and the blood gushed noisily out.[12] He was stretched in the dust like Typhon, whom Zeus's thunderbolts consumed. The dark earth round about groaned loudly as he fell.

Then the Greeks came in crowds, when they saw him fallen

---

12 At the end of the inconclusive duel between Hector and Aias in book vii. of the *Iliad*, the two men exchange gifts, Hector giving Aias a sword and Aias giving Hector a belt (303–305). Homer says nothing more about these presents, but the later stories were that Achilles used the belt to tie Hector's body to his chariot, and that Aias used the sword to kill himself.

in the dust. Before this, no one had come close to him, because the sight of him frightened every man. As soon as he was dead, however, they fell down at once beside him, and, lying face down, they poured quantities of dust upon their heads, and the laments of the grieving men went up to the glorious sky. Just as when men drive away the young lambs of fleecy sheep to provide a meal for themselves, and the robbed ewes leap high and bleat steadily about the strong pens; so they, all together, groaned loudly around Aias that day. Loud echoes came from shadowy Ida, the plain, the ships, and the vast sea.

Teucer was strongly resolved to meet his sad doom beside   500
Aias, but others kept him from the great sword. In his misery, he collapsed by the dead Aias, shedding many tears. They fell faster than those of a child who pours ashes down over his head and shoulders at the hearth, overwhelmed with sorrow at his day of orphanhood. The mother who raised him is dead, and he had no knowledge of his father. So Teucer wailed for his dead brother, creeping about the corpse. He spoke words of sorrow like these:

"Aias, strong of spirit, why was your heart so hurt that you brought about your own ruin and death? Was it that the Trojans may have some respite from their trouble and may come and kill the Greeks, now that you are dead? When they are being killed, they will no longer have the courage they used to have in war. You were their protection against harm. And the goal of going home no longer pleases me, now that you have died here. I want to die in this place myself, so that the life-bringing earth can cover me along with you. I do not feel so much concern for my parents, if they still exist and, still living, still dwell in Salamis, as I do for you, who are dead. Because you were my glory."

He said this with deep groans. Glorious Tecmessa groaned in accompaniment. She was noble Aias' wife. Even though she was his captive woman, he married her and put her in charge of all the things which dowered wives look after in their homes for their legally wedded husbands. Taken in his mighty embraces, Tecmessa had borne him a son, Eurysaces, the perfect image of his father. (He was still small and had been left in his bed.) Tecmessa collapsed by the corpse of her husband with deep groans, pressing her body into the dust and defiling her beauty. In the great sorrow of her heart, she cried out these words of grief:

"How wretched I am, now that you are dead—not killed by enemy hands in battle, but by yourself. So an unforgettable anguish assails me. I did not expect you to die in Troy and leave me looking on a day so full of groans. But the malevolent fates have poured all this evil upon me. How I wish that the fertile earth had gaped open for me first, before I saw your cruel doom. No other disaster has ever come to me worse than this, not even when you first dragged me far away from my native land and my parents, along with the other captive women. I was full of sadness, because I had previously been a revered queen, and now the day of slavery had come upon me. But not even my pleasant country nor my parents who are gone concern me as much as your death. In my misery, all your planning was of ways to please me. You made me your wife to share your thoughts, and said that when you got home from Troy you would immediately make me queen of delightful Salamis. But a god failed to accomplish this for us. You are vanished and gone. You feel no concern for me now, or for your son. His heart will have no joy in a father, and he will not succeed to your lordly power. Others will make a wretched slave of him, since when their father is no more, children are cared for by far inferior men. Grim orphanhood makes life heavy for children, and troubles pour in upon them from every side. And miserable me—the day of slavery will soon come upon me, because you have died before me, you who were for me a god."

When she had said this, Agamemnon, who felt kindly toward her, said to her:

"Tecmessa, no man will ever make you a slave while noble Teucer and I are still living. We will always honor you with the greatest privileges; we will honor you and your son like gods, just as though Aias, who was the Greeks' strength, were still alive. How I wish that he had not brought grief to all of Greece by destroying himself with his own hand. The vast army of our enemies did not have the power to subdue him in war."

So he spoke, and his heart ached within him. The soldiers all around groaned piteously, the Hellespont re-echoed their laments, and a terrible sorrow spread over them. Sorrow, moreover, took hold of shrewd Odysseus himself at Aias' death, and with aching heart he spoke like this among the sad Greeks:

"My friends, how true it is that never yet has there been anything worse than anger, which fosters evil quarrels among men. It is this which even now stirred up great Aias; his heart was full of anger against me. How I wish the Trojan youths had never given me the glorious victory connected with Achilles' armor. Pained to the heart on this account, the brave son of sturdy Telamon perished by his own hands. I am not myself, however, in any way to blame for his anger. It was rather some sad Fate which destroyed him. If the heart within me had ever expected him to be overwhelmed with wrath in his mind, I should never have come to compete for victory. Nor should I have allowed any other Greek who wanted to compete to do so. Instead I should have personally taken up the divine armor and gladly presented it to him and given him anything else he wanted. And even as it was, I did not, myself, in the least think that he would be hurt and angry afterwards. I was not, after all, fighting him for his wife or his country or great wealth. I looked on it as a dispute over ability. Contests over this are always pleasant for sensible men. But Aias, for all his excellence, under the influence of a supernatural power did wrong in the eyes of a hateful Fate. It isn't right to take an annoyance deeply to heart. It is the part of a sensible man, even if many sorrows come upon him, to endure them with a stubborn spirit and not give way to grief."

So spoke the famous son of godlike Laertes. When they were all sated with laments and dismal sorrow, then Nestor spoke to the still melancholy Greeks:

"My friends, we see now how the Fates in their pitiless spirit have been quick to inflict upon us sorrow upon hateful sorrow. Aias is dead, and powerful Achilles, other Greeks as well, and my own son Antilochus. But it is not proper to wail and be troubled in spirit all our days for men killed in battle. Instead, we must for-

600

get lamentation that has grown unseemly, because it is better to do all that is proper for dead mortals—give them their funeral pyre and their grave marker and solemnly bury their bones. A corpse is not raised up by laments, nor does it know how to notice anything, when the pitiless Fates open their jaws for it."

This was the advice he gave. The godlike kings, their hearts full of sorrow within them, immediately gathered in a group around Aias, and, big though he was, they carried him swiftly to the ships, since many were helping to lift him. They cleaned off the dried blood and the dust which, with his armor, covered his mighty frame, and then they veiled his body with a shroud. Then the men brought vast quantities of wood from the Idaean hills and heaped it everywhere around the body. Many were the logs they placed about him, many the sheep and the well-made robes, fine herds of cattle, horses proud of their swift feet, gleaming gold, and innumerable arms of warriors, all that the glorious man had previously taken from the men he had killed. Besides these, they put around him transparent amber. Men say that amber is the tears of the daughters of Helios, god of divination. They shed these tears for dead Phaethon, grieving for him by the stream of great Eridanus, and Helios, fashioning an imperishable honor for his son, made the tears amber as a great possession for human beings. It was this substance that the Greeks threw upon Aias' broad pyre, exalting the glorious fallen hero. Then, deeply groaning, they put around him precious ivory and lovely silver, great jars of ointment, and all the other things that increase glorious and splendid wealth.

Then they threw on the power of strong fire, and a breeze came from the sea. The goddess Thetis sent it to consume great sturdy Aias. His body burned by the ships through the night and the morning under the blowing wind. Just as, I suppose, long ago Enceladus was subdued by Zeus's grim lightning on the tireless sea beneath Thrinacia, and the whole island was filled with smoke from it. Or just as Heracles, crushed by the tricks of Nessus, gave his living frame to be burned in the fire, daring so great a deed, and all of Oeta groaned round about as he burned alive, and his spirit left the famous hero Heracles and was mingled with the air. He himself was accepted among the gods when the earth had opened for his weary body. So Aias, forgetful of battle, lay with his armor in the fire, while the vast army lamented on the beach. The Trojans were gay; the Greeks, sorrowful.

When the destroying fire had completely consumed the heroic body, they quenched the pyre with wine. They put his bones into a golden box and heaped up over them a vast mound of earth, not far from the Rhoetaean headland. Then they scattered at once to their nimble ships. Their hearts were sad, because they honored him equally with Achilles. Black night rushed upon them, bringing sleep to men. They had their dinner and awaited the dawn, sleeping only a little while and barely closing their eyes. They were dreadfully afraid that the Trojans might attack them by night, now that Telamonson was dead.

✷✷✷

BOOK SIX

The Arrival and the Victories of Eurypylus

D AWN, LEAVING OCEAN'S STREAM and the bed of Tithonus, mounted the great heaven, and her bright light was spread everywhere. The earth and the sky began to laugh. And men, who perish easily, turned to work and took up their various tasks. The Greeks poured into the assembly at the summons of Menelaus. When the whole army was gathered together, then he arose among them and spoke to the assembled men:

"Kings, descended from gods, listen to what I have to say. The heart in my breast is greatly disturbed, as the soldiers die who came to this grim war for my sake. Their home will not receive them back, nor will their parents. The doom of a supernatural power has crushed many of them. I wish the heavy might of intolerable death had swooped upon me before I gathered the army here. As it is, a supernatural power has imposed upon me pains without end, as I look upon many evils. What man could find joy in his heart when he looks for a long time on deeds of battle that leave him helpless? I urge that all of us who are still left fly at once on our fast ships, each one to his own country. Aias is dead, and powerful Achilles. With them killed, I do not expect us to escape destruction, but to be destroyed by the cruel Trojans—all for me and the bitch Helen. I feel no concern for her, but I do for you, when I see you being killed in battle. Let her go to her doom with her worthless lover. A supernatural power took all the good sense from her mind when she left my home and bed. Priam and the Trojans will concern themselves with her affairs. As for us, I urge that we go home at once, since it is far better to escape from hateful war than to die."

So he spoke, testing the Greeks, but the heart in his breast was full of other thoughts.[1] His jealous spirit was brooding over killing Trojans, breaking from their foundations the town's high walls, and, above all, sating Ares with the blood of glorious Alexander fallen among the dead. (Nothing is more full of loathing than jealousy.) These, then, were the thoughts he had as he sat down in his place. Next the spearman Diomedes Tydeusson rose among them and was quick to rebuke Menelaus, dear to Ares:

"You cowardly son of Atreus, why has wretched terror come upon you? Why do you say such things among the Greeks? You talk like a child or a woman, whose strength is feeble. But the splendid sons of the Greeks will not be persuaded by you. They will throw all Troy's towers to the ground first. Boldness is a great glory to men; flight is a disgrace. And if any man here is persuaded to do as you command, I'll cut off his head at once with the dark iron and throw it out as food for the high-soaring birds. Come now, those who are interested in stirring up men's courage, be quick to urge all the soldiers among the ships to sharpen their spears and get their shields and all their other gear in good order. Then have all the men and horses who are eager for battle take a quick meal. In the plain, Ares will very soon pass judgment on our courage."

So spoke Tydeusson, and then resumed his former seat. Then Calchas, the son of Thestor, made a speech like this to them, standing in the center, where it is proper to address a meeting:

[1] This idea of testing the army's morale by proposing that the war be abandoned and everyone return home appears in the second book of the *Iliad*, where the suggestion is made by Menelaus' brother Agamemnon. The picture of Menelaus as greatly concerned about all the deaths he has caused is altogether in keeping with the picture of him given in both the *Iliad* and the *Odyssey*.

"Listen to me, my friends, you Greeks steadfast in war. You are aware that I know how to announce prophecies clearly. Even before now, I said that in the tenth year we should sack lofty Troy. The immortals are now causing this to happen, and victory is at the Greeks' feet. We must, however, send Tydeusson and the good soldier Odysseus to Scyros at once in a black ship. They will persuade Achilles' powerful son and return with him. He will bring a great light of help for us all."

So spoke the wise son of Thestor. The soldiers around him were noisy in their joy, because they believed in their hearts that Calchas' statement was true, just as he said. Then the son of Laertes addressed the Greeks:

"My friends, there is no reason to make a long speech to you today. Grief brings weariness. I know that when men are tired a speaker gives no pleasure, nor even a singer whom the deathless Pierian Muses love. At a time like that, what men want is brevity. So now I pray that I may carry out the task which has the approval of all the Greeks in the army, particularly with Tydeusson accompanying me. With both of us going, we will bring war-loving Achilles' powerful son. Our words will persuade him, even though his mother, with many a wail, may try to keep him in their halls. I am confident in my own mind that the son of a mighty sire is a warrior."

When he had finished, shrewd Menelaus said to him:

"Odysseus, you are a great benefactor of the sturdy Greeks. If the powerful son of great-souled Achilles, because of your persuasions, comes from Scyros to help us who long for him, and if one of the heavenly gods gives victory in answer to our prayers, and if I reach the land of Greece, I will give him as a wife my splendid daughter Hermione. I will also gladly provide many precious gifts along with her. I do not expect him to look with haughty disdain upon either his wife or his fine father-in-law."

So he spoke, and the Greeks approved his words. Then the assembly was dissolved, and the men scattered to their ships, eager for a meal, which provides strength for men. When they finished and were completely satisfied, then the son of Tydeus, along with wise Odysseus, drew a fast ship into the great sea. Quickly they put into it provisions and all the gear, and they went aboard themselves. With them were twenty men skilled in rowing, when the 100 winds are adverse and when a calm makes smooth all the broad ocean. When they had taken their seats at the well-made benches, they struck the great surface of the sea. An abundance of foam boiled around them, as with their oars on both sides they made their way over the water. The ship sped on, as the sweating oarsmen rowed. Just as when very weary oxen under the yoke vigorously drag forward a wooden wagon whose turning axle squeaks under the burden, and sweat streams down to the ground from the necks and shoulders of both the toiling oxen; so the men worked hard, then, at the heavy oars, and they made their way very rapidly over the broad sea.

The other Greeks stopped watching their progress and sharpened the javelins and spears that they used in battle. The Trojans within the town were fearlessly preparing for war, full of eagerness and praying to the blessed gods to be relieved from slaughter and to have respite from their toil.

In answer to their desires, the gods brought them a great protection against disaster—Eurypylus, of the stock of powerful Heracles. A numerous army followed him, skilled in pursuit, all those who live by the streams of long Caïcus and put their trust in their stout spears. The young men of Troy thronged around him in great delight. Just as when tame geese shut in a pen see the man who throws them their food, and they stand quacking around him and fawn on him, and his heart is warmed as he watches; so the Trojans were glad when they looked upon powerful Eurypylus. His bold heart was pleased, too, at the men who gathered around him. Women marveled from doorways at the glorious man. He moved swiftly, outstanding among his army, like a lion that comes among jackals in the mountains.

Paris welcomed him and honored him as he had honored Hector. He was, indeed, his cousin and came from the same stock. His mother, Astyoche, was the glorious sister of Priam. She had lain in the mighty embraces of Telephus, who himself had been born to bold Heracles by fair-haired Auge without her father's knowledge. While Telephus was small and still eager for milk, he was fed at one time by a nimble doe who loved him equally with her own fawn and offered him her udder. This was Zeus's plan, since it was not appropriate for a son of Heracles to die wretchedly. Paris, then, with most willing heart, led Telephus' glorious son through the city's broad squares to his home. They passed by the monument of Assaracus, the tall house of Hector, and the holy shrine of Athena, near which were Paris' home and the inviolate altar of Zeus, the household guardian. Paris questioned Eurypylus eagerly about his brothers, his parents, and his other relatives, and Eurypylus gave him a full account. The two men conversed thus with each other as they went along.

They came to the great and wealthy house. There, of course, Helen sat like a goddess, wearing the beauty of the Graces. Four servants were busy around her, and there were others as well outside of her splendid room, working at all the tasks that belong to slave women. Helen marveled greatly as she looked at Eurypylus, just as he did when he looked at her. They spoke words of greeting to each other in the fragrant house. Then slaves placed two chairs close to the queen, and Alexander quickly sat down, and Eurypylus sat beside him.

His soldiers made their camp in front of the city, where the stout-hearted Trojan guards were. They quickly placed their gear on the ground and beside it stationed their horses, still breathing hard from their painful work. Then they threw into feeding troughs the things that swift horses eat.

Then night rushed upon them, and the earth and sky grew dark. They took their meal in front of the steep wall, Cetaeans and Trojans both, and there was much talk as they ate. Everywhere strong fires blazed before their tents. The shrill shepherd's pipe raised its music, and clarionets fitted with clear-toned reeds, and all around was the lovely sound of the lyre. The Greeks watching from afar marveled at the sound of men and horses, of clarionets, lyres, and the pipe that has its place at shepherds' feasts. Each commander, therefore, ordered the men at his quarters to guard the ships by turns until dawn, afraid that the noble Trojans might come and set fire to the ships, since they were then feasting out in front of their high wall.

So likewise in the halls of Alexander brave Telephusson feasted with the famous kings. Priam and the other Trojan men prayed earnestly one after another that he would join in battle against the Greeks and bring a grim doom upon them. He undertook to do it all. When they had had their dinner, they went severally to their homes. Eurypylus lay down there in a handsome room a little apart, where previously noble Alexander himself used to sleep beside his famous wife. It was a splendid room—far the best of all those in the palace. There he went and lay down. His hosts took their rest elsewhere until Dawn of the fair throne.

At Dawn's coming, Telephusson leapt up and went with all the other kings in Troy to the wide camp. The soldiers at once eagerly put on their armor, all of them longing to be among the foremost in the toil of battle. So, too, Eurypylus put upon his huge frame his armor, which was like flashing lightning. There were many designs on his glorious shield, representing everything that bold and mighty Heracles had done in times past.

On it there were two snakes, their tongues darting in their 200 grim jaws, terribly intense and looking as though they were moving to strike. Heracles, although only a baby, was subduing one snake with one hand and the other with the other. His mind and heart were fearless, because he was like Zeus in strength right from the beginning. The stock of the heavenly gods is not at all ineffectual and helpless, but its strength is vast even while still in the womb.

The strong Nemean lion had been represented on the shield, too, suffering greatly under the powerful arms of mighty Heracles. There was a bloody froth around its savage jaws, and it looked as though it were breathing its last.

Next to it had been worked the form of the Hydra and its many necks. Its tongues darted terribly. Some of its grisly heads had been destroyed and lay on the ground, but the few remaining necks were producing many more heads. Heracles and bold Iolaus were hard at work, both of them full of mighty thoughts. One was swiftly cutting off the eager heads with a toothed sickle; the other was burning the wounds with red-hot iron, and the beast's strong attack was being stopped.

Next in order was fashioned a strong and tireless boar, frothing at the jaws. Great, sturdy Heracles was carrying it alive to Eurystheus, just as though it were real.

A swift deer had been beautifully fashioned. It had been doing vast damage to all the vineyards of the wretched people in the neighborhood. The mighty hero held it by its golden horn, even though it breathed out a blast of deadly fire.

Nearby were the loathsome Stymphalian birds. Some, hit by arrows, were breathing out their lives in the dust, others, still interested in getting away, were swooping through the gray sky. Angry Heracles was shooting one arrow after another at them, and he looked like a man full of zeal.

The great stable of godlike Augeas had been skillfully fashioned on the indestructible shield. Powerful Heracles was bringing against it the deep stream of divine Alpheus, and the nymphs nearby were marveling at this great deed.

Some way off was the fire-breathing bull. Invincible though it was, Heracles was forcing it down with his strength, holding its mighty horn, and the muscles of both his arms were strained by the pressure. The bull appeared to be bellowing.

Near it Hippolyte was represented on the shield, wearing the beauty of the gods. In his eagerness to rob her of her beautiful belt, Heracles was dragging her with his powerful hands down from her swift horse by the hair. The other Amazons were standing apart, trembling with fear.

Nearby were the grisly man-eating mares of Diomedes in the land of Thrace. Heracles killed them at their loathsome mangers, and their evil-minded king along with them.

On the shield, too, was the body of tireless Geryon, lying dead by his cattle. His heads had been subdued by Heracles' club and lay in the dust, covered with blood. Before him, his dog Orthros had been laid low, the most destructive of all dogs. His strength was like that of grim Cerberus, who was, of course, his brother. Close by lay the herdsman Eurytion, covered in blood.

Nearby had been formed the gleaming golden apples of the Hesperides on their untouchable tree. Beside it the dreadful dragon lay subdued. The Hesperides were cowering here and there, frightened by great Zeus's bold son.

And, of course, Cerberus was on the shield—a vast horror even for immortals to see. Echidna had borne him to tireless Typhoeus in a horrible cavern close to black, grim night. He was a hideous sort of monster who, at the fated gates of sad Hades, kept back the throng of dead in their dark pit. Zeus's son subdued him easily with blows and brought the bewildered animal beyond the steep streams of Styx, boldly dragging him by force against his will to an unaccustomed place.

Apart from this, the long valleys of the Caucasus had been fashioned. Heracles, having shattered on every side the bonds of Prometheus, along with the very rocks that held them, was setting the great Titan free. Close by lay the grim eagle, his body pierced by the painful arrow.

The powerful Centaurs had been pictured also, shown in their great strength around the hall of Pholus. Wine and Eris, goddess of strife, had roused these monsters to fight Heracles. Some of them lay beaten among the pine trees which they held in their hands as weapons of battle. Others were still fighting enthusiastically with long firs, and had not stopped from the conflict. The heads of all were drenched in gore, as they were struck in the pitiless battle—just as though it were real. Blood had been mixed with the wine; and all the food, the mixing bowls, and the fine polished tables had been trampled in common ruin.

In another place, again, Heracles, angry because of his dear wife, was subduing Nessus with his arrow by the streams of Evenus, after he had fled from that battle.

The great strength of powerful Antaeus had been shown on the shield. He could never get his fill of wrestling bouts, and Heracles had lifted him high and crushed him in his mighty arms.

By the streams of the broad Hellespont lay the great and terrible monster struck by Heracles' pitiless arrows. Heracles was untying the harsh bonds of Hesione.

The broad shield of Zeus-nourished Eurypylus, of course, also contained other wonderful deeds of brave Heracles. Eurypylus looked like Ares when he darts among the ranks of men. The Trojans flocked around him and were delighted at the sight of the arms and the man who wore the appearance of a god. Paris spoke to him and urged him to battle:

"I am glad you have come, because I have hope in my heart that all the Greeks will perish miserably along with their ships. I have never seen such a man among the Trojans or among the warlike Greeks. I beg you by great and mighty Heracles, whom you resemble in size and strength and glorious appearance, remember him, fill your thoughts with deeds worthy of him, and boldy defend the Trojans, if somehow we may have a rest from being slaughtered. You, I think, are the only man to keep evil doom away from our falling city."

He spoke, vigorously urging him on. Eurypylus said to him:

"Priamson, great of soul, formed like the blessed ones, these things have been fixed on the knees of the gods—what man will die in the great conflict and what man be saved. But I will stand before your city, just as is proper, and as I have the strength to fight. Moreover, I take this oath as well: not to return until I have either killed or perished."

These were his brave words, and they brought the Trojans great pleasure. Then Eurypylus selected Alexander and brave Aeneas, Polydamas of the good ashen spear, glorious Pammon, Deiphobus, too, and Aethicus, who surpassed all the other Paphlagonians in standing his ground against a crowd in battle. He chose all these men, skilled in the work of war, so that among the foremost they might fight the enemy in battle. They moved very quickly out in front of the crowd and eagerly hurried from the town followed by many soldiers. Just as if they were fine swarms of bees pouring noisily with their leaders from a covered hive when spring days come; so the men followed them on their way to battle. As they moved, a great noise from the men and their horses went up to the sky, and their wonderful armor resounded. Just as when the rushing power of a great wind moves the deep barren sea to its foundations, and dark waves, roaring against the beach, soon spew out seaweed from the sounding surf, and noise rises along the barren shores; so the vast earth resounded loudly under the rushing army.

The Greeks on their side poured out in front of their wall around glorious Agamemnon. There was a cry of soldiers calling to each other to meet the deadly battle and not to await rebuke by cowering beside the ships when men were pressing on to fight. They met the charging Trojans just as calves meet cows coming from the scrub to the farmyard, on their way downhill from the spring meadow, when the plowlands flourish thick with crops, the earth is heavy with abundant flowers, and the cups are full of the milk of cows and sheep. There is much lowing here and there, as cows and calves mix together, and the cowherd among them is glad; so a din arose, as these armies rushed against each other, because men were shouting terribly on both sides. They joined in vast battle. Tumult roamed among them, along with grim Slaughter. Shields, spears, and helmets clashed in close combat. Around them the bronze gleamed like fire. The battle bristled with spears, and everywhere the black earth was wet with the blood of slaughtered men and swift-footed horses who were strewn among the chariots. While some still writhed from spear blows, others fell on top of them. A hideous shouting swept through the air; a brazen fight had fallen on them both. Some were fighting with dangerous stones, some with freshly sharpened javelins or arrows, others with battle axes or with double-edged axes, with mighty swords, or with spears for close fighting, and there was a similar variety in their shields.

The Greeks first pushed the Trojans away from them a little. But their ranks charged back and drenched the battle in blood as they leapt upon the Greeks. Eurypylus roamed the whole army like a black tempest and boldly killed Greeks. Zeus gave him strength beyond telling, showing favor to glorious Heracles. There it was he struck Nireus, a man like the gods fighting against the Trojans. Eurypylus hit him a little above the waist with his long spear, and he fell to the level earth. The blood gushed out of him and drenched his famous armor, his glorious beauty, and his luxuriant hair. He lay with the dead in the dust and blood, like a vigorous shoot of fissile olive that a strong river in its noisy course drags away by the roots along with the river bank, quite undercutting the whole trench in which it stood, and it lies there heavy with flowers; so this day the handsome frame and lovely splendor of Nireus was stretched out over a great expanse of earth.[2]

Eurypylus boasted loudly over the man he had killed:

"Lie now in the dust. You wanted your admired beauty to help you, and it gave you no help at all. You wanted to escape, but I robbed you of your life. Poor fool, you did not even realize you had come against a better man. In battle, beauty is no match for strength."

When he had said this, he was planning to be quick about taking the splendid armor from the man he had killed. But Machaon came against him, angry because of Nireus, who had met his doom close to him. He struck Eurypylus with his cruel spear on his broad right shoulder, and, strong though he was, the blood rushed out. Even so, however, Eurypylus did not run away from the terrible turmoil, but, just like some lion or wild boar in the hills, he raged in the midst of the fighting, hoping to overpower the man who was attacking him and who had beaten him to the thrust in the crowd. These were his thoughts as he charged upon Machaon. He struck Machaon swiftly on the right buttock with his heavy long spear. But Machaon did not retreat or try to avoid his attacker, even though the blood was gushing out. Instead, he quickly lifted up a huge stone and threw it down upon

400

[2] Nireus is mentioned in Homer's catalogue of ships (*Iliad* ii. 671–75) as having brought to Troy three ships from Syme (a small island near Rhodes). Homer says he was the handsomest man in the Greek army at Troy, next to Achilles, "but he was weak, and a small force accompanied him . . ." His mother, according to Homer, was Aglaïa. This word is used here by Quintus as a common noun (in the translation, "splendor"), and he may conceivably have meant to remind the reader of the Homeric genealogy. The mother's name appears later in this book of Quintus (492), and at the beginning of the next book Quintus notes the combination in Nireus of beauty and physical weakness.

the head of brave Eurypylus Telephusson. His helmet, though, was quick to protect him from cruel hurt and death. The hero Eurypylus was now filled with anger at this mighty man, and in his deep passion he drove his spear at once through Machaon's chest. The bloody point went right through to his back. He fell as a bull falls under the jaws of a lion, and his bright armor rang loudly about his body. Eurypylus quickly drew out the cruel spear from the wounded flesh and uttered a loud boast:

"You poor wretch, your heart had no sense in it at all. Though a person of no account, you came against a far better man. And so heaven's evil doom has won you. You will have your profit, when the birds feast on your flesh now that you have been killed in battle. Why, did you still hope to return home and escape the strength of my hands? You are a doctor, with a fine knowledge of healing drugs. Relying on these, perhaps, you expected to escape the evil day. But not even your father himself, from windy Olympus, will save your heart now from death, not even if he pours over you nectar and ambrosia."[3]

So he spoke, and Machaon, still breathing a little, said to him:

"Eurypylus, it is not fated for you, either, to live for long, but close beside you in the Trojan plain stands deadly Doom, and so the words you utter now are evil."[4]

As he said this, his life left him, and he went at once to Hades. Even though he was no more, famous Eurypylus said to him:

"Lie there on the ground right now. I, for my part, am not concerned about the future, even if dismal destruction is at my feet this very day. We men do not live forever; doom is ready for us all."

After he said this, he stabbed the corpse. Teucer gave a great cry when he saw Machaon in the dust. He had been standing far off from him, fully occupied with the toil of battle. The fighting was heavy on those in the center, and man rushed upon man. Even

[3] Machaon and Podalirius, the two doctors in the Greek army, were sons of Asclepius, son of Apollo.
[4] The dying man's prophecy of the imminent death of his killer is a motif Homer used in describing the deaths of Patroclus and of Hector in the *Iliad* (xvi. 851–54; xxii. 359–60).

so, however, Teucer did not disregard the glorious fallen hero and Nireus who lay beside him—although he noticed Nireus after he had seen godlike Machaon in the dust. He gave a loud shout at once and called to the Greeks:

"Hurry, you Greeks, and do not give ground to the hurrying enemy. Our disgrace will be unspeakable if the Trojans drag off to Troy with them glorious Machaon and godlike Nireus as well. Rather, we must fight with right good will against the enemy, so that we may save the bodies of our dead or die ourselves beside them. This is right for men: to defend their own and not leave them as spoil for others. Not without sweat does glory grow among men."

So he spoke, and sadness fell upon the Greeks. The two armies fought around the bodies, and many men were killed by the war god, making the earth red. The conflict was even. Podalirius was slow to become aware of the sad death of his brother, struck low in the dust. He had been sitting by the swift ships, healing the wounds of men who had been hit with spears. He put on all his armor, his heart full of anger for his brother. The strength grew amazingly in his breast, and he was eager for dismal war. The black blood boiled fiercely in his heart, and he leapt swiftly among the enemy, brandishing a long-pointed javelin in his nimble hands.

He soon killed Agamestor's glorious son Clitus, whom a fair-haired nymph bore beside the streams of Parthenius. This river moves like olive oil through the land, and it pours its beautiful flowing waters into the Euxine Sea. Another glorious man he killed beside his brother's body was Lassus, whom divine Pronoe bore by the streams of the river Nymphaeus, very close to a broad cave. This is an amazing cave that men say is a holy place of the nymphs themselves, all those who live around the high mountains of the Paphlagonians and all who live around the rich vineyard country of Heracleia.[5] That cavern befits gods. It is fashioned of stone and huge to behold. Water cold as ice goes through the cave,

[5] A number of the features of this cave also appear in Homer's cave of the nymphs of Ithaca in the *Odyssey* (xiii. 103–12): the stone bowls, the weaving apparatus, the flowing water, the two entrances, one for gods and one for mortals, one facing Boreas, one Notus.

and everywhere in its deepest recesses there are what appear to be mixing bowls of stone on the rough rocks, as though fashioned by the hands of men. Beside them are Pans and lovely nymphs as well, looms and distaffs, and all the other works of human craftsmanship. These things are a great marvel to human beings who go inside the sacred cavern. There are two ways in it for going up and down. One is turned toward the blasts of noisy Boreas, the other faces Notus, the bringer of rain. This latter is the way by which mortals go under the broad cavern of the gods. The other is the way of the blessed ones. It is not an easy path for mortals, because chaos stretches far and wide, all the way to the pit of haughty Hades. But the blessed ones may look upon these things.

While, then, the men fought around Machaon and Nireus, Aglaïa's famous son, a great crowd perished on both sides. At last, though, after a tremendous struggle, the Greeks rescued them and quickly brought their bodies to the ships. A few of them did, that is, because the greater number were involved in the evil hardship of savage war, and they remained in the battle of necessity. When a great many had fulfilled their black dooms in the bloody and painful fighting, then it was that many of the Greeks fled to the protection of their ships. These were all those upon whom Eury- 500
pylus rolled a huge disaster by his attack. A few with Aias and the two powerful sons of Atreus remained in the conflict. Soon they would all have perished at the hands of their enemies as they moved about in the throng, had not Aias, son of Oïleus, struck brave Polydamas with his spear on the left shoulder near the breast. The blood gushed out, and he retreated a little. Famed Menelaus struck Deiphobus by the right breast, but his swift feet carried him away. Then glorious Agamemnon killed a great throng from the deadly multitude and, raging with his spears, set out after glorious Aethicus, but he escaped to his comrades.

When the inspiring leader Eurypylus noticed them all withdrawing together from the hateful conflict, he at once left the soldiers he had driven to the ships and swiftly darted against the two strong sons of Atreus and against Aias, Oïleus' stout-hearted son, who was not only a fast runner but also excellent in battle.

These were the ones he rushed quickly upon, his spear of vast length in his hands. With him came Paris and brave Aeneas, who was quick to hit Aias on his strong helmet with a huge rock. Aias was stretched out in the dust, but did not breathe out his life. A fated day had been prepared for him on his return, by the Capherean Rocks. Brave attendants snatched him up, still breathing a little, and carried him to the Greek ships.

Then, of course, the splendid kings, the Atreussons, were left alone. A deadly crowd of men stood around them, throwing missiles at them from every side, whatever they had the strength to take in their hands. Some poured on deadly darts, some stones, and others javelins. The Atreussons in the center kept turning this way and that, just like boars or lions in the middle of an enclosure on that day when lords collect people and huddle them cruelly together, preparing evil death from the strong wild beasts, and the beasts inside the enclosure devour whatever slaves come close to them; so the Atreussons in the center kept killing men who rushed at them. But not even so, eager though they were to fend off the Trojans, would they have had the strength to do so, except that Teucer came, and brave Idomeneus, Meriones, and Thoas, and godlike Thrasymedes. They had previously run away from the bold strength of Eurypylus and, shunning heavy disaster, would have retreated to the ships, but they became terrified for the Atreussons and so advanced against Eurypylus. A destructive battle began.

Then Teucer of the good ash thrust his spear at the shield of Aeneas, but he did not wound his handsome flesh, because his vast shield of four oxhides protected him from damage. But even so, he was frightened and retreated a little. Meriones charged upon noble Laophoon Paeonson, whom fair-haired Cleomede bore by the streams of the Axius. He came to holy Ilios with noble Asteropaeus to help the Trojans. He it was whom Meriones stabbed with his jagged spear above the genitals, and the spear point quickly drew out his entrails. Most speedily his spirit rushed to the dark. Then Alcimedes, brave comrade of Aias Oïleusson, made a cast into the crowd of sturdy Trojans. First uttering a prayer, he threw a cruel stone from his sling into the terrible uproar of the enemy, and the soldiers scattered in flight, terrified both by the stone and by the whistling it made. A fatal doom carried it against Hippasides, Pammon's bold charioteer, who was holding the reins in his hands. It struck him on the temple and knocked him at once from the chariot, down in front of his own wheels. The tires of the swift chariot rolled over the wretched body of the fallen man, when the horses lunged to retreat. A terrible death quickly subdued him, and he left his whip and reins far off. Grief fell upon Pammon. Necessity had now made him both a king and also a driver of the swift car. He would have met with death and his final day if some Trojan, coming up through the bloody tumult, had not taken the reins in his hands and saved the lord, hard pressed now by the deadly hands of the enemy.

Nestor's sturdy son struck with his spear godlike Acamas above the knee, as he charged at him. Loathsome pains came upon him from this cruel wound, and he withdrew from battle, leaving the sad conflict to his comrades, because he had no further interest in fighting. Then an attendant of famous Eurypylus hit Deïopites, sensible comrade of Thoas, a little below the shoulder. The painful spear came close to his heart, and a cold sweat oozed from his frame along with the blood. Then, as he turned to swift retreat, powerful Eurypylus overtook him and cut his tendons. His unwilling feet remained right where he had been hit, and his precious life left him. Then Thoas struck Paris a swift blow on the right thigh with his sharp spear, and he retreated a little to get his bow, which he had left behind. Idomeneus picked up the largest stone he could lift in his hands and struck the arm of Eurypylus, causing his deadly spear to fall to the ground. He at once withdrew to get a spear, since the one he was carrying had been knocked from his hand. The Atreussons, therefore, had a slight respite from battle. But attendants quickly came to Eurypylus, bringing him a long hard spear that had loosed the limbs of many. Taking this, he attacked the Greek army with raging strength, killing whomever he met, and subdued a great crowd.

Neither the Atreussons nor any other of the Greeks, who

600 like close combat, remained firm at this point. A dreadful fear seized all of them, because Eurypylus charged upon them all, bringing disaster. He clung to their heels and kept up the slaughter. Then he called to the Trojans and to his mounted comrades:

"My friends, with courage in our hearts, we must fashion for the Greeks death and annihilating doom. Why, just like sheep to the fold, they are now returning to their ships. Let us all remember deadly fighting, in which we have been expert from boyhood."

So he spoke, and they rushed in a body against the Greeks. The Greeks were much afraid and turned to run from the difficult fighting. The enemy followed them as white-toothed dogs chase wild deer up through long valleys and a forest. They threw in the dust many who were full of eagerness to escape the cruel onset of deadly slaughter. Eurypylus killed noble Boucolion, Nesus, Chromius, and Antiphus. Some of these lived in rich Mycenae, others in Sparta. Famous though they were, he killed them. From the crowd, he destroyed vast tribes of men. I have not the strength to tell them all, much though I should like to, not even if the heart in my breast were of iron. Aeneas killed Pheres and Antimachus, both of whom had come with Idomeneus from Crete. Glorious Agenor killed noble Molus, who had come from Argos and was subject to king Sthenelus. Molus had lagged far behind in the flight from the battle, and Agenor hit him with a freshly sharpened javelin in the lower part of his right leg. The point rushed onward and cut through the broad sinew and cruelly shattered the man's bones. Doom was mixed with the pain, and the man died.

Then Paris struck Mosunus and brave Phorcys, two brothers who had come from Salamis in Aias' ships and never saw their return. Besides these he killed Cleolaus, Meges' good attendant, hitting him on the left breast. Evil night took hold of him and his spirit flew away. The stricken man's anguished heart, still throbbing fast within his breast, shook the feathered arrow.[6] Paris was

[6] No physiological phenomenon in Homer has been more widely criticized and even ridiculed than his statement that when Alcathous was struck in the heart by Idomeneus' spear, the heart in its last throbbing shook the butt end of the spear (*Iliad* xiii. 442–44). In imitating this marvel, Quintus at least changed the missile to an arrow.

quick to shoot another arrow at bold Eëtion. The bronze sped through his jaw. He shrieked, and tears were mixed with his blood. Man killed man, and a wide area was closely packed with Greeks who had fallen in troops, one upon another.

The Trojans this day would have burned the ships with fire, had not swift night rushed down, bringing a thick mist. Eurypylus, and with him the sons of Troy, withdrew a little from the ships to the streams of the Simois, where they pitched their camp, full of joy. The Greeks among their ships fell upon the sand and groaned, full of deep sorrow for the men who had been killed, because black fate had overtaken many of them in the dust.

BOOK SEVEN

The Coming of Achilles' Son
Neoptolemus to Troy

W HEN HEAVEN HAD HID the stars, and brightly shining Dawn arose, and the cloud of night had withdrawn, then some of the strong, warlike Greeks went eagerly against Eurypylus and into the mighty conflict in front of the ships. Others, there by the ships, buried Machaon and Nireus. Nireus was like the everliving gods in handsome beauty. He was lacking in physical strength, however, because the gods do not grant men everything together, but as a result of some fate, evil always stands close beside good. So with lord Nireus: physical weakness was associated with lovely beauty. But the Greeks did not neglect him. They buried him and wailed at his tomb just as they did for glorious Machaon, whom they had always honored equally with the blessed immortals for his sound ideas. Quickly, then, they raised over them both a funeral mound.

During this time, deadly war was still raging in the plain. A great noise and din arose from both sides, as shields were broken with stones and spears. But while they were toiling in the hard fighting on the plain, Podalirius continued to lie in the dust, steadily refusing to eat anything and groaning deeply. He would not leave his brother's grave, and his rash mind kept straying to the thought of suicide. Sometimes he put his hand to his sword, then again he searched for a fatal drug. His comrades held him back, speaking earnestly to him, but he had no rest from his pain. He would have destroyed his life with his own hands on his noble brother's fresh grave, if Nestor Neleus' son had not become aware of him. He was filled with concern for him in his great trouble. He found him sometimes collapsed upon the sad mound, sometimes pouring dust upon his head, beating his breast with his powerful hands, and calling on his brother's name. The slaves and comrades as well were lamenting around their lord. Evil sorrow held them all. Nestor spoke with soothing words to the deeply grieving man:

"Check your wretched lament and your terrible sorrow, my son. It does not befit a sensible man to collapse by one who is no more and wail like a woman. You will not raise him up again to the light, because his soul has flown out of sight into the darkness, the destructive fire has devoured his body, and the earth has received his bones. Just as he grew up to flourishing life, so, too, he died. Endure your great grief, just as I endured the loss of my son at the enemy's hands. He was not in any way inferior to Machaon, but was surpassing good with the javelin and excelled in intelligence. No other young man loved his father as he loved me. He died for me, eager to save his father. But though he is dead, I brought myself to eat promptly, to stay alive, and to look upon the Dawn, knowing well that all of us mortals move along the same path to Death. For all of us is set the gloomy goal of sad doom. But, since we are mortal, it befits us to endure all that god gives us, both good and bad."

So he spoke, and the unhappy Podalirius answered him, the sad tears still flowing down and wetting his splendid cheeks:

"Sir, uncontainable grief for my brilliant brother overwhelms my heart. He brought me up when our father died and joined the gods in heaven.[1] He held me in his arms as though I were

---

[1] Quintus says "went to heaven." Quintus did not mean by this what a modern speaker might, but is referring to the deification of Asclepius. Nestor in his reply refers to a "saying among men" that the souls of the good go to heaven,

his own son. Gladly he taught me the healing of disease. We liked to share one table and one bed, and we enjoyed our possessions in common. So grief beyond forgetting assails me, and now that he is dead I no longer want to look upon the fine light of the sun."

So he spoke in his sorrow, and the old man said to him:

"A heavenly power has given to all human beings equally the evil of bereavement, and the earth will cover all of us. We do not, of course, travel the same path in life, nor the sort of one that each man desires, because, up above, goods and evils lie on the knees of the gods, infinite in number, all mixed into one. No one of the immortals looks upon these things, but they have been made invisible, covered with a marvelous mist. Fate alone lays hands upon them and, without looking, sends them forth from Olympus to earth. They are carried every way, as though by blasts of a wind. And frequently great disaster overwhelms a good man, and prosperity he does not deserve falls upon a bad one. Man's life is blind. This is why no one walks with security, but our feet often stumble. Our winding path turns sometimes to sad trouble, sometimes to good. No man is wholly prosperous from beginning to end, but the fortunes that men encounter differ. Since we live only a little while, it is not right to live in sadness. Rather, hope always for better things; don't keep your heart set on what is mournful. For there is a saying among men, you know, that the souls of the good go to a heaven that is imperishable forever, and the souls of the bad go to darkness. Your brother has two claims: he was kindly to mortals, and he was the son of an immortal. I think he has gone up to the race of the gods, by the will of your father."

With these words, Nestor raised him up from the ground against his will, encouraging him with his words, and led him away from the dismal tomb. Podalirius kept turning around and groaning terribly. And so they reached the ships.

The other Greeks and the Trojans were in the painful toil of fighting, because the battle was still in progress. Eurypylus, with a stubborn spirit like Ares', was subduing hosts of the enemy with

---

those of the bad to the darkness. This idea of a system of rewards and punishments after death is entirely foreign to Homer's notions about the fate of the dead.

his tireless hands and eager spear. The earth was becoming packed   100
with corpses of men killed on both sides. Eurypylus stood among
the corpses fighting boldly, his hands and feet spattered with
blood. He did not stop from the deadly conflict, but overpowered
with his spear stout-hearted Peneleos, as he came to meet him in
the pitiless fighting, and he killed many around him. Eurypylus
was not one to turn his hands away from the battle, but he angrily
followed the Greeks, just as in old times mighty Heracles attacked
the Centaurs on the tall peaks of Pholoe, greatly raging in his
strength, and killed them all, very swift though they were, and
powerful, and skilled in deadly pursuit; so Eurypylus over-
whelmed by his attack host upon host of Greek soldiers. Massed
together, they fell in the dust in throngs and were spread out
everywhere. Just as when many banks are cut away on both sides
as a great river presses upon them in a sandy place, and the river
rushes on to the swelling sea, its fierce current boiling, and the
cliffs everywhere roundabout re-echo, the long streams roar as
the banks continue to collapse, and all the dikes give way before
the river; in the same way many glorious sons of the warlike
Greeks fell down in the dust beneath Eurypylus' hands, as he
overtook them in the bloody turmoil.

Some got away—all those whose speed of foot saved them.
And even so, they rescued Peneleos from the noisy confusion and
brought him to the ships, even though they were trying by speed
of foot to avoid hateful dooms and pitiless fate. They ran in a body
to the protection of the ships, and no man had the strength of spirit
to fight against Eurypylus, because Heracles sent wretched rout
upon them, exalting in every way his tireless grandson. The
Greeks stayed cowering down inside their wall, just like goats
under a projecting cliff, afraid of a terrible freezing wind that
swoops down bringing much snow and chill hail. Although the
goats are hurrying to pasture, they do not go beyond the hill in
the face of the blast, but they wait out the storm gathered together
under shelter and in ravines, and feed in flocks under the shadowy
scrub until the evil blasts of wind stop; so the Greeks in the pro-
tection of their walls awaited, fearfully, the attack of Telephus'
powerful son.

145

He would soon have destroyed the swift ships and the army, if Athena Tritogeneia had not put courage into the Greeks, late though it was. They poured a steady stream of destructive missiles upon the enemy from their high wall and killed man after man. The walls grew wet with hideous gore, and there were shrieks from stricken men.

In this way, then, they fought night and day—Cetaeans, Trojans, and stubborn Greeks, sometimes in front of the ships, sometimes around the high wall, since the conflict was beyond control. Even so, however, they stopped the slaughter and grim fighting for two days, because a message from the Greeks came to king Eurypylus proposing that they intermit the battle and give to the funeral pyre the men who had been killed in action. He agreed at once, and so they stopped the hard fighting, and each side buried the dead who had fallen in the dust.

The Greeks mourned for Peneleos beyond all the others. They erected a monument over the dead man, very wide and high, conspicuous even for future generations. At some distance from this, they buried the mass of the dead heroes, their hearts pained with great sorrow. They heaped up one funeral pyre for all and gave them a common grave.

So the Trojans, too, on their side buried their dead. But destructive Eris did not stop, but still kept urging the bold strength of Eurypylus to attack the enemy. And he had not yet withdrawn from the ships, but he stayed there, trying to increase the evil conflict against the Greeks.

Meanwhile, Odysseus and Diomedes made a fast run in their black ship and arrived at Scyros. They found Achilles' son in front of his home, sometimes hurling darts and spears, sometimes exercising his fast horses. They were glad to see him occupied with the work of deadly war, even though his heart was much oppressed by his father's death (for he had already heard of this). They went quickly to him, marveling because they saw that his handsome person was like bold Achilles'. He spoke first, and said:

"Gentlemen, a fine good day to you on your arrival at my

house. Tell me where you are from and who you are and what need of me brings you through the barren waves."

So he spoke, questioning them. Glorious Odysseus said in reply:

"We are friends of the splendid fighter Achilles, to whom, men say, wise Deidameia bore you. We ourselves, too, see your perfect resemblance to that man, and he was like the mighty immortals. I am from Ithaca, he from horse-feeding Argos. You may perhaps have heard the name of the warrior Diomedes and also of shrewd Odysseus, the man who now stands in person before you. It is a prophecy that brings me. Be quick to have pity on us. Come to Troy and protect the Greeks. In this way there will be an end to the war, and the glorious Greeks will give you gifts beyond telling. I myself will give you the arms of your godlike father. You will have great delight in wearing them. They are not like the arms of mortal men, but are equal, I fancy, to the arms of the god Ares. Much gold has been fitted everywhere about them, covered with elaborate designs. Hephaestus himself, among the gods, found his heart glow as he made these immortal arms. You, too, will marvel when you see them. Earth and heaven and the 200 sea have been worked on the shield, and in a vast circle all around it living creatures have been fashioned, looking just as though they were moving. It is a marvel even to immortals. Of mortals, no one ever yet looked upon such arms among men or carried them, except your father, whom all the Greeks honored like Zeus. I was especially fond of him and full of good will toward him. When he was killed, I brought his body to the ships, sending pitiless doom on many of the enemy. It was because of this that glorious Thetis gave me his splendid arms. I'll gladly give them to you in your turn, when you reach Ilios—indeed, I want to give them. And when we sack Priam's city and return home in the ships to Greece, Menelaus will make you his son-in-law at once, if you wish, in return for your help. He will also give you possessions beyond telling, and gold to take along with his fair-haired daughter, all that ought to accompany a wealthy king."

In answer to these words, Achilles' sturdy son said:

"If the Greeks are summoning me because of prophecies, let us tomorrow set out at once over the wide depths of the sea, in case I may become a light of help for the Greeks in their longing. For the present, let us go into the house to the sort of hospitality it is proper to prepare for guests. My marriage the gods will take care of later."

So speaking, he led the way, and they followed him with great pleasure. When they came to the large house with its beautiful courtyard, they found Deidameia, sad at heart and wasting away, just as the snow melts on the mountains when the south wind blows shrill and the sun shines steadily; so she was wasting away because her splendid husband had fallen in battle. Although she was still mourning, the distinguished kings spoke their greetings to her, and her son came close and told her clearly the lineage and name of each. The reason for their coming, however, he concealed until morning, so that in her grief tearful misery might not take hold of her, and she might not by her entreaties try to check him when he was eager to go. They had their meal at once and refreshed themselves with sleep, all those who live in the plain of Scyros Island, round which the waves of the sea roar loudly as the Aegean breaks on its shores.

But no delightful sleep took hold of Deidameia. She kept thinking of the names of cunning Odysseus and godlike Diomedes. They were the pair who had made her a widow by persuading war-loving Achilles' bold mind to go to meet the enemy's war cry. Inflexible Fate encountered him, ruined his return, and brought infinite sorrow to his father Peleus and to Deidameia herself. On this account, a great dread pervaded her heart for her son, eager to be off to war's tumult, lest sorrow on top of wretched sorrow come to her.

The Dawn mounted to the great heaven, and the men quickly rose from their beds. As soon as Deidameia noticed this, she threw herself upon Neoptolemus' broad chest, wailed wretchedly, and shrieked to the sky. Just as a cow in the hills bellows endlessly, as she searches in the valleys for her calf, and the tall peaks of the steep mountain re-echo; so as she wailed the lofty house resounded everywhere from its innermost depths. In her great misery, she said:

"My child, where are your brave thoughts flying to now? Are you planning to accompany your guests to Troy, the town of tears? Many men are being killed there in miserable conflicts, even though they are experts in war and ugly battle. You are still young and have no knowledge yet of those arts of war which keep off for men the evil day. Listen to me and stay in your own halls, that no evil report may come to my ears from Troy of your death in battle. I do not think you will come back here again from the fighting. Why not even your father escaped destructive doom, but he was killed in action, although he was better than you and better than the other heroes and had a goddess for a mother. He died through the guile and devices of these men here, who are now urging you to go to the cruel war. This is why my heart trembles. I'm afraid that with you gone too, my son, it will be my lot to be left desolate and to suffer miserable troubles. There is no pain yet discovered that comes harder upon a woman than when, after her husband's death, her children perish, and she is left in her home bereaved by harsh death. Immediately men cut away her lands, ravage all she has, and pay no heed to her rights. So true it is that nothing has been made that is weaker or more wretched than a widow woman in her halls."

She said this with many a loud wail. Her son spoke this to her in reply:

"Be of good cheer, my mother, and dismiss this evil omen. No man is destroyed by war beyond his Fates. And if I am fated to be destroyed for the sake of the Greeks, then I pray I may do something worthy of my ancestors before I lie dead."

So he spoke, and his grandfather, old Lycomedes, came close to him and spoke to the young man so eager for fighting:

"Oh my son, stout of heart, so like your father in your strength, I know that you are staunch and strong. But even so, I am naturally afraid, not only of the bitter war but also of the wretched waves of the sea, because sailors are always close to

death. Be afraid, my son, when you come to sail later on, either
from Troy or elsewhere. Be afraid of what often happens at the
300 season when the sun comes together with murky Capricorn,
throwing behind him the archer, the drawer of the bow, when the
winds set in motion wretched winter weather, or when the stars
are carried along the wide stream of Ocean, as Orion comes down
to the darkness. Fear in your heart, too, the equinox and its diffi-
culties, when storm winds from somewhere, swooping over the
great gulf, clash along the broad depths of the sea. Or when the
setting of the Pleiades comes, fear them, also, in their eagerness to
sink into the sea, and fear the other stars which are a terror to toil-
ing men, both in their setting and in their rising on the wide surface
of the sea."

With these words, he kissed his grandson and did not try to
keep him from his journey. The boy was longing for the din of
battle. He had a lovely smile on his face and wanted to go at once
to the ship. His mother, however, continued to hold him back in
the palace, tearfully conversing with him when he was in a hurry
to be on his way. Just as when someone mounted on a race horse
holds him back when he is eager for the race, and he champs the
restraining bit, neighing, and his chest grows wet with froth, and
his feet, longing for the race, do not stand still, but there is a great
noise as he keeps moving his nimble feet in one spot, the mane
streams out from the impetuous animal, he lifts his head high, he
gives many a snort, and the mind of his master is pleased; so the
mother of brave Achilles' splendid son tried to hold him back, and
his feet were impatient, and she took pride in her son, even in
her sorrow.

When he had kissed her affectionately a thousand times, he
left her there alone, grieving piteously in her dear father's halls.
Just as a swallow wails around a building, greatly distressed over
her parti-colored young that a terrible snake has devoured, for
all their cheeping, and brought pain to the devoted mother bird,
and she sometimes flies around the desolated nest, sometimes flits
in the beautiful porticoes, crying very plaintively because of her
young; so Deidameia wailed for Neoptolemus. Sometimes she

collapsed with a loud cry on her son's bed, and then again would weep by the door jambs. If there was any toy within the rooms with which he had delighted his childish mind when he was little, she placed this in her bosom. If she saw any javelin that he had left behind, she smothered it with kisses, and, with many a wail, she did the same to anything else she saw that belonged to her brave son.

He could no longer hear his mother's lavish expressions of grief, but was well on his way to the swift ship. His legs carried him rapidly on, and he looked just like a gleaming star. Accompanying him on either side were the son of Tydeus and brave Odysseus, together with twenty other men. The spirits of these men were full of good sense, and Deidameia, feeling that they were the best men she had in her halls, gave them to her son to be his ready attendants. They were busy around Achilles' bold son this day, as he hastened through the city to the ship. He moved laughing among them. Thetis and her Nereids were glad, and dark-haired Poseidon himself rejoiced as he looked upon the sturdy son of noble Achilles and saw how eager he was for tearful war, even though still a boy, still beardless. Strength and courage urged him on, and he went rapidly from his native land. He looked like Ares when, angry at enemies, he goes into the bloody turmoil of battle, and his heart is filled with a great rage, his brow is grim, his eyes flash like fire, his cheeks, clad at once in beauty and chilling terror, seem dreadful as he rushes on, and even the gods themselves are afraid; such was Achilles' fine son. The people in the town prayed to the immortals that they bring back safe from cruel war their noble king. The gods heard their prayers. Neoptolemus stood out above all who accompanied him.

On their arrival at the shore of the deep-thundering sea, they found oarsmen within the polished ship arranging the sails and making hurried preparations on the ship. They went on board at once themselves. The men untied the cables and raised the anchor stones which, with their great strength, are standard equipment on ships. Poseidon, the husband of Amphitrite, gladly gave them fair sailing, because he was much concerned for the Greeks, who

were being hard pressed by the Trojans and great-souled Eury-
pylus. Odysseus and Diomedes, sitting one on each side of
Achilles' son, delighted him with stories, talking about the deeds
of his father: all that he had contrived on the broad sea and in the
land of Telephus, who fought hand to hand, and all he did to the
Trojans, winning glory for the Atreussons around Priam's city.
The boy's heart glowed, and he was eager to win for himself his
fearless father's honor and glory.

Noble Deidameia, however, aching for her son, was weeping
sad tears in her halls, and the heart in her breast was melting away
because of her cruel troubles, just as soft lead or a lump of wax
melts on coals. She kept looking over the vast sea and did not ever
stop groaning. A mother is troubled about her son, even if he will
be home for dinner.[2] But the sails of Neoptolemus' ship, as it went
on its long journey, were disappearing now and seemed like a mist.
She groaned and lamented all day long.

The ship ran over the sea with a following wind, barely
touching the surface of the noisy ocean. On each side the dark
waves roared about the keel. Quickly the ocean-going vessel made
her way across the great gulf. Then the darkness of night fell upon
her, but she continued on her way over the sea's depths with the
400   wind and with the pilot's guidance. When the Dawn in her
splendor came into heaven, the peaks of the Idaean hills appeared
to them, Chrysa, the Sminthian shrine, the promontory of Sigeum,
and the tomb of brave Achilles. The son of Laertes was shrewd
enough not to show this to Neoptolemus, and so avoided making
him unhappy. Swiftly they passed by the Calydnian Islands and
left Tenedos astern. Now the shrine of Eleus appeared, where the
tomb of Protesilaus is, shadowed over by tall elms. (Whenever
these trees, as they grow up from the earth, catch sight of Ilios,
their tops wither immediately.) The wind helped the rowers bring
the ship close to Troy. They reached the place where the other
Greek ships were drawn up on the shore. The Greeks were then
hard at work in the wretched battle, fighting around the wall that

---

[2] The text is doubtful, and possibly something is lost. The idea may be
"even if he has been invited out to dinner."

they had themselves previously built to protect the ships in war and the powerful army as well. This wall was now on the verge of being knocked to the ground and destroyed by the hands of Eurypylus. But Diomedes, son of powerful Tydeus, was quick to notice that the high wall was under attack. He jumped at once from the swift ship and called out boldly, with all the power he could command:

"My friends, truly a great disaster is rolling upon the Greeks today. We must put on our bright armor at once and go into the turmoil of a hard battle. For the able Trojan soldiers are fighting now at our towers. They will soon shatter the high wall and burn our ships with fire—a most terrible thing. There will be no return for us then, no matter how much our hearts long for it, but we shall ourselves soon perish beyond our fate and lie in Troy far from our children and our wives."

So he spoke, and all together they dashed with great speed from the swift ship. Fear took them all as they looked upon the situation—all except bold Neoptolemus. He was like his father in courage, and a passion for battle fell upon him. They soon reached the quarters of Odysseus, which were closest to their dark-prowed ship. Many changes of armor lay there, belonging to shrewd Odysseus and to his godlike comrades, all that they had taken from men they had killed. Then the able men put on beautiful armor, while those whose spirit was feeble in their breasts put on the inferior. Odysseus put on the armor he had brought from Ithaca. He gave to Diomedes Tydeusson those beautiful arms that he had previously stripped from powerful Socus.[3] The son of Achilles in his turn put on his father's armor, and he looked exactly like him. Because of Hephaestus' hands, the armor fitted easily about his limbs, even though it was monstrous for others. For him, though, all the armor taken together seemed light. The long Pelian spear did not burden him at all, and, huge though it was, he easily lifted this weapon that still longed for blood.

[3] Odysseus' fight with Socus is described in the eleventh book of the *Iliad* (426–58). Socus, angry because Odysseus has just killed his brother, attacks and wounds Odysseus, but Odysseus then kills him as he tries to get away.

All the Greeks who saw him wanted to come close to him, but they could not, because the heavy turmoil of battle was pressing them hard all around the wall. Just as when by a desert island in the broad sea men who have been cut off from human beings are miserable, because opposing squalls of wind pen them up for a very long time, and they run wretchedly about their ship, and all their provisions are failing, and then a whistling wind blows fair for them to their delight; so the Greek army, oppressed before, rejoiced at the coming of Neoptolemus in his strength, hoping that they would have a breathing space from their painful labor. His eyes were gleaming like those of a reckless lion in the high mountains which, wrathful at heart, rushes at hunters who have just approached its cave, intent on dragging out the whelps left alone far from their parents in a shady glen, and the lion, high up on some crag, catches sight of the destructive hunters and rushes upon them, its savage jaws roaring terribly; so the glorious son of fearless Achilles stirred up his spirit against the brave Trojans.

First of all, he swooped to the place in the plain where the fighting was especially fierce. He suspected that the Greek wall would be easier for the impetuous enemy attack in this place, because it had been equipped with weaker parapets. The others went with him, full of eagerness for war.

They found stout-hearted Eurypylus and his companions attacking a tower, thoroughly convinced that they would soon shatter the high walls and destroy the Greeks. But the gods did not accomplish their desire. Instead, Odysseus and powerful Diomedes, godlike Neoptolemus and glorious Leonteus pushed them back from the wall with showers of missiles. Just as when dogs and hard-working herdsmen chase powerful lions away from a farm, vigorously and noisily assailing them from every side, and the lions, with glaring eyes, turn this way and that, filled with a deep longing to gulp in their jaws calves and cows, but nonetheless they give way before the attack of the stout-hearted dogs, for the herdsmen rush upon them vigorously; [so Eurypylus and his men grudgingly drew back][4] a little, as far as one may throw a very

[4] A guess to fill a gap.

154

large stone. Eurypylus would not allow the Trojans to retreat far from the ships, but kept urging them to stay very close to the enemy until he took the ships and destroyed all the Greeks. Zeus had given him infinite strength. Moving quickly, he took up a stubborn, jagged rock, rushed up, and hurled it against the high wall. All the foundations of the lofty wall cracked terribly all around. Fear seized all the Greeks, as though the wall had already 500 collapsed in the dust. But even so, they did not rush away from the ruinous turmoil, but held their ground like jackals or wolves, shameless ravagers of sheep, whom hunters in the mountains with their dogs drive from their caves, eager to inflict a speedy and painful death on their whelps, and they do not give ground at all under the force of missiles, but stand firm and protect their young; so the Greeks stood firm in the conflict, defending the ships and themselves. Eurypylus, bold in battle, made great threats against them all in front of the swift ships:

"You cowards, men with feeble spirit in your breasts, you would not have driven me in fear from your ships with your missiles, except that your wall protected you from my attack. Now, just like dogs cowering before a lion in the forest, you stay within your walls to fight me, avoiding complete destruction. If you ever come away from your ships into the Trojan plain, eager for battle as before, no one will protect you from evil death, but all of you together will lie in the dust, destroyed by me."

So he spoke, talking of things that were not to be done. He had no realization, either, that not far off great trouble was rolling upon him, sent from the hands of brave Neoptolemus, who was soon to destroy him with his eager spear. Neoptolemus was not even at that time aloof from the mighty conflict, but he was killing Trojans from the wall. They were in retreat, frightened by the missiles from above, and of necessity were crowding in confusion around Eurypylus, for an anguish of fear seized them all. Just as when children crowd about their father's knees, frightened by the thunder of great Zeus that breaks among the clouds, when the upper air resounds terribly; so the sons of Troy took refuge with the great king among the Cetaean men, afraid of Neoptolemus and whatever he hurled from his hands. Calamity was flying straight on, bringing tearful war upon the heads of the enemy.

The Trojans, their hearts struck with helplessness, thought that they saw great Achilles himself as well as his arms. But they kept a miserable silence within them, so that no awful fear would come to the mind of the Cetaeans or their lord Eurypylus. And so, although infinitely afraid, they stayed where they were, one here another there, between disaster and chilling terror. Shame and wretched fear alike held them. Just as when men going on foot along a rocky path see a torrent rushing down from a mountain, and the noise resounds about the cliff, and they have no desire to go down into the noisy stream, although they are in a hurry, because they see destruction at their feet and are afraid and lose interest in their journey; so the Trojans stayed where they were under the Greek wall, though they were eager for flight.[5] Godlike Eurypylus kept urging them on into the tumult. He was quite sure that the huge man would grow weary of hand and strength as he slaughtered so many in the battle. But Neoptolemus did not stop fighting.

Then Athena, looking down upon their hard fighting, left the high halls of Olympus that is fragrant with incense and moved over the mountain peaks. In her great hurry, she did not touch the ground with her feet, but the holy air carried her. She looked like a cloud and moved faster than the wind. She reached Troy quickly and set foot on the hill of windy Sigeum. From there she looked at the men's hand-to-hand combat and gave much glory to the Greeks.

The son of Achilles had far more boldness than the others and more strength as well. These are the qualities that, when they occur together, produce great distinction for men, and he was preeminent in both, because he had Zeus's blood and was like his dear father. So, fearless as he was, he killed many men close to the towers. Just as a fisherman at sea, eager for a catch, fashions

---

[5] Zimmerman and the manuscripts give "eager to fight." This seems unsuitable to the context, and I have preferred a conjecture of Köchly. Possibly something has been lost.

destruction for fish by bringing the power of fire within his ship, and, as it is kindled by his breath, the gleam of fire shines around the ship, and the fish dart from the dark water, wanting to see the gleam—their last, because he kills them with a sharp-pronged trident as they rush up, and his heart is made glad by the catch; so the glorious son of the great soldier Achilles subdued hosts of the enemy around the stone wall as they rushed against him. All the other Greeks were fighting hard, too, at the other parapets. The broad shore and the ships roared, and the high walls resounded with the din of missiles. Weariness beyond telling was over-powering the armies of both sides and making slack the limbs and the strength of the men. It had not, however, affected at all the glorious son of stubborn Achilles. His stout heart was quite un-wearied, and wretched fear had not touched him in the slightest. He fought on; in strength he was like an ever-flowing, unweary-ing river, which the onset of a tremendous fire does not ever frighten as it comes, even if a great raging wind drives on the holy strength of Hephaestus. If the fire comes close to the stream, it is quenched, and its dreadful force has no power to touch the un-wearying water; so neither the cruel fighting nor any fear touched the limbs of brave Peleusson's noble son. He stood firm in his place and encouraged his comrades. Never a missile of the many that were being thrown reached his handsome flesh. They darted in their numbers to no purpose, like snowflakes around a crag. He was completely protected by his broad shield and stout helmet, glorious gifts of the god. Exulting in them, the powerful son of Achilles ranged about the wall with loud cries, vigorously order- 600 ing the fearless Greeks into battle. He was far the best of all, and he had a spirit that still could not get enough of deadly attack, and, of course, he had it in mind to avenge his father's cruel death. The Myrmidons rejoiced in their king, and there was a horrible shout-ing around the wall.

Then Neoptolemus killed the two sons of wealthy Meges, who was the son of Dymas and had splendid sons. They were very skillful at throwing the javelin, driving a horse well in war, and handling properly a long spear. Periboea bore them to Meges at one birth by the banks of the Sangarius. Celtus and Eubius they were called. But they did not enjoy their vast wealth for long, because the Fates granted them a very short term of life. Just as they both saw the light on the same day, so they both died at the hands of bold Neoptolemus, one struck in the heart by a javelin, the other on the head by a cruel stone. The crushed helmet was shattered about his head and wrecked his brain. A thousand other companies of the enemy were killed around them.

The mighty work of war continued until the time when men unhitch oxen from the plow, and the immortal day was done. The army of fearless Eurypylus withdrew a little from the ships. Those who were close to the towers also had a little breathing space. The sons of Troy themselves had respite from the noisy tumult. There had been dreadful fighting around the wall. All the Greeks would have perished at their ships, if Achilles' powerful son had not that day kept back the great army of the enemy and Eurypylus himself.

The old man Phoenix came to Neoptolemus at once and, when he caught sight of him, he marveled at his likeness to Peleus-son. He felt great joy and unspeakable sorrow simultaneously: sorrow at the remembrance of swift-footed Achilles, and joy because he saw his powerful son. He cried in his happiness, because the races of men do not ever live free from lamentation, even if sometimes they feel joy. He embraced him just as a father might embrace a son who, through the gods' will, has endured troubles for a long time and then comes to his home, to the great delight of his father; so Phoenix embraced Neoptolemus, kissed his head and chest, and in his admiration spoke to him like this:

"Greetings, my child, noble son of Achilles. At one time, when your father was little, I used to enjoy taking care of him in my arms. Through the splendid plan of the gods, he grew rapidly, like a flourishing young tree. I used to take delight in looking on his person and his strength. He was most helpful to me. I used to honor him like an especially dear child, and he honored me as much as he honored his own father. Indeed, as far as feelings went, I was a father to him and he a son to me. If you saw us, you would think we were of one blood, our thoughts were so much alike. In ability he was far the better, since in person and in strength he was like the blessed gods.

"You are exactly like him, and I can feel that he is still alive among the Greeks. Sharp pain for him surrounds me all my days, my old age is miserable, and I am oppressed in spirit. I wish the heaped-up earth had covered me while he was still living, because it is a glory for a man to be buried by the hands of one who cares greatly for him. Well, my child, my sad heart will never forget him, but don't you harry your heart at all with sadness. You must help the hard-pressed Myrmidons and the horse-taming Greeks, filled with wrath at the enemy for your noble father's sake. Great will be your glory for subduing Eurypylus, who cannot have his fill of battle. You are and will be as much better than he is as your father was superior to his unhappy parent."

When he had finished, the son of brown-haired Achilles said to him:

"Sir, mighty Fate and haughty Ares will pass judgment on our ability in war."

This is what he said, and he wanted to rush outside the wall that very day in the armor of his father, but night checked him. Bringing to men release from work, she rushed from the Ocean stream, her body clothed in darkness.

The sons of the Greeks were filled with happiness and were glorifying Neoptolemus by the ships equally with powerful Achilles, because he had restored their courage by his readiness to go into conflict. For this reason, they were honoring him with splendid prizes, offering gifts beyond telling, which increase a man's wealth. Some gave gold and silver; some, slave women; some, quantities of bronze; some, iron; others gave red wine in jars, swift-footed horses, the military gear of men, and well-made robes, the beautiful work of women. Neoptolemus' heart glowed within him at these gifts. Then they gave their attention to dinner in the huts, glorifying Achilles' godlike son equally with the unwearying heavenly gods. Agamemnon, in his great exultation, spoke to him like this:

"You are beyond doubt the son of bold Achilles, my child.

You have his sturdy strength, his appearance, and his size and courage, and the heart within you is the same. So you warm my spirit. I have every hope of destroying the enemy companies and Priam's famous city with your hands and your spear. You are like your father, and I can feel I see him by the ships, when, in anger over Patroclus' death, he shouted at the Trojans.[6] He, however, is now with the immortals, but he has sent you today from the blessed ones to defend the Greeks when they were being killed."

700   When he said this, Achilles' sturdy son replied:

"Oh, Agamemnon, I wish I had found him still alive, so that he could see for himself if his son pleased him and brought no shame to his father's strength. I think it will be this way, if the carefree heavenly ones keep me safe."

So the sensible Neoptolemus spoke, and the people who were there to honor him marveled at the glorious man. When they had their fill of the dinner and feasting, then the sturdy son of brave Achilles rose from dinner and went to his father's quarters. Quantities of armor belonging to men Achilles had killed were stored here. Everywhere around him the captive women were taking care of the desolate quarters just as though their lord were still alive. When he saw the Trojan armor and the slave women, he groaned, and love of his father took hold of him. Just as when in the thick scrub and glens covered with brush a savage lion has been destroyed by hunters, and then the cub comes to the dusky cavern and looks and looks everywhere about the empty cave, and when it sees in heaps there the bones of many animals that have been killed in the past, horses or cattle, then it feels great sorrow for its parent; so at this time the child of brave Peleusson felt a chill sorrow in his heart. The slave women crowded around him with admiration, and Briseis herself, when she saw Achilles' son, was sometimes very glad at heart—sometimes, too, sad at the remem-

---

[6] After Patroclus' death—and when there is danger that Hector may drag away his body—Achilles, at the urging of the goddess Iris, goes to the trench which surrounds the Greek camp and gives a great shout. The Trojans withdraw in panic, frightened by the sound and by the sight of the supernatural fire which blazes from Achilles' head, and the Greeks rescue the body of Patroclus (*Iliad* xviii. 165-232).

brance of Achilles. Speechlessness took hold of the heart in her breast, as though fearless Achilles himself were still alive.

The Trojans, too, on their side were themselves happily glorifying the mighty man Eurypylus in their quarters, just as they had done for glorious Hector when he had killed Greeks in defense of his city and all its property. But when sweet sleep came upon mortals, then the sons of Troy and the brave Greeks, except for the guards, lay down to rest, heavy with sleep.

BOOK EIGHT

The Death of Eurypylus

WHEN THE LIGHT of the sun was spread over the earth, coming from the edges of the world, where Dawn has her cave, then on either side the Trojans and the sturdy sons of the Greeks armed themselves, eager for conflict. Achilles' noble son urged the Greeks to meet the Trojans with fearless spirit, while Eurypylus, of course, great and strong, urged on the Trojans. He had every hope of knocking the wall to the ground, destroying the ships in a terrible fire, and killing the army with his own hands. But his hope was like the empty air, and the Fates of death, standing close to him, were filled with laughter at his futile plans.

Then Achilles' fearless son spoke out boldly to the Myrmidons, exhorting them to fight:

"Listen to me, men, and put a warlike spirit in your breasts, so that we may become a relief from wretched war for the Greeks and a disaster to our enemies. Let no one of us be afraid. Boldness produces mighty strength in abundance for men, while fear destroys both physical and mental power. Come, all of you steel yourselves for battle, so that the Trojan army may have no rest, but may think that Achilles is still alive and with the Greeks."

With these words he put upon his shoulders the armor of his

father, gleaming all over. Thetis' heart was made glad, as she looked from the sea upon the great strength of her grandson. He swept quickly out in front of the lofty wall, driving his father's immortal horses. Just as when the sun appears from the boundaries of Ocean, shining its marvelous fire upon the earth, the fire that brings painful disease to men, when the Dog Star Sirius accompanies the sun's team and chariot; so did the powerful hero, Achilles' son, move against the Trojan army. Immortal horses carried him, which Automedon, who was in charge of them, had given to him when he wanted to force the army away from the ships. The horses rejoiced at carrying their lord who resembled Achilles, and their immortal hearts were confident that he was a hero no whit inferior to his father. So, too, the Greeks gathered around mighty Neoptolemus with loud laughter, full of eagerness, like annoying wasps which someone disturbs, and they fly out of their hollow, longing to wound human flesh. All the wasps in the nest are irritated and cause great trouble to persons hurrying by; so they poured out from the ships and the wall, longing for battle. A wide space was crowded with them. The whole plain shone with the arms of men in the bright gleam of the sun above. Just as a cloud moves through the vast sky, driven by the hard blasts of Boreas, when there is snow and the difficult season of winter, and darkness covers the whole heaven; so the earth was full of these armies as they came together from each side not far from the ships. Dust rose high into the broad heaven, the arms of the men and the numerous chariots rattled, the horses neighed as they rushed here and there to battle. His own courage ordered each man, urging him into the cruel conflict.

Just as when two winds drive high waves wildly before them, roaring dreadfully along the broad surfaces of the sea and shattering their blasts upon each other, when a terrible storm rages on the wide depths of the sea, and furious Amphitrite moans roundabout with horrible waves which rush this way and that, mountain-high, and as they rise up everywhere there is a terrible roaring on the deep; so the armies on each side came together in war with a dreadful eagerness. Eris, goddess of strife, and their own strength impelled them. They clashed together like thunder or lightning, which make a great roar in the sky whenever the blustering winds contend and, blowing furiously, crash the clouds together, because Zeus is very angry at men who are doing things contrary to honored Themis, goddess of right; so they assailed each other, and spear clashed with spear, shield with shield, and man attacked man.

First of all the mighty son of the good soldier Achilles killed brave Melaneus and glorious Alcidamas, sons of able Alexinomus, who lived in hollow Caunus close by the clear lake under snowy Imbras beside the foothills of Tarbelus. And he killed Cassander's son, swift-footed Menes, whom glorious Creusa bore near the mouth of the broad river Lindus, where the boundaries of the war-like Carians are, and the heights of famous Lycia. He also killed the fighter Morys, who had come from Phrygia, and along with him he killed Polybus and Hippomedon, hitting one under the heart and the other on the collarbone. He went on destroying one man here, another there, and the earth groaned with Trojan corpses. The Trojans gave way before him, just like dry brush which a blast of pernicious fire easily destroys, when Boreas, the north wind, rises in the autumn; so the Trojan ranks collapsed, as he rushed upon them.

Aeneas subdued Aristolochus, a stubborn fighter, hitting him on the head with a stone. It shattered the skull along with his helmet, and the spirit immediately left his bones. Tydeusson killed swift Eumaeus, who lived on steep Dardanus, where Anchises has his bed and where he subdued Cytherean Aphrodite in his arms. Then Agamemnon killed brave Stratus. He did not come home to Thrace from the war, but perished far from his native country. Meriones destroyed Chlemus, Pisenor's son, dear and faithful comrade of Glaucus. He used to live by the mouth of the Limyrus, and the men dwelling in the vicinity honored him as king when Glaucus had been killed and lorded it no more over all those who lived around the site of Phoenix, the steep peak of Massicytus, and the crag of Chimaera.

Man killed man in the turmoil. Among them, of course, Eurypylus sent evil dooms upon many of the enemy. The first man he killed was the stubborn fighter Eurytus, next Menoetius of the flashing belt, godlike comrades of Elephenor, and by their side he killed Harpalus, who was the comrade of wise Odysseus. Now Odysseus was hard at work in a distant place and had no power to defend his fallen attendant. But his comrade, spirited Antiphus, angered by Harpalus' death, made a cast at Eurypylus. He did not wound him at all, because the mighty spear went a little off its course and fell upon brave Meilanion. His mother bore him by the mouth of the broad Caicus. She was called Cleite, had beautiful cheeks, and was married to Erylaus. Eurypylus, angry at his comrade's death, rushed immediately upon Antiphus. But his swift feet carried him safely into the crowd of his comrades, and the mighty spear of brave Telephusson did not destroy him. He was destined to die a dreadful death later on at the hands of the man-killing Cyclops, for this was the way, I assume, it pleased loathsome Fate.[1] Eurypylus then made an attack on the other side, and as he steadily advanced a great crowd fell under his spear. Just as tall trees, brought low by the might of iron, fill up the ravines in the shaggy mountains and lie every way on the ground; so the Greeks were brought low by the spears of brave Eurypylus—up until Achilles' son came against him, with proud thoughts in his heart. The two of them shook their long spears in their hands, eager to attack each other. Eurypylus first questioned him and said:

"Who are you and where have you come from to fight against me? I assure you pitiless Fates are carrying you to Hades. No man has escaped me in cruel conflict, but all those who have come here eager to fight me—on them all I have cruelly sent a painful death. The dogs are dividing the bones and flesh of all of them by the streams of Xanthus. But tell me, who are you, and whose horses are those in which you take such pride?"

When he said this, Achilles' powerful son said to him:

[1] In the second book of the *Odyssey*, the first person to speak in the Ithacan assembly is an old man named Aegyptius, and Homer tells us that his son Antiphus had gone to Troy with Odysseus and had been the last of Odysseus' companions eaten by the Cyclops Polyphemus (17–20). When the Cyclops' cannibal meals are described in Book xix, none of the victims are named.

"Why, when I am hurrying into the bloody turmoil, do you who are my enemy question me as if your thoughts were friendly and ask me to tell of my lineage? There are very many men who know it. I am the son of stout-hearted Achilles, who in days gone by struck your father with his long spear and drove him to run away. The evil Fates of death would have taken hold of him, if my father had not been quick to heal the painful damage.[2] The horses that carry me are those of my godlike father. Harpuia bore them after union with Zephyrus, the west wind. Their feet run even over the restless sea, barely touching it with their hooves, and they speed like the winds. And now, since you have learned the lineage of my horses as well as my own, make an effort to get direct knowledge also of the force of my tireless spear. Its lineage comes from the heights of lofty Pelion, where it left its stump and forest."

With these words, the splendid man leapt from his chariot to the ground, brandishing his extremely long spear. Eurypylus, on the other side, took in his powerful hands a huge rock and sent it flying against Neoptolemus' golden shield. But the stone's on-rush did not shake him at all; he stood like a vast crag on a tall mountain that not even the force of all the rivers swollen with rain can push aside, because it is so firmly rooted; so the mighty son of Achilles stood fast with steady courage. Not even this, however, caused Eurypylus with his bold strength to fear Achilles' irrepressible son. His own boldness and the Fates were inciting him.

The hearts in the breasts of both of them seethed, and the bright armor rattled upon them. They came at each other like savage wild beasts whose conflict increases in the mountains, when they are struck to the heart by dismal hunger, and they both make wild rushes, busy with a freshly killed ox or a stag, and the

---

[2] Telephus himself is not named in Homer, though Odysseus, while conversing with the ghost of Achilles in the world of the dead, reports to him as an especially impressive feat that Neoptolemus killed Eurypylus Telephusson (*Odyssey* xi. 519-20). In post-Homeric story, Telephus becomes of some importance. The Greeks attack Teuthrania, mistakenly believing that they are at Troy, and in this conflict Achilles wounds Telephus. Telephus is told by an oracle that he can be cured only by the weapon which injured him. He goes to Achilles, begs for help, and Achilles sprinkles on the wound some rust from the spear he had used against Telephus, and so Telephus is healed.

glens re-echo as they fight; so these men attacked each other, joining in pitiless conflict. On both sides of them the long ranks of the two armies were hard at work in battle, and a savage conflict rose around them. Like swift blasts of wind, the two men clashed with their spears, eager to shed each other's blood. The battle goddess Enyo stood close beside them and kept urging them on. They did not pause in their attack, but struck each other's shields, and sometimes their greaves and their plumed helmets. Many a blow reached flesh, because the fierce work of war was driving on the bold heroes. Eris' heart was delighted as she watched them. Abundant sweat flowed from them both, but they stood their ground with strength unimpaired, for they were both of divine blood.

The gods [watched them] from Olympus [with divided thoughts],[3] for some were glorifying Achilles' mighty son, and some godlike Eurypylus. And the two heroes fought on, tireless as crags of high mountains, and both shields rang loudly from the blows of the spears. But at last, after great effort, the long Pelian spear went through Eurypylus' throat, and the red blood gushed   200 swiftly out of him. The soul flew from his body through the wound, and a deadly darkness fell upon his eyes. He collapsed on the ground in his armor, just like a flourishing pine or fir torn up by the roots by the force of the cold north wind; so much ground did the body of Eurypylus cover as he fell. The earth of the Trojan plain rang loudly, the body lost its color, pallor spread over it and quenched its beautiful flush of red. Exulting over it, the powerful hero Neoptolemus boasted loudly:

"Eurypylus, you were certain, I fancy, that you would destroy the Greek ships and the Greeks themselves and give us all a miserable death. But the gods brought no fulfillment to your desire. My father's great spear subdued you to me, stubborn fighter though you are. No mortal who comes against me will escape this spear, not even if he be of solid bronze."

He spoke and quickly drew the long spear from the body. The Trojans were terrified as they looked upon the stout-hearted

3 A guess to fill a gap.

hero. He removed Eurypylus' armor at once and gave it to his swift comrades to carry to the Greek ships, while he himself jumped into his fast chariot drawn by the tireless horses and advanced. Just as a thunderbolt comes along with lightning from unwearying Zeus through the vast air, and even the immortals, except for great Zeus, fear it as it comes down, and, rushing to the earth, it shatters trees and rocky hills; so he rushed rapidly upon the Trojans, preparing trouble for them. Men were struck dead on every side, all whom the immortal horses reached; the surface of the earth was covered with them and grew red with the abundant gore. Just as when myriads of leaves in the glens on a mountain fall in thick showers and cover the earth; so on this day a host of Trojans beyond telling was laid low on the ground by the hands of Neoptolemus and the spirited Greeks. Over their hands flowed quantities of dark blood from men and from horses, and the rims of the chariot wheels grew wet as they moved around their axles.

The sons of Troy would have gone inside their gates, like heifers running from a lion or pigs from a storm, if grim Ares had not come down from Olympus without the knowledge of the blessed ones, eager to defend the war-loving Trojans. His horses carried him into the tumult: Aethon and Phlogius, Conabus and Phobus as well. A Fury fierce of face had borne them to the blustering north wind. They were fire-breathing creatures, and the bright air groaned under them as they hurried to battle. Quickly Ares arrived at Troy. The earth re-echoed loudly about the feet of the divine horses. He came very close to the clamor of battle, brandishing his mighty spear, and called loudly to the Trojans, ordering them to face their enemies in the conflict. They all marveled when they heard the divine voice, because they did not see the immortal form of the deathless god, or his horses either, for he was hidden in a mist. But the famous intelligence of godlike Helenus understood the wonderful voice darting clear enough from somewhere upon Trojan ears. His heart, of course, rejoiced, and he called out loudly to the retreating army:

"Poor wretches, why do you run in fright from the bold son of war-loving Achilles? He too is a mortal person, and he has no strength like that of Ares, who is giving us great help in answer to our longing. He shouts to us, giving us vigorous orders to fight against the Greeks in the turmoil. Come, my friends, bear up with spirit and put boldness in your breasts. I do not think another better protector in war will come for the Trojans. What is better than Ares for battle, when he gives protection to armed men? This is the way he has now come as our helper. Take thought for battle yourselves, too, and cast fear away."

So he spoke, and they stood and faced the Greeks. Just as, in the scrub, dogs who have previously run away from a wolf turn to fight it vigorously when the shepherd earnestly sets them on with his words; so the sons of Troy, in the terrible confusion of the fighting, put aside their fear, and man fought boldly face to face with man. The soldiers' armor rang from the blows of swords and spears and missiles. Spear points sank into flesh, and dreadful Ares grew wet with the abundant blood. One man after another fell in the turmoil, as the two armies fought on. The scales of battle were even. Just as when, on the slope of a great vineyard, men trim with the iron the rows of vines, working fast, and in their competition their work prospers equally, because they are equal in age and strength; so for these two armies the grim scales of battle were even. The Trojan hearts were bold, they put their faith in the might of fearless Ares and stood their ground, while the Greeks, of course, put their faith in the son of the stubborn fighter Achilles. The mutual slaughter went on, and deadly Enyo, the battle goddess, roamed among them. Her arms and shoulders were spattered with grisly gore, and a dreadful sweat flowed from her limbs. She was not helping either side, but was enjoying the even conflict, her heart full of awe for Thetis and glorious Ares.

Then Neoptolemus killed far-famed Perimedes, whose home was by the Sminthian grove. Next he killed Cestrus and the stubborn fighter Phalerus, strong Perilaus, and Menalces of the fine ashen spear. Iphianassa bore him near the foot of holy Cilla to the craftsman Medon, skilled in the arts of craftsmanship. He remained at home in his dear native land and got no profit from his son. Later, when he was dead, collateral heirs divided his home

and all that his craft had made.[4] Deiphobus killed Lycon, a stub-
300   born fighter, hitting him a little above the groin. All his entrails
and his whole belly poured out around the long spear. Aeneas
killed Dymas, who used to live at Aulis and had followed Arcesi-
laus to Troy. But he did not ever see his dear country again.
Euryalus destroyed Astraeus with a blow of his cruel spear. The
deadly point flew straight through his chest and, cutting the pas-
sages of his stomach, brought the man doom; his food was mixed
with his blood. Not far from him, great-souled Agenor killed
Hippomenes, brave Teucer's noble comrade, with a swift blow on
the collarbone. His spirit leapt from his body along with his blood,
and grim night covered him. Sorrow fell upon Teucer at his com-
rade's death, and he shot a swift arrow, aiming straight at Agenor.
But he failed to hit him. Agenor just barely avoided it, and the
arrow fell upon brave Deiophontes, who was close beside him. It
struck his left eye, cut the pupil, and came out through his right
ear. The Fates pushed the cruel arrow where they pleased. He
leapt up, still upright on his feet, and Teucer hit him with a second
arrow sent whistling at his throat. It rushed straight through and
cut the tendons of his neck, and a painful doom overtook him.

Man was fashioning death for man, the Dooms and Destiny
were rejoicing, savage Eris, filled with enthusiasm, gave a tremen-
dous shout, and Ares shouted terribly in answer to her. He in-
spired the Trojans with great boldness, quickly turned the Greek
ranks, and routed them. He did not, however, frighten Achilles'
son. He stood his ground, fought boldly on, and killed one man
after another. Just as a young boy flings out his hand at flies that
come around the milk, and they, subdued by his little blow,
breathe out their spirit on all sides near the milk pail, and the boy
is delighted at his accomplishment; so the illustrious son of pitiless
Achilles found pleasure among the dead bodies and gave no heed
to Ares, who was urging on the Trojans, but took vengeance here
and there as the army attacked him. Just as the peak of a great
mountain stands firm against the onrushing blasts of the wind; so
he stood firm and fearless.

4 Or possibly "all his farm lands."

His enthusiasm angered Ares, and he was about to fight him in person, face to face, throwing off the holy cloud that hid him. But Athena leapt to shadowy Ida from somewhere on Olympus. The divine earth and the noisy streams of Xanthus trembled, she shook them so. Fear shattered the spirit of the Nymphs, who were afraid for Priam's city. Lightning flashes hovered around her immortal armor, terrible snakes breathed fierce fire from her indestructible shield, her divine helmet touched the clouds above her. She would have rushed into conflict with swift Ares, if Zeus's mighty will had not frightened them both by thundering terribly from the high heaven. Ares drew back from the combat, for the anger of great Zeus was now quite clear to him. He made his way to wintry Thrace, and his proud spirit was concerned no more for the Trojans. Noble Pallas, too, remained no longer in the Trojan plain, but she went to the holy land of Athens.

The mortals' thoughts were still on deadly battle, but strength was failing the sons of Troy, and the Greeks, full of desire for fighting, kept on their heels as they retreated. Just as winds follow after ships speeding under sail into the great swell of the sea, or as the power of fire advances upon scrub, or as nimble dogs, eager for the chase, follow the deer on the mountains; so the Greeks advanced against their enemies. Achilles' son was urging them on, killing with his great spear whomever he met in the turmoil. The Trojans were routed and went into their city with its lofty gates.

And so the Greeks had a little rest from war, when they had driven the troops of Trojans into Priam's city, just as shepherds at sheep farms drive in the lambs. Just as when oxen have a rest, after they have grown very tired pulling a load up to a difficult height, panting hard under the yoke; so the Greeks had a rest, when they had grown weary in arms. They were still eager to fight, however, and encircled the town and its towers. The Trojans pulled tight the bolts on their gates and awaited on their walls the power of the attackers. Just as when shepherds wait out a dark storm at the sheepfolds, when a blustery day of winter comes, with lightning, rain, and heavy snow all together and, although they are eager to go to the pasture, do not hurry out until the great storm abates and the wide, loud-roaring rivers subside; so the Trojans, afraid of the enemy's attack, waited on their walls. The Greek army streamed rapidly toward the town. Just as when long-winged starlings or jackdaws swoop down in clouds upon olive fruit, longing for the pleasant food, and men are unable to put them to flight by their shouts until they have eaten, for hunger encourages their reckless spirit; so the powerful Greeks then streamed around Priam's city and fell upon the gates, eager to pull down the vast work of the brave earthshaker Poseidon.

Much afraid though they were, the Trojans did not forget to fight, but stood on their towers and continued the work of war without ceasing. Arrows leapt incessantly from their strong walls into the crowd of the enemy, together with stones and swift javelins, because Apollo had given them an enduring strength. His
400 heart wanted to protect the warlike Trojans now, even though Hector was gone.

Then Meriones shot a bitter arrow and struck Phylodamas, friend of strong Polites. He hit him just under the jaw, and the arrow was fixed in his throat. He fell like a vulture which a man destroys by knocking it from its crag with a barbed arrow; so swiftly he fell from the tall tower. The spirit left his limbs, and the armor rattled on the corpse. Exulting at this, Meriones, the son of powerful Molus, shot another arrow, his heart full of desire to hit long-suffering Priam's son Polites. But Polites leaned aside quickly and avoided it, and the arrow did not wound his handsome flesh. Just as when on the deep sea a ship is being driven forward by the wind, and a sailor catches sight of a rocky ledge in the waves and, intent on avoiding it, turns the ship aside by moving the rudder with his hand, so that she goes where his spirit bids, and a little effort keeps off a great disaster; so he, seeing the deadly missile in time, escaped doom.

They fought on steadily, and the walls, the lofty towers, and the parapets, where the Trojans were being killed with arrows by the vigorous Greeks, were growing red with blood. The Greeks, too, were not free from the troubles of war, but of course many of them, also, were making the earth red. There was great destruction, and men were being hit on both sides. Grim Enyo, sister of War, found pleasure in urging on the conflict. The Greeks would now have broken the gates and walls of Troy, their strength was so enormous, except that famed Ganymede, looking down from heaven, raised a quick cry, because he was much afraid for his country:

"Father Zeus, if I am really of your stock, and at your commands left glorious Troy to live among the deathless gods and have life immortal, then listen to me now, when my heart is full of sorrow. I will not endure to look upon my city burned up or my race destroyed in cruel conflict. There is no worse pain than this. If it is the will of your heart to do this, do it apart from me. My pain will be lighter if I do not see it with my own eyes. That is the most piteous and abominable thing, when a man sees his country brought low by the hands of enemies."

So, with deep groans, spoke the glorious heart of Ganymede. And then Zeus personally covered Priam's famous city in a continuous bank of huge clouds, and the ruinous battle was darkened. No longer was any man able to see where the wall stood. Its entire length was covered in thick clouds. All around them there were lightning flashes and the noise of thunder from heaven. The Greeks marveled as they heard the noise of Zeus, and Nestor, Neleus' son, called out loudly among them:

"Distinguished leaders of the Greeks, our legs will no longer be firm beneath us now that Zeus is vigorously defending the bold Trojans. A great disaster is rolling upon us. We must go at once to our ships and abandon the toil of battle and the cruel turmoil. In his great anger, he may burn us all. We must obey his portents. All men should always obey him, since he is far the greatest of mighty gods and feeble men. When he was angry at the proud Titans, he poured down from heaven the power of fire, and all the earth was burned beneath it, and the broad stream of Ocean boiled from its depths, reaching up to its very boundaries. The streams of the longest-flowing rivers were dried up, and all the races reared by the life-giving earth were destroyed, all those that the infinite sea feeds, and those fed by the waters of the ever-flowing rivers. Above them the vast sky was hidden in ashes and smoke, and the earth was afflicted. On this account, I am afraid of the might of Zeus this day. We must go to the ships, because he is protecting the Trojans today. Hereafter he will give glory to us too. Sometimes one gets a good day; sometimes a bad one. And, I fancy, we are not yet fated to take the famous city, if Calchas' story was really true that he told before among the assembled Greeks, saying that we would destroy Priam's town in the tenth year."

So Nestor spoke, and they left the glorious city behind them and withdrew from battle, fearing Zeus's attack. They had confidence in the man who was an expert in old stories. Even so, they did not neglect the men who had been killed in action. They rescued them from battle and gave them burial, because the cloud did not cover them, but only the tall city and the unscalable wall, where many sons of Troy and of Greece had been destroyed by Ares. They went then to the ships, took off their armor, and washed away the dust, the sweat, and the gore, going into the waves of the strong-flowing Hellespont.

Helios drove his tireless horses under the dark, and the night was spread over the earth, turning men from their tasks. The Greeks were honoring the bold son of the good fighter Achilles as they had honored his father, and he was dining merrily in the quarters of the kings. No weariness weighed him down at all, because Thetis had removed the painful aches from his limbs and made him like an unwearied man to look upon. When his mighty heart was satisfied with the meal, he went to his father's quarters, where sleep enfolded him. The Greeks slept before the ships, making regular changes of guards, because they were terribly 500 afraid that the Trojan army or that of their close-fighting allies might set fire to the ships and rob them all of their return. So likewise in Priam's town the peoples of Troy slept by turns around the gates and the wall, fearful of a fierce attack by the Greeks.

✳ ✳ ✳

BOOK NINE

The Return of Philoctetes to the Greek Army

WHEN THE DARKNESS of night was done, and Dawn arose from the bounds of the earth, and the vast sky gleamed brightly, then the warlike sons of the sturdy Greeks looked up along the plain, saw Ilion's height cloudless, and greatly wondered at yesterday's marvel. But the Trojans still refused to take a stand in battle before the high wall. A great fear possessed all of them, and they fancied that glorious Peleusson was alive. Among them Antenor prayed to the king of the gods:

"Zeus, ruling from Ida and the gleaming heaven, hear me as I pray and turn away from our city this powerful man whose mind is full of deadly plans, whether he is Achilles, and he did not go to Hades' house, or is some other Greek like that man. Many people are dying in the city of Priam, descendant of gods, and there is no rest from evil, but death and doom are constantly on the increase. Father Zeus, you are not concerned at all for the Trojans who are being killed by the Greeks, but even you, forgetful of your son Dardanus the godlike, are vigorously helping the Greeks. If the spirit in your breast has this desire, that the Trojans perish miserably at the Greeks' hands, do it quickly and do not fashion sorrows for us over a long time."

So he spoke in earnest prayer, and Zeus heard him from heaven and quickly fulfilled part of his request, but the other part he was not going to fulfill. He granted his request that many Trojans perish along with their children, but did not grant his request that he turn Achilles' brave son away from the city of wide squares. Instead, he roused him up all the more, because his spirit was inclined to show favor and honor to Nereus' gracious daughter Thetis.

These, then, were the plans of Zeus, far the greatest of all the gods. Between the city and the broad Hellespont, the Greeks and the Trojans were burning the men killed in action and their horses as well. The slaughter of battle had stopped, because powerful Priam had sent the herald Menoetes to Agamemnon and all the other Greeks, urging that the dead be burned, and they had agreed, out of respect for those who had been killed. (No wrath follows them.) When they had finished their work on the numerous funeral pyres for the dead, then the Greeks went to their quarters, and the Trojans went to the halls of rich Priam. They were filled with great sorrow for fallen Eurypylus, because they had honored him equally with Priam's sons. They buried him, therefore, apart from the others who had been killed, in front of the Dardanian Gate, where the eddying river sends its long streams when it is swollen by the rain from Zeus.

The son of fearless Achilles went to the wide tomb of his father. Tearfully he kissed his dead parent's well-made gravestone and, with deep groans, spoke to him like this:

"Greetings, my father, even though you are now down under the ground. I shall never forget you, though you are gone to Hades' house. How I wish I had found you alive among the Greeks. Sharing mutual joys in our hearts, we should then, perhaps, have taken from holy Ilios wealth beyond telling. But as it was, you did not see your son, nor did I see you still living, for all my longing. But even so, even though you are far away among the dead, the enemy have shuddered much at your spear and your son in battle, while the Greeks have enjoyed seeing him like you in build and nature and in deeds as well."

So he spoke and wiped the hot tears from his cheeks. He went quickly then to the ships of his father, not alone, for twelve Myrmidons went with him, and among them was the old man Phoenix, groaning dismally for splendid Achilles.

Night came over the earth, and stars rushed into heaven. When the men had eaten, they went to sleep. Then the Dawn rose, and the Greeks put on their suits of armor. The gleam from them sparkled far off, reaching even into the upper air. They rushed quickly outside the gates, all together, like snowflakes that fall thick and fast from the clouds in the cold season of winter; so they poured out before their wall, and a terrible cry arose. The earth groaned loudly around them as they moved.

The Trojans marveled when they heard the shout and saw the army. Every man's heart felt crushed within him, and he had a presentiment of doom. They saw the army of the enemy all around them, like a cloud. The armor of the moving men clanged, and the dust rose steadily from their feet. Then some god put boldness into Deiphobus' heart and made him quite fearless—or his own spirit urged him into the turmoil—so that with his spear he might drive from his country the destructive army of the enemy. He made a bold speech among the Trojans:

"My friends, come, put a warlike spirit in your breasts, keeping in mind all the miseries that the end of a difficult war brings to men who have been taken prisoner. We are not merely fighting for Alexander or for Helen, but for our city and ourselves, for our wives, our dear children, and our aged parents, for all the splendor and wealth of our lovely land. I pray that I may fall in battle and my dear land cover me before I see her under the spears of the enemy. I think no other disaster has been created among wretched men that is worse than this. And so, push hateful fear from you, and all of you around me strengthen yourselves for pitiless conflict. Achilles is no longer alive to fight against us, because the destructive fire devoured him. It is some other Greek who has now roused their army. And men who are fighting for their country 100 ought not to be afraid of Achilles or any other Greek. Let us not, therefore, fear the turmoil of war, even though, in our efforts, we have suffered much already. Haven't you yet learned this in your hearts, that, after hard work, men find feasting and wealth; that, after harsh winds and a severe winter, Zeus brings on through the air a bright day for men; after serious illness, strength comes back; and, after war, peace? All things change in time."

So he spoke, and with enthusiasm they quickly got themselves ready for war. There was a din everywhere through the town, as the men armed themselves for cruel battle. Then, of course, for this man a wife, fearful of the fighting, tearfully piled equipment beside her eager husband; for this one, little children, hurrying about their father, brought all his gear. And the soldier sometimes, I fancy, was pained at their sorrow, and then again smiled proudly at his children. His heart now was all the more eager to do his work in battle on behalf of his children and himself. For another man again, his old father, with skillful hands, put about his body defenses against evil conflict, with many an exhortation to his dear son to yield to no man in battle, and he showed his son a battered chest with many a sign of fighting long ago.

When at last they were all equipped in their armor, the Trojans poured out of the city, full of desire for dismal war. Cavalrymen rushed against swift cavalrymen, the troops of infantry assailed infantry, and chariots came face to face with chariots. The earth resounded, the the men rushed into conflict, and each commander shouted out orders to his men. As they quickly came together, there was a clashing of arms all around and a harsh, confused shouting from both sides. Many missiles from both sides flew swiftly. The soldiers' shields rang loudly under the blows of spears, javelins, and swords. Many men were struck with swift blows of battle-axes, and the soldiers' gear was wet with blood.

Trojan women watched the cruel conflict from the wall, and the limbs of all were trembling, as they offered prayers for children, husbands, and brothers. Grey-haired old men sat with them, looking on. Their hearts were eaten by cares for their dear sons. Helen, however, stayed at home alone with her servants, for shame beyond telling held her back.

The men fought steadily on in front of the wall. Dooms were

glad around them, and pernicious Eris was shouting with loud cries to both sides. The dust grew red with the blood of the men being killed, and men of both armies were dying in the tumult. There it was that Deiphobus killed Hippasides, the powerful charioteer of [Nestor], and he fell from the swift chariot among the dead. Distress seized his lord, because he was afraid that, since his hands were now busy with the reins, Priam's brave son would kill him too. But Melanthius did not ignore him. He jumped quickly onto the chariot, shook the long reins, and called out commands to the horses. He had no whip, but drove by hitting them with his spear. Priam's son abandoned them and went into a crowd of others, where he soon brought many men their day of doom. He boldly attacked the enemy, always like a deadly storm. Countless numbers fell under his hands, and the earth was packed with corpses. Just as when on the tall mountains a woodcutter leaps into a wooded ravine and busily destroys a fresh-sprouting forest to make charcoal by burying quantities of felled timber underground along with fire, and the trees fall on every side and cover the slopes, and the man is pleased with his work; so the Greeks, dying in troops under Deiphobus' swift hands, collapsed upon one another. Of the others, some fought on with the Trojans, others fled to the broad stream of Xanthus. Deiphobus drove them into the water and did not stop his killing. Just as when on the shores of the Hellespont that teems with fish hard-working fishermen drag a bulging net to land, and, while it is still in the water, a man takes a curved stick in his hand, jumps in, and brings cruel doom to the swordfish, killing one after another every one he comes upon, and the water grows red with blood; so under Deiphobus' hands the streams of Xanthus were stained red with blood around him, and the corpses were crowded thickly.

Of course the Trojans were not fighting a bloodless battle either. Achilles' mighty son was killing them in other ranks. Thetis, I fancy, rejoiced as much over her grandson, while she watched, as she grieved for Achilles. Beneath his spear a great army fell in the dust along with their horses, and he kept pursuing them and killing. He killed famous Amides, who encountered him. Amides was riding on his horse, but got no profit from his splendid horsemanship. Neoptolemus hit him with his bright spear in the belly, and the point went right through to his spine. His entrails poured out, and a deadly Doom speedily took hold of him as he fell at the feet of his fast horse. Neoptolemus killed Ascanius and Oenops, dealing one a great blow with his spear at the orifice of the stomach, and hitting the other under the throat, which is an especially critical spot for men. He killed also all the many others whom he came upon. Who could name all the men who perished in battle at the hands of Neoptolemus? And yet his limbs did not ever grow tired. Just as when a young man on a flourishing farm works all day long with his sturdy hands and pours down upon the ground a huge olive crop, knocking the olives swiftly down with his stick, and he covers the ground under the trees; so a great crowd fell under the hands of Neoptolemus.

In another part of the field, Diomedes Tydeusson, Agamemnon of the good ashen spear, and the other princes among the Greeks were fighting enthusiastically in the pitiless conflict. The noble Trojan officers also felt no fear, but they too were fighting with spirit and steadily trying to check their retreating men. Many, however, were disregarding their commanders and running from the battle, frightened by the power of the Greeks.

At last, Achilles' mighty son noticed the Greeks who were steadily dying one after another by the streams of Scamander, and he abandoned those whom he had previously been killing in their flight to the city and ordered Automedon to drive to the place where a great host of Greeks was being destroyed. He obeyed at once and with the whip sped the horses, divinely strong, to the conflict. They flew swiftly, carrying their powerful lord through the bodies of the dead. Just as Ares goes into ruinous war mounted on his chariot, and the earth trembles around him as he speeds on, and the divine armor resounds on the god's chest and shines like fire; so Achilles' powerful son went to meet noble Deiphobus. Clouds of dust rose about his horses' hooves. When he caught sight of Deiphobus, the sturdy hero Automedon recognized who he was. He spoke to his lord at once like this, identifying the famous warrior:

"My lord, it is the army of Deiphobus. He, too, in the old days was afraid of your father. But now some god or some supernatural power has put brave spirit in his heart."

So he spoke. Neoptolemus made no reply, but urged him to drive the horses still faster, that he might most quickly keep disgraceful doom from the dying Greeks. When they came close to each other, then Deiphobus, though filled with the deepest desire for battle, stopped just like dreadful fire when it comes close to water. He was filled with amazement as he looked upon stouthearted Achilles' horses and the huge son no whit inferior to his father. The spirit in his breast wavered, impelled now to run away, now to fight against the hero. Just as when a wild boar on the mountains chases jackals away from its newborn young, and a lion appears in another spot, rushing from somewhere, and the boar's vigorous attack is halted, and it no longer wants to go forward, nor, of course, to retreat, and it whets its frothy teeth in its jaws; so Priam's son stood his ground with his horses and chariot, his mind full of thoughts, and his hands moving on his spear. The son of pitiless Achilles said to him:

"Priamson, why are you in such a frenzy against the inferior Greeks who are afraid of your attack and run away when you charge upon them? You imagined you were far the best of soldiers. If you really have courage in your heart, test my irresistible spear in battle."

So he spoke and, driving the horses and chariot of his father, he swooped upon him as a lion swoops upon a deer. He would have killed him and his charioteer as well with his spear, had not Apollo been quick to pour down from some part of Olympus a black cloud, snatch him from the deadly combat, and set him down in the city, where the other Trojans, too, were going in their flight. The son of Achilles struck empty air with his spear and said:

"You dog, you have escaped my power. It was not your

strength that protected you in your eagerness, but some god who concealed you by pouring night over you, and so saved you from evil."

So he spoke, and then Cronosson, high above, dispersed the dark cloud like a mist and scattered it into the lofty sky. At once the plain appeared and all the surrounding country. Neoptolemus saw the Trojans far off by the Scaean Gates, and naturally, like his father, he went against the enemy, who ran before his advance. Just as sailors are afraid of a terrible wave rushing upon them, a wave that has been roused by the wind and comes on swiftly, very wide and high, and the sea is raging with the storm; so an evil fear of his onset enveloped the Trojans. Neoptolemus spoke like this, urging on his comrades:

"Listen, my friends. Put fearless boldness in your hearts, such as brave men ought to have who are eager to win with their hands a distinguished victory and to get glory from the din of war. We must take courage and fight beyond our strength, until we sack the famous city of Troy and win our desire. It is a disgrace to remain here for so long a time and accomplish nothing and be as feeble as women. I would rather be dead than be called unwarlike."

So he spoke, and they rushed into the work of war with even greater boldness and attacked the Trojans. They, too, fought bravely around their city and at times also, inside the gates, from their walls. The dreadful war was unceasing, the Trojans being eager to keep off the terrible enemy army, the sturdy Greeks wanting to sack the town. A ruinous misery possessed them all.

Then it was that Leto's son Apollo wrapped himself in clouds and leapt from Olympus, longing to help the Trojans. The swift winds carried him rapidly on, and, since he was wearing arms of gold, the pathways on high gleamed like lightning as he came down. His quiver rattled about him, the upper air resounded terribly, and the earth rang loudly when he put his tireless feet by the stream of Xanthus. He gave a dreadful shout that put boldness into the Trojans and made the Greeks afraid to stand their ground in the bloody conflict.

Poseidon, the mighty Earthshaker, did not fail to notice all

300

this. He breathed courage into the Greeks, now hard pressed, and the battle became deadly through the plans of the immortals. A thousand companies of men died on each side. Apollo, of course, was filled with anger at the Greeks and was planning to shoot Achilles' son in the very spot where he had shot Achilles. But birds of omen, shrieking on the left, together with many other signs, were restraining his spirit. His anger was not, however, going to regard the portents any longer—a fact that did not escape Poseidon, the god of the black hair. He [quickly] covered himself in a miraculous mist [and rushed toward Apollo].[1] The dark earth shook around the feet of the moving god. In his desire to check Apollo, he spoke to him like this:

"Check your anger, and do not kill the huge son of Achilles. Olympian Zeus himself will not be pleased at his death, and it will bring great pain to me and all the sea gods, just as we were pained before, because of Achilles. Withdraw into the divine upper air. You may anger me, and I will at once break open a wide gulf in the great earth and immediately put all of Ilios itself and its walls as well under the wide darkness. You will yourself be pained at this."

So he spoke. Apollo, full of awe of his father's brother and frightened for the city with its vigorous people, withdrew into the broad heaven, and Poseidon withdrew into the sea. But the human beings fought on, killing one another, and Eris took pleasure in the conflict. But then, at the suggestion of Calchas, the Greeks drew back to their ships and gave up all thought of fighting. It was not fated that the city of Ilios be conquered until strong Philoctetes joined the Greek army—a man skilled in sad war. Calchas had become aware of this either from the flight of birds of good omen or by examining the inward parts of animals. He was a man not unskilled in divination, but knew everything, like a god.

Relying on Calchas and withdrawing from the pains of war, the Atreussons dispatched to the pleasant island of Lemnos in a swift ship Diomedes, Tydeus' sturdy son, and the stubborn fighter Odysseus. They soon arrived at Hephaestus' city, going over the

[1] A guess to fill a gap.

broad Aegean Sea to Lemnos, land of vines. Previously in this place the women had contrived a terrible destruction for the husbands of their youth. They were extremely angry, because their husbands were not honoring them at all, but were sleeping with captive Thracian women whom they had won by their spears and their manliness when they had sacked, at one time, the land of the warlike Thracians. Jealousy fell upon the wives' hearts, and their anger swelled greatly, and with their own hands they recklessly killed the husbands they had loved, showing them no pity, although they were the men they had married in their youth. A terrible madness takes hold of a man or a woman when he falls victim to the disease of jealousy, for powerful pains urge one on. These women, implanting in their minds a fearless spirit and a great strength, brought ruin on their husbands in a single night and made the whole city a city of widows.

When Odysseus and Diomedes reached the land of Lemnos and the stone cavern where Philoctetes, the son of glorious Poeas lay, wonder came over them, as they looked upon the hero lying on the hard ground and groaning with hideous pains. Round about him, by his couch, were strewn the feathers of many birds. Others had been sewn together and put around his body as a protection against bitter cold. Whenever melancholy hunger seized him, he shot an irresistible arrow, wherever his mind directed it. In part he ate the prey, and in part put them over his grisly wound to keep off the black anguish.[2] His dry locks of hair streamed around his head, like those of a fierce wild beast that the snare of a painful trap has caught by the foot as it went swiftly through the night. Under pressure of necessity, it cuts off the tip of its foot with its destructive teeth and so arrives at its cave, its heart suffering at once from hunger and cruel pains; so evil suffering overpowered Philoctetes in his wide cavern. His whole body was wasted away; he was nothing but skin and bones. His cheeks were filthily squalid, and he was hideously dirty. Pain beyond curing overwhelmed him, and the eyes of the terribly suffering hero were sunk deep under

---

[2] The text is doubtful. There may well be a line lost which contained a reference to leaves used for his wound. Cf. Sophocles, *Philoctetes*, 649–50.

his brows. He never stopped groaning, because severe pains kept gnawing at the base of his black wound. It had putrefied on the surface and penetrated to the bone. Just as when on a cliff that juts into the dashing sea the water of the vast ocean overwhelms a rock crag by cutting it away at the base, strong though it is, and as it is lashed by the wind and the blustering storms holes are hollowed out in it, eaten away by the sea; so the wound in his foot kept growing larger from the putrefying poison which a fierce water snake had injected in him with its cruel fangs. (Men say its bite is loathsome and incurable whenever the power of the sun dries it out as it crawls around on dry land.) So the wound was wearing out the supremely great hero, overpowered as he was by obstinate pain. The floor of the vast cave was spattered with the purulent discharge that dripped steadily from the wound onto the ground— a great marvel even for men of later generations. Beside his bed stood the long quiver, full of arrows. Some he used for hunting, some against enemies, and these he smeared with the deadly poison of the noxious water snake. In front of the quiver, there was placed nearby the great bow fitted with curving horns, the work of Heracles' tireless hands.

When he caught sight of Odysseus and Diomedes coming to his wide cave, he resolved at once to send against them both his cruel arrows, remembering his terrible anger because they had previously abandoned him and his loud groans and left him alone on deserted shores of the sea. He would have immediately executed the desire of his bold spirit if Athena had not dispersed his melancholy anger as he looked upon the familiar men. They came close to him, both of them looking like men in deep distress. The two of them sat beside him in the hollow cave, one on each side, and questioned him about his ruinous wound and severe pains, and he explained his miseries to them. They kept giving him words of encouragement and told him that his horrible wound would be healed after all his cruel trouble and pain, if he came to the Greek army. The army itself, moreover, they said, was in great distress at the ships, the Atreussons themselves as well as the others. No one of the Greeks in the army was responsible for his troubles,

400

they said, merely the cruel Fates. "No man can avoid them as he moves over the earth. They always move unseen by the side of toiling men all their days, sometimes in their pitiless spirit harming the race of mortals, at other times again exalting them, because they are the ones who contrive for mortals quite all that is sad and pleasant, just as they themselves desire." As Philoctetes listened to Odysseus and godlike Diomedes, his spirit quickly and easily gave up its obstinate anger, although he had been terribly angry before, at all that he had suffered.

Swiftly and joyfully they carried him and his weapons to the ship and the roaring beach. They thoroughly wiped his body and the cruel wound with a porous sponge and washed the wound well in quantities of water. He received a little relief, and they busied themselves at once in preparing a good meal, which he was glad to have. They ate along with him, on board the ship. Ambrosial night came on, and they fell asleep quickly, remaining until dawn on the shore of the island of Lemnos. With dawn, they busied themselves with the cables and raised from the sea the curving anchors. Athena sent a wind blowing astern of the slim-prowed ship. They spread their sails at once with both the sheets, steering their sturdy ship straight. Under the breeze, she ran swiftly over the level sea. The black wave broke with a roar around her, and the gray froth boiled everywhere about her. Shoals of dolphins darted around her, making their way swiftly along the pathways of the gray sea.

Soon the heroes reached the Hellespont, that abounds in fish, where the other ships were. The Greeks were delighted when they saw the men who had been much longed for in the army, and they were naturally pleased to disembark from the ship. Philoctetes, Poeas' bold son, kept his thin hands on the other two, and they led him to the glorious earth, limping badly and supported by their powerful arms. Just as in the forests an oak tree or a fat pine tree cut halfway through by a strong woodcutter still stands for a little while—as much, that is, as the woodcutter left when he cut away at the resinous trunk, so that the pitch, set on fire, might provide a torch in the mountains—and the tree, heavily burdened, is bent down by wind and weakness onto flourishing young trees, and they hold up its weight; so Philoctetes, weighed down by intolerable pain, leaned upon the bold heroes who brought him into the crowd of Greek soldiers.[3]

As they looked upon him, every man felt pity for this archer suffering from a loathsome wound. But quicker than swift thought, Podalirius, equal to the heavenly gods, made him hale and sound, carefully sprinkling many drugs over his wound and making proper invocation of his father's name. The Greeks raised a quick shout, all of them together glorifying Asclepius' son. They zealously washed Philoctetes clean and anointed him with olive oil. His pernicious despondency and pain disappeared, through the will of the immortals, and the Greeks were glad at heart as they looked upon him. He had relief from his misery, color succeeded to his pallor, great strength to his wretched weakness, and all his frame filled out. Just as when a grainfield grows strong with ears of grain, although it had previously been wasting away, and the rain of a hard winter had fallen heavily upon it and swamped it, and then, made strong by the winds, it smiles, flourishing on a carefully worked farm; so the whole body of Philoctetes, previously so afflicted, at once took on a flourishing appearance. He had left in the rounded hull of the ship all the cares that had been overwhelming his spirit.

The Atreussons looked with wonder on the man who had, as it were, returned from the dead. They thought this was the work of the immortals. This was, indeed, the truth, just as they thought. Noble Athena Tritogeneia shed over him size and grace. He took on at once exactly the appearance he had had before among the Greeks, before he was laid low by misfortune. Then all the princes together brought the son of Poeas to the quarters of rich Agamemnon and glorified him with the honor of a banquet. When they had had their fill of drink and fine food, then Agamemnon of the good ashen spear spoke to him:

"My friend, do not now put terrible anger into your heart

---

[3] An obscure passage with many difficulties of detail. As Köchly says, *locus vexatissimus*. The text may be defective, and there may be lacunae.

because we abandoned you years ago on the island of Lemnos, when our minds were deluded by the will of the gods. We did not do this apart from the blessed ones, but the immortals themselves, I fancy, wanted to inflict many evils upon us in your absence, because you are an expert in destroying with your arrows enemies who fight against you. [The paths of human life][4] over all the earth and over the great sea are hidden from our eyes by the will of the

500 Fates. The paths have many branches, are numerous and crooked, turn in all directions. Men are carried along them by the Fate of a supernatural power, like leaves swept along by the blasts of the wind. The good man often lights upon an evil path, the man who is not good, on a good one. No man upon the earth is able to avoid them, any more than he can have his free choice. The sensible man must endure his misery with a stubborn mind, even if the winds carry him along a hard way. Since, then, this act of ours was foolish and wrong, we will in return make recompense with great gifts, if ever we take the fine citadel of Troy. For the moment, take seven women, twenty fast prize-winning horses, and twelve tripods. Your heart will find pleasure in these all your days. Moreover, in my quarters you will always have a king's honor at the feast."

So he spoke, and gave the hero the splendid gifts. The son of stout-hearted Poeas said to him:

"My friend, I am no longer angry at you, nor at any other Greek, if, perhaps, there was also someone else involved in the wrong done me. I know how pliable the minds of good men are. It is not right to be always hard and headstrong, but sometimes to be formidable and sometimes gentle. But let us now go to our beds, because if a man is eager to fight, it is better for him to sleep than to linger at banquets."

With these words, he hurried away to his comrades' quarters. They quickly and with great joy in their hearts got a bed ready for their war-loving king, and he lay down gladly until the dawn.

Divine night withdrew, the light of the sun reddened the hills, and men were busy with all their tasks. The Greeks were

[4] A guess to fill a gap.

full of enthusiasm for ruinous war. Some sharpened their polished spears, some their arrows, some their javelins. With the dawn, they prepared a meal for themselves and fed their horses, and all ate. Among them, the sturdy son of noble Poeas spoke like this, urging them on to the work of war:

"We must now give our thoughts to battle. Let no man of us remain by the ships until he has destroyed the famous walls of Troy, with its fine towers, and burned the town."

So he spoke, and the spirits in their breasts were greatly cheered. They put on their armor, took their shields, and all together, equipped with ashen spears, oxhide shields, and double-crested helmets, they rushed from the ships. One man pressed close to another in the ranks, and you could not say that one man was separate from another, as they rushed on. The moving men were thus closely packed and, as it were, fitted together.

BOOK TEN

The Death of Paris

Τ

HE TROJANS, FOR THEIR part, were outside of Priam's town, all of them with their arms, their chariots, and their fast horses. They were burning the bodies of the men killed in action and were fearful of an attack by the Greek army. So when they saw the Greeks rushing toward the town, they quickly raised the mound of earth over the dead, working fast because they were terribly frightened by the sight of the Greeks. In their distress of spirit, Polydamas, who was outstandingly intelligent and sensible, spoke to them:

"My friends, Ares is raging against us in a way that we can no longer withstand. We must consider how to find some way to deal with the war. The Greeks are staying here, and they are winning. I propose that we now mount our well-constructed towers and stay there, fighting night and day, until the Greeks return to fertile Sparta or, remaining here by our wall, get tired of sitting here ingloriously. They will have no strength to break our high walls, no matter how hard they work; what has been made by gods is not weak, but imperishable. Moreover, we shall not, I fancy, have any lack of food or drink. Large supplies have been stored within the halls of wealthy Priam. These will provide food in abundance for

a long time, even if another army three times as big comes here
eager to defend us in our need."

So he spoke, and Aeneas, Anchises' bold son, rebuked him:
"Polydamas, how is it that men say you are a man of sense?
A person who suggests that for a long period we suffer miseries in
the town! The Greeks will not get tired of their long stay here,
but they will continue to press us hard, when they see us taking a
defensive position. We shall have a painful death in our city, if
they fight on around it here for a long time. No one will offer us
fine grain from Thebe if we are shut up in the town, and no one
will bring us wine from Maeonia. We will die wretchedly from
the pangs of starvation, even if our great wall does protect us. If
we are going to escape evil death and dooms and not die in tor-
ment from the miseries of starvation, we must fight in arms along
with our children and our old fathers. Then, too, perhaps Zeus will
give us some help, because we are descended from his glorious
blood. And if we are to meet our end hated by him as well, it is
better to die a quick and glorious death fighting for our country
than to stay inside the walls and die with suffering."[1]

So he spoke, and they all shouted their approval as they heard
him. At once, then, the armies were fenced round against each
other with helmets, shields, and spears. From Olympus, the eyes
of tireless Zeus looked upon the Trojans arming themselves for
war against the Greeks, and he roused up each man's spirit, so that
he might intensify in both armies incessant fighting. For truly
Alexander, fighting for his wife, was soon to die at Philoctetes'
hands.

Eris, mistress of turmoil, brought them into one place. She
was not visible to anyone, because a blood-stained cloud enveloped
her shoulders. She moved here and there, stirring up great tumult,
going now into the gathering of the Trojans, now among the
Greeks. Fear and Terror were boldly busy around her, glorifying

[1] The cautious Polydamas again, as in Book Two, plays the role Homer
gives him in the *Iliad*. Aeneas here has the role which Hector has in Homer and
which Quintus gave to Paris in Book Two. Since Hector loses his life as a result of
disregarding Polydamas' advice, Quintus would have followed Homer more close-
ly if he had had Paris oppose Polydamas here in the book where he is to be killed.

the stout-hearted sister of their father. The goddess was full of eagerness and, just now small, reared up huge. The arms of adamant she held were spattered with gore, she brandished her deadly spear high in the air, the black earth moved under her feet, she breathed out a terrible blast of fire and kept up a great shouting, urging on the men. They came quickly together and joined battle, for a dreadful goddess was leading them to a great task. Just as the winds howl, blowing fiercely at the beginning of spring, when the tall trees and the forest put forth their leaves, or as when blazing fire roars in the dry scrub, or as the vast sea rages wildly under the shrieking winds, and there is a tremendous whistling, and the limbs of sailors tremble beneath them; so the vast earth resounded under them as they rushed on. Then they fell to fighting and man charged upon man.

Aeneas first killed a Greek, Harpalion, son of Arizelus. His mother Amphinome bore him in the land of the Boeotians, and he had come to Troy along with glorious Prothoenor to help the Greeks. He it was whom Aeneas then hit under the soft belly and took from him his spirit and sweet life. Beside him he killed Hyllus, son of brave Thersandrus, hitting him on the throat with a barbed javelin. Glorious Arethusa had borne him beside the waters of Lethaeus on the island of Crete. His death brought great pain to Idomeneus.

But Achilles' son soon killed twelve Trojans with his father's spear: Cebrus first of all, Harmon, Pasitheus, Ismenus, Imbrasius, Schedius, Phleges, and besides these Mnesaeus, Ennomus, Amphinomus, Phasis, and Galenus. The last used to live on steep Gargarus and was outstanding among the sturdy Trojans in battle. He had come to Troy with a huge army, because Priam Dardanusson had promised to give him many fine gifts of great beauty— fool, he took no thought of his doom, for he was to die quickly in the ruinous war, before he brought home Priam's splendid gifts.

And then a destructive Fate turned against the Greeks Eurymenes, comrade of stout-hearted Aeneas. A great boldness in his heart roused him, that he might destroy many before he fulfilled his fated day and died. He killed men here and there, like a pitiless wild beast, and the Greeks were quick to give way before him, raging terribly on his life's last day and reckless of doom. There would have been no end to his work in that battle, if his arms had not grown weary and the point of his spear had not been completely bent back. There was no strength left in the handle of his sword, but Doom shattered it. Meges hit him with a spear in the throat, the blood spurted from his mouth, and Fate stood quickly by his side along with the pain.

When Eurymenes had been killed, two attendants of Epeius, Deïlion and Amphion, were planning to take off his armor. But in their turn these eager men were cruelly destroyed beside the corpse by the bold strength of Aeneas. Just as when in a vineyard someone destroys among the drying grapes wasps that are darting at the fruit, and they breathe out their lives before they have tasted the fruit; so Aeneas destroyed them quickly, before they had taken the armor as booty.

Tydeusson killed Menon and Amphinous, fine men both, and Paris killed Demoleon Hippasusson. He had previously lived in the Laconian land, by the streams of the deep-flowing river Eurotas, and had come to Troy under the command of Menelaus the swift fighter. Paris killed him by hitting him under the right breast with an arrow and took the life from his limbs.

Teucer killed Zechis, Medon's famous son. He used to live in Phrygia, land rich in sheep, in the sacred cave of the fair-haired nymphs. Once upon a time when Endymion was asleep there beside his cattle divine Selene saw him from on high and came down from heaven. Keen desire for the young man led her, pure and immortal though she was. A memorial of their marriage bed has been created under the oak trees and has lasted up to the present day. Cow's milk had been poured around it in the woods, and men still look with wonder upon it. Seeing it from a considerable distance, you would say it was grey milk, but the cave sends forth white water, and, when it gets a little distance off, the streams congeal, and there is earth like stone.[2]

Meges, son of Phyleus, attacked Alcaeus and pierced him

[2] A number of details in this marvel are uncertain.

under his panting heart with a spear, quickly destroying the life he loved. His wretched parents did not, for all their longing, receive him back again from melancholy war. Fair-girdled Phyllis and Margasus they were, and they lived by the streams of clear Harpasus. This river gives trouble when it unites with the Maeander its noisy stream and copious swell, raging constantly with turbulent flood.

The son of Oïleus stabbed at close range Glaucus' noble comrade Scylaceus of the good ashen spear. The cruel point went a little above his shield and drove through his broad shoulder, and the blood spurted over the oxhide shield. The wound did not, however, overpower him, because his fated day received him by the walls of his dear native city after his homecoming. When the swift Greeks had sacked tall Ilios, then he escaped from the war and arrived in Lycia all alone, without his comrades. Close to the city, the women gathered and asked him about their children and their husbands, and he, of course, told the fate of all. Then they formed a circle around him and stoned him to death; so he got no benefit from returning home to his native country, but groaned loudly as the stones covered him. The missiles formed his grim tomb, close to the sanctuary and monument of mighty Bellerophon, in Tlos, near the famous rock of the Titaness. But after he had fulfilled his fated day and died, he has since been honored like a god through the commands of glorious Apollo Letoson, and his honor has never faded.

Besides these, Philoctetes, the son of Poeas, killed Deïoneus and Antenor's son Acamas of the good ashen spear. He also brought low a great throng of other men, for he was raging among the enemy like tireless Ares, or a noisy river that overflows and destroys the long dykes, when, violently stirred up around rocks, it comes down dangerously from the hills, mixed with rain, a stream with a strong current that flows all the year round, and the projecting bluffs cannot hold back its boiling floods; so no man had the courage to approach Poeas' brave son, not even if he caught sight of him at a distance, for the courage in his breast was tremendous.

He was equipped, too, with the elaborately decorated weapons of brave Heracles. On his shining belt were fierce and savage bears, terrible jackals, and leopards with grim smiles on their faces. Near these were spirited wolves, boars with white tusks, and powerful lions—all terribly like living creatures. And there were conflicts everywhere around the belt, accompanied by dreadful slaughter. So many were the decorations set around his belt.

Other designs adorned his huge quiver: Zeus's son, windfooted Hermes, was there, killing great Argus by the river Inachus —Argus, whose eyes slept by turns. Strong Phaethon was there by the river Eridanus, after he had been thrown from his chariot. A black smoke hovered in the air from the earth that was on fire— all as if real. Godlike Perseus was killing fierce Medusa, where the bathing places of the stars are, the ends of the earth, and the sources of deep-flowing Oceanus, in the West, where the night meets the tireless setting sun. On it, too, Prometheus, the great son of tireless 200 Iapetus, was hanging in unbreakable bonds on a crag of the lofty Caucasus, and an eagle was tearing his liver, which was constantly growing. He was just like one who is groaning. The famous hands of Hephaestus had fashioned these decorations for mighty Heracles, and he gave them to Poeas' son to wear because he was an especially intimate friend.

Philoctetes, glorying in this armor, was destroying hosts. Finally, Paris rushed at him courageously, wielding in his hands his cruel arrows and curving bow. His final day was coming to meet him. He shot from the bowstring a swift arrow, and the string hummed as the arrow darted away. It did not leave his hands to no purpose, although it missed Philoctetes, who barely avoided it. The arrow struck Cleodorus, a very famous man, a little above the breast and drove through all the way to the shoulder. The reason was that he did not have his shield which kept grim destruction from him, but was drawing back unprotected, because Polydamas had struck the shield from his shoulders by cutting through the baldric with a strong ax. He was withdrawing, fighting with his cruel spear, when the arrow came from another quarter and fell upon him. This is the way, I suppose, that a supernatural power wanted to bring grim destruction upon Cleodorus. He was the son of wise Lernus, whom Amphiale bore in the rich land of the Rhodians.

When Paris had overpowered Cleodorus with his cruel missile, then it was, doubtless, that noble Poeas' powerful son stretched his bow with eager speed and gave a loud cry:

"You dog, how sure I am that I will give you death and destructive doom, since you are eager to match yourself with me. All those who are being hard pressed in war because of you who are their ruin will then have a breathing space. With you dead here, then there will be a quick release from destruction, because you have been their disaster."

With these words, he drew the well-twisted bowstring close to his breast, the bow was bent to a circle, the pitiless arrow was aimed, and under the hero's strong pull the terrible point projected only a little over the bow. The string rang loud, as the arrow rushed away with a harsh whistle. The glorious man did not miss, although he did not by any means destroy Paris' life. He still had strength in his spirit, because the arrow did not then fall on a critical spot, but cut with a glancing blow the flesh of his handsome arm. Then Paris aimed his bow again. But the dear son of Poeas was too quick for him and hit him above the groin with a barbed arrow. Paris did not stay to fight any longer, but rushed quickly away, like a dog which is seized with terror of a lion and draws back, even though he has been attacking before; so Paris, his heart pierced with dreadful pain, withdrew from the war.

The soldiers, however, kept rushing confusedly together, killing one another. The conflict was bloody, and men were being killed on both sides. Corpses were soon piled upon corpses, like raindrops or hail or flakes of snow when, at Zeus's orders, Zephyrus and winter sprinkle the high mountains and the woods; so they, destroyed on both sides by pitiless doom, fell in crowds and were piled one upon another.

Paris was moaning terribly, wretched in spirit because of his wound. Doctors were quick to busy themselves about the distracted man. Then the Trojans returned to their city, and the

Greeks soon arrived at their dark ships, because black night had caused them to stop the turmoil of fighting and now took the weariness from their limbs by pouring over their eyelids sleep, the protector from distress.

But swift Paris lay sleepless until dawn. Although many were eager to help him with all sorts of cures, no one succeeded, because it was fated that at Oenone's hands he escape doom and death—if she were willing. He was quick to believe the prophecies and went, though much against his will; a deadly need brought him face to face with the wife of his youth. Unpropitious birds came toward him and uttered cries over his head, while others darted on his left. As he looked at them, doubtless sometimes he was afraid and sometimes hoped their flight was not significant. But they were revealing to him a dreadful and painful death.

He reached the home of famous Oenone. All her maids marveled when they saw him, as did Oenone herself. He fell quickly at his wife's feet, [mastered by his painful wound, that kept getting worse],[3] black above and black within, until it went through the bone and reached the fat marrow. The terrible poison was rotting the man's belly where his flesh had been wounded. He was in misery, his heart pierced with loathsome pain. Just as when a man's chest is on fire from sickness and a terrible thirst, and his pounding heart grows parched, and the bile boils and burns around it, and his torpid soul hovers on his dry lips, longing at once for life and for water; so the spirit within his breast was burning up with pain. Feebly, he spoke to her like this:

"My revered wife, do not hate me in my misery because in other days I left you desolate in our halls. I did not want to, but Fates I could not escape led me to Helen. I wish that I had died in your arms, and had lost my life before I shared her bed. By the gods who dwell in heaven, by your bed and the wedded love of our youth, please make gentle your spirit and keep away the horrible pain by putting healing drugs on the deadly wound. They are fated to push the pains from my spirit—if you are willing. It rests with your heart, whether you resolve to save me from a

[3] A guess to fill a gap.

hateful death or not. But be quick to pity me, cure the power of the arrows with their swift doom, while I still have strength and can move my limbs. Although you cannot forget your grim jealousy, still do not abandon me to die under a pitiless doom, now 300 that I have fallen at your feet. Your act would not please the Prayers of Repentance, who are themselves daughters of Zeus the thunderer, and, when they are angry at haughty human beings, they incite a cruel Fury and her wrath to follow them. But quick, my queen, keep evil dooms away from me, even if I did do some wrong in my folly."

So he spoke, but he had no success in winning over her somber heart. She taunted him in his great misery and said:

"Why have you come to me? You abandoned me in our halls years ago for the sake of Helen, Tyndareus' daughter, the woman of trouble, and you cared nothing for my loud wails. Go and sleep by her side and take your merry joy. She is surely far better than the wife you wed in your youth. People say she is ageless. Hurry to her with your entreaties and don't, with tears in your eyes, make your pitiful and miserable requests to me. I wish I had the courage of a wild beast in my heart, to devour your flesh and then lap up your blood for the sort of anguish you gave me, when you put your trust in follies. You miserable Paris, where now is your love goddess, Cytherea of the beautiful crown? How is it Zeus has forgotten his son-in-law? Keep them as your saviors, but get out of my halls. You're a disastrous ruin for the blessed ones and for men. Because of you, you man of sin, grief took hold of even the immortals, some for grandsons dying, some for sons. Leave my house and make your way to Helen. Hers is the bed by which you must whimper, suffering night and day and pierced with loathsome pain, until she cures you of your terrible anguish."

With these words she sent the moaning Paris from her halls, now so dear to him. Poor fool, she was not aware of her own lot. When he died, the Fates of death were speedily to follow after her, too. For so the doom of Zeus had spun for her.

Paris hurried away over the rough heights of Ida to his last path, where his terrible doom led him, limping wretchedly and with great pain in his spirit. Hera noticed him, and her immortal heart was cheered as she sat there on Olympus, where Zeus's garden is. Four handmaids were sitting close to her. Once upon a time, bright-eyed Selene, subdued by Helios, had borne them in the broad sky. They are imperishable and not like one another, but in appearance quite distinct one from another. [One is in charge of the spring, one of autumn, one has summer as her portion][4] and the other gives her care to winter and Capricorn—for man's life goes through its changes in these four portions which these handmaids take care of in turn. Well, these things doubtless may well be a concern to Zeus in heaven. The handmaids and Hera were talking of all the things a destructive Doom was planning in her deadly mind: arranging a loathsome marriage of Helen and Deiphobus and the cruel wrath and anger of Helenus on account of the woman; how the Greeks were going to seize him on the high mountains, while he was angry at the Trojans, and bring him to their swift ships; how at his suggestion mighty Tydeus' son Diomedes, accompanied by Odysseus, was going to move quickly over the great wall, bring a painful death to Alcathous, and seize Athena Tritogeneia, well disposed and willing, who had been a protection for the city and for the Trojans themselves. Not even any of the gods, though infinitely angry, had power to sack Priam's prosperous town while she, a goddess free from care, stood before it. No man had made her immortal statue out of iron, but Cronosson himself had thrown it down from Olympus to the city of wealthy Priam.[5]

These were the things Zeus's wife was chatting about with her handmaids, and many other topics besides. But Paris died on Ida and did not come home for Helen to see him. The nymphs raised loud wails around him, because, I think, they still remembered him in their hearts and all the things that, ever since his childhood, he used to talk about with them when they gathered together. And the nimble countrymen who tended cattle moaned

[4] A guess to fill a gap.
[5] The theft of this old statue of Athena, the Palladion, was one of the important episodes in the latest stages of the Trojan War. It is one of the mysteries of Quintus' poem that he does not include this event in his narrative.

for him, sad in spirit, and the mountain glens re-echoed their groans.

Then it was that a herdsman told long-suffering Priam's wife about Paris' dreadful fate. Her heart shuddered with fear as soon as she heard this, her limbs grew slack beneath her, and she uttered a lament like this:

"You are dead, my dear child, and you have left me sorrow upon sorrows, inescapable forever, because you were far the best of all my sons, after Hector. And so I shall weep in misery for you as long as the heart still beats in my breast. These sufferings have not come to us apart from the blessed ones, but some Fate planned these ruinous things. How I wish I had not endured them, but had died first, in peace and prosperity. [As it is, I continue to look upon disaster after disaster,][6] expecting to behold other evils even worse: my sons killed, my city ravaged and burned with fire by the stout-hearted Greeks, my daughters-in-law and my daughters, along with the other women of Troy, dragged away with their children, suffering the violence of war captives."

So she spoke, wailing. Her husband had not yet heard anything. He was sitting by Hector's tomb, and his tears were falling upon it. Hector was the one he had honored particularly, beyond his other children, because he was the bravest and protected the country with his spear. Priam's wise heart was full of pain for Hector, and he had not yet heard anything. But Helen raised a loud, continuous wail, although the things she cried out among the Trojans were not the same as the desires she had in her heart. She said to her own spirit:

"My husband, you were a great disaster to me, to the Trojans, and to yourself, and now you have died miserably. You have left me in the midst of loathsome evil, expecting to see still worse disasters. How I wish that the Harpies had snatched me away long ago, when I followed you because of the pernicious Fate of some supernatural power. As it is, the gods have given disaster to you and to me, and my lot is grim. Everyone shudders at me beyond telling; everybody hates my heart, and I know of no place where

6 A guess to fill a gap.

I can find refuge. If I run away to the crowd of Greeks, they will   400
immediately outrage my body. If I stay here, Trojan women and
Trojan men will surround me on all sides and quickly destroy me.
And no earth will cover my corpse, but the dogs will tear it, and
the swift tribes of birds. How I wish that Fate had killed me,
before I saw these disasters."

So she spoke, not by any means wailing for her husband so
much as she was lamenting for herself, remembering the wrong
she had done. The Trojan women moaned around her, as though
for Paris, but with other thoughts in their hearts, some thinking of
their parents, some of their husbands, some of their sons, and some
of their valued brothers.

Oenone alone was torn with sorrow from the depths of her
noble heart. She did not wail among the women of Troy; but apart,
in her own halls, she lay on the bed of her husband of long ago,
groaning deeply. Just as in the scrub on the highest mountains ice
forms and covers many ravines, and then when it melts in the
blasts of Zephyrus the tall heights grow wet, water streams down
them, and the ice in the glens, thick though it is, melts into the
cold water of a flowing spring; so she, most wretched with hateful
sorrow, was wasting away in pain for the husband she had wedded
in her youth. With terrible groans, she said to her own spirit:

"Why was I so foolish? My life is hateful to me. I fell in love
with an ill-fated husband, and I had hoped that, even when worn
by old age, we would reach life's final threshold always at one in
our thoughts. But the gods arranged otherwise. How I wish the
black Fates of death had snatched me, when I was about to be
separated from Alexander. But even if he abandoned me during
his lifetime, I will dare a great deed to die beside him, since the
light of day gives me no pleasure."

As she said this, pitiful tears rolled down from her eyes, and,
remembering the husband of her youth who had now met his
doom, she wasted away like wax before a fire—in secret, because
she stood in awe of her father and the well-dressed servants. And
then night was poured over the glorious earth from broad Ocean-
us, bringing to mortal men release from labor. Then, while her

father and the slaves slept in the halls, she broke through the gateways and rushed out like the wind. Her legs carried her swiftly. Just as when in the mountains a heifer is filled with great love for a bull, and her spirit rouses her to rush swiftly on speeding feet, and in her longing for love she feels no fear of the herdsman, but her unrestrainable impulse carries her on, in the hope she may see somewhere in the scrub the bull with feelings like her own; so Oenone, running swiftly, went over the long paths on speeding feet, seeking to climb upon the terrible funeral pyre. Her knees did not grow weary at all, but, as she rushed on, her feet carried her ever faster. A ruinous Doom and Cypris, goddess of love, were urging her on. She had no fear of shaggy wild beasts who met her in the night, though she was terrified of them before. She strode over all the rocks and slopes of the rough mountains, made her way through all the gullies; and Selene, goddess of the moon, looking down on her from on high, remembered, I fancy, noble Endymion, and so she was filled with pity for the speeding girl and shone out brightly above her to illuminate the long paths.

So she made her way along the mountain and reached the place where the nymphs were wailing around the body of Alexander. A vigorous fire still enveloped him, because shepherds had come together from various places on the mountain and had heaped up a great fire, for the last time showing their regard and their sorrow for the man who had been at once their comrade and their king. They were standing around him uttering laments. When Oenone saw him clearly before her, she gave no expression to her grief, overwhelmed though she was, but covered her beautiful face with her robe and leapt at once upon the pyre. A loud lament arose, as she burned beside her husband. The nymphs all around marveled, when they saw her throw herself down along with her husband. And a nymph spoke like this in her own heart:

"Truly, Paris was a wicked man. He abandoned the noble wife of his youth and took a wanton to his bed, bringing grim pain to himself and the Trojans and his city. A foolish man, he had no regard for the feelings of his wise wife in her misery, while she honored him above the light of the sun, even though he disliked her and did not love her."

So a nymph spoke in her heart, while Paris and Oenone burned in the center of the pyre, forgetful of the dawn. The herdsmen around them were marveling, just as when in other days all the Greeks marveled when they saw Evadne, wife of Capaneus, lay her body beside her husband who had been destroyed by Zeus's cruel thunderbolt.

But when the destructive blast of fire had consumed them both, Oenone and Paris, and reduced them to a single heap of ashes, then they quenched the fire with wine, placed their bones in a golden jar, and quickly fashioned a monument around them. They put over them two gravestones, which are turned away from each other, still showing toward each other a cruel jealousy.

✳ ✳ ✳

BOOK ELEVEN

Indecisive Fighting Around the Walls of Troy

THE TROJAN WOMEN were lamenting in the town, but could not go to Paris' grave, since it lay at a great distance from the lofty city. The young men were outside the city, steadily busy with the work of war. The slaughter of battle did not stop, even though Alexander had fallen, because the Greeks were rushing upon the Trojans right up to the town, and the Trojans themselves came outside of their wall, under pressure of necessity. Eris and Enyo, full of groans, were moving among them, looking like terrible Furies, and both of them breathed deadly destruction from their mouths. Dooms with ruthless spirit were raging terribly beside them. In another spot, Terror and Ares were urging on the soldiers. Fear followed after them, spattered with bloody gore. Some men were steadfast when they saw him, but others ran away. Everywhere lances, spears, and arrows of men were pouring from all directions, eager for evil slaughter A din arose from the struggling men, as both armies fought in the destructive battle.

There Neoptolemus killed Laodamas, who had been raised in Lycia by the beautiful river Xanthus. (Once upon a time, divine Leto, wife of Zeus the thunderer, revealed this river to men. She broke open with her hands the rough plain of far-famed

Lycia when, in the suffering of childbirth, she was overwhelmed by the great anguish produced in the travail of the divine birth.) After him, he killed Nirus in the conflict, hitting him with a spear that went through his jaw. The bronze cut through his mouth and his vocal tongue. Holding in his mouth the irresistible spear point, he bellowed, and as he screamed the blood flowed around his cheeks. The cruel spear, thrust with the strength of a mighty hand, pressed him down to the ground, and his life left him. Then Neoptolemus hit glorious Evenor a little above the flank and drove the spear point into the center of his liver; so he got a quick and painful death. He killed Iphition and Hippomedon, sturdy son of Maenalus, whom the nymph Ocyroe bore beside the river Sangarius. He did not return for his mother to greet him, but an evil Doom robbed her cruelly of her son and brought great grief for him to her heart.

Aeneas killed Bremon and Andromachus. Andromachus was raised in Cnossus, Bremon in holy Lyctus, but both of them fell from their swift chariots in one spot. Andromachus gasped out his life pierced in the throat by a long spear, while Bremon breathed his last struck in a painful spot at the base of the temple by a cruel stone hurled by a very mighty hand, and black fate enfolded him. The horses were terrified, and flying far from their charioteers they wandered among the heaps of corpses until they were seized by noble Aeneas' attendants, whose spirits were delighted by the fine booty.

Then Philoctetes struck with a deadly arrow Peirasus, as he ran from the battle. The arrow shattered the curving tendons in the back of his knee and wrecked the man's power of movement. When one of the Greeks saw that he was lamed, he quickly struck a cruel blow on the sinews of his neck and robbed him of his head. The earth received the headless body. The man still longed to speak, but the rolling head was carried far away, and his spirit quickly left him.

Polydamas struck with his spear Cleon and Eurymachus, who had come from Syme under the command of lord Nireus. Both of them were skilled in devising tricks for catching fish with a grim hook and in throwing nets into the glorious sea and with cunning hands on shipboard to wield a trident against fish with speed and accuracy. This day, however, their deeds at sea did not keep destruction from them.

Eurypylus, steadfast in battle, killed famous Hellus. His mother, fair-cheeked Clito, bore him near the Gygaean Lake. He was stretched on his face in the dust, and his arm, together with his long spear, fell some distance from him. It had been cut from his powerful shoulder by Eurypylus' grim sword, and the arm was still eager to raise the spear for battle. But all in vain, for no man controlled it for its task, but it merely moved convulsively. Just as the tail cut off from a fierce snake rises up, but there is no strength in it for the difficult task of pursuing the man who wounded it; so the right arm of the stouthearted man was eager to use the spear for fighting, but there was no strength in it any more.

Odysseus killed Aenus and Polyidus, both Cetaeans, destroying one with the spear and the other with the cruel sword. Sthenelus killed glorious Abas, hurling a javelin at him that flew through his throat and reached the tendon at the nape of his neck. The painful wound took all the strength from the man's limbs and destroyed his life.

Diomedes killed Laodocus, Agamemnon killed Melius, Deiphobus brought down Dryas and Alcimus. Agenor killed Hippasus, for all his great fame. He came from the river Peneius, but he did not give his parents any fine return for bringing him up, because a supernatural power destroyed him.

Then Thoas killed Lamus and brave Lyncus, Meriones killed Lycon, and Menelaus killed Archelochus. He used to live under the ridge of Corycia and the crag of clever Hephaestus. This is a marvel to mortals, because there burns within it a fire untiring and unquenchable night and day. Around the fire palm trees flourish and bear great quantities of fruit, although their roots are burned along with the rocks. The immortals, I fancy, fashioned this for future generations to see.

100   Teucer was eager to hit with a swift arrow noble Hippomedon's son Menoetes, coming at him. Mind, hand, and eyes di-

rected the arrow from the curving bow, and it leapt from his nimble hands toward the wretched man. The string still sang from it, I fancy, when Menoetes, struck fair, was in his death throes. Doom was carried along with the arrow to a critical spot, his heart, just where the mind and strength of men lie, and the ways to death are swift.

Euryalus threw far from his sturdy hand a great stone and shook the quick-moving ranks of the Trojans. Just as when a man who is guarding a field becomes angry at noisy cranes and rushes at them in great vexation and, whirling a sling of fine ox sinews in his nimble hand, hurls a stone at them, and the whistling rush of it scatters the long lines that are spread out in the sky, and they are frightened and dart away with a tremendous din, one crowded against another, although they had previously been flying in good order; so the enemy were terrified by the terrible missile of vigorous Euryalus. A supernatural power carried it to good purpose: it shattered about his eyes the head and helmet of mighty Meles, and an accursed doom overtook him.

Man killed man, and the earth was groaning around them. Just as when a violent wind swoops down furiously, and under its howling blast the tall trees in a wide grove fall everywhere, torn up by the roots, and all the earth roundabout resounds; so they fell in the dust, their armor rattled noisily, and the earth roundabout re-echoed loudly. Their thoughts were set on terrible battle, as they brought doom to one another.

Then it was that noble Apollo came close to Aeneas and brave Eurymachus Antenorson. They were fighting the powerful Greeks, standing very close together in the conflict, just like two strong matched oxen yoked to a wagon, and did not stop fighting. The god spoke to them quickly, taking the appearance of the prophet Polymestor, whom, once upon a time, his mother had borne by the river Xanthus to be a servant of Apollo the far-shooting god.

"Eurymachus and Aeneas, divine stock, it does not befit you at all to give ground before the Greeks. Not even mighty Ares himself would find pleasure in meeting you, if you are willing to fight in the turmoil, because the Fates have spun a long life for you both."

After saying this, he mingled with the winds and disappeared. Their minds, however, were conscious of the god's power, because a great courage was immediately shed over them, and their spirits were raging in their breasts. They leapt among the Greeks like dangerous wasps which, their hearts filled with terrible anger, fall upon bees that they see moving about the drying grapes in autumn or hurrying from their hive; so the sons of Troy leapt swiftly among the brave Greeks. The dark Dooms rejoiced at their fighting, Ares laughed, and Enyo gave a hideous shriek, and their bright armor rang loudly upon them.

Aeneas, Eurymachus, and the other Trojans killed great crowds of the enemy with their invincible hands, and the soldiers were falling just like the grain in the season of warm summer, when the reapers assail it swiftly with nimble hands after they have divided up the large sections of a vast field; so beneath the Trojans' hands thousands of ranks fell. The earth around them was filled with corpses and flowed with blood. Eris' heart was warmed as they died. The Trojans did not stop in the least from the evil turmoil, but advanced like lions upon sheep. The Greeks' thoughts were on miserable flight, and all those who still had unimpaired strength in their legs ran from the deadly battle. The son of brave Anchises followed steadily behind the enemy, striking them in the back with his spear, and Eurymachus was with him. The immortal heart of the god Apollo was warmed as he looked on from above. Just as when a man finds pigs coming into a field of ripe grain before it has been cut by the harvesters and sets strong dogs upon them, and they are afraid when they see the dogs rushing up and no longer think of food, but turn all together to miserable flight, and the dogs are soon at their heels and bite them pitilessly from behind, and the pigs run off squealing loudly, and the lord of the field is glad; so Phoebus was warmed when he saw the great host of the Greeks running away from the battle. They had no further concern for the work of men, but prayed to the gods that their feet would carry them swiftly.[1] Their only hope of returning home now lay in their feet. Eurymachus, Aeneas, and their comrades with them were raging with spears and attacking them all.

Then a certain man among the Greeks, either because he was extremely confident of his strength or through the will of Fate desirous to kill him, checked his horse that was in flight from the noisy battle and eagerly wheeled him round toward the conflict to fight against the enemy. But stouthearted Agenor was too quick for him and gave him a painful cut on the muscle of the arm with his two-edged ax. The bone in the smitten arm yielded to the might of the iron, and it easily cut the sinews. The veins spurted blood, and the man collapsed on the horse's neck. Soon, however, he fell down among the corpses, but he left his strong hand still clinging stubbornly to the pliant reins, just like the hand of a man still alive. It caused great astonishment, hanging from the reins as it was and all covered with blood. It was Ares' plan that it should frighten the enemy. You would say it was still engaged in the work of war and still longing to be driving the horse, and the horse was carrying it as a kind of token of his dead master.

200

Aeneas killed Aethalides, hitting him with a spear above the waist. The spear went through by his navel, dragging his guts. He was stretched in the dust, clutching in his hands spear point and guts at once. He groaned terribly, howled, and bit the earth with his teeth; then life and anguish left him.

The Greeks were terrified, just like oxen that have been willingly at steady work under yoke and plow, when a gadfly, longing for blood, strikes them in the flank with his thin proboscis. The oxen, greatly tormented, run away from their work, and the man is troubled for them, both because of the work and out of concern for the oxen, lest the pitiless iron share of the plow may bound at them from behind, land on their feet, and cut the sinews; so the Greeks were in flight, and the spirit of Achilles' son was troubled for them. He gave a great cry, trying to check them:

[1] A doubtful reading, a conjecture by Zimmermann. The manuscripts give "work of gods."

"You cowards, why are you running away? You're like worthless starlings frightened by the attack of a hawk. Get some courage in you. It is far better to die in battle than to choose impotent flight."

So he spoke, and they listened to him and were quick to put a bold spirit in their breasts. He rushed upon the Trojans with proud thoughts, brandishing a swift spear in his hands. The hosts of Myrmidons, of course, followed him with the might of a storm wind in their hearts, and the other Greeks had a respite from the rout. Neoptolemus, with a spirit like his dead father's, killed man after man in the conflict. The Trojans gave ground, withdrawing like waves which boil over a beach and are rolled in numbers by a blast of Boreas as they rise up from the sea, and another wind, rushing against them from some other quarter and raging in a great storm, pushes them away from the beach, although Boreas is still blowing slightly; so the son of godlike Achilles pushed back the Trojans who had previously been advancing upon the Greeks —only a little, however, because the strength of bold Aeneas did not permit them to run away, but forced them to remain courageously in the terrible conflict. Enyo made the battle equal on both sides.

The son of Achilles did not brandish his father's spear at Aeneas, but turned his spirit elsewhere, because Thetis of the splendid robe, out of regard for Cytherean Aphrodite, turned her grandson's courage and great strength against troops of other soldiers. So, then, Neoptolemus was killing many Trojans, and Aeneas was destroying thousands of companies of Greeks. As the men were being killed in the battle, the birds rejoiced, eager to devour the entrails and flesh of men, while groans came from the nymphs of the beautiful river Simois and from the daughters of Xanthus.

When they were busy with the toil of battle, the restless winds raised a great dust storm. It darkened all the vast sky above, like a fog that reduces visibility to zero. It concealed the ground and destroyed the men's ability to see. But even so, they fought. They recklessly killed anyone they laid hands on, even if he was a great friend. There was no way to determine in the tumult whether the man who approached was a friend or an enemy. The soldiers felt helpless. All would have become confused, and all alike would have died miserably, falling on one another's deadly swords, if the son of Cronos from Olympus had not protected them in their distress. He drove the dust away from the battlefield and lulled the pernicious winds. They continued to fight, but, of course, their work was much easier, because they could see whether they should kill the man who was near them in the tumult or avoid him. Sometimes the Greeks held back the Trojan throng, sometimes the Trojans held back the Greek lines. There was a terrible battle. Missiles coming from both sides were falling like snowflakes. Fear seized the shepherds watching the conflict from a spot on the Idaean hills. One of them, raising his hands to the sky, prayed to the heavenly ones that all the enemy perish at the hands of Ares, and that the Trojans have a respite from the groans of war and see, sometime, the day of freedom. But the gods paid no heed to him; cruel Fate had other plans. She has no awe of mighty Zeus or of any other immortal. Her terrible mind does not care in the slightest what destiny she spins for men at their birth, for men or for cities, with her thread that none can escape. Through her all things either waste away or grow. It was through her will that toil and conflict arose for the Trojan horsemen and the Greeks who fought hand to hand. They were unceasingly fashioning for each other slaughter and pitiless doom. They felt no fear, but fought enthusiastically, for courage draws men to battle.

When many had died in the dust, then it was that the Greek strength was made the greater by the will of wise Pallas Athena. She came very close to the fighting and was a great defense for the Greeks, being eager to sack Priam's famous town. And then glorious Aphrodite, who was greatly saddened by Alexander's fall, came quickly and personally rescued famed Aeneas from the battle and deadly fighting, pouring a thick mist around him.[2] It was

[2] Aeneas seems to have been something of an embarrassment to the Greek poets who dealt with the Trojan War, since he was an important Trojan leader who, tradition agreed, had survived the fall of the city. Homer was careful to

not fated for that man to fight against the Greeks any longer in the tumult before the high wall. Aphrodite was afraid that Athena might kill Aeneas even contrary to the Fates, and so she was careful to avoid wise Athena Tritogeneia, who longed with all her heart to help the Greeks. Previously she had not even spared Ares himself, who was far superior to Aeneas.[3]

300 The Trojans no longer stood fast on the battle front, but their spirits were afraid, and they drew back, because the Greeks leapt upon them like savage wild beasts and were full of great eagerness for war. As the men were killed, the rivers and the plain were filled with corpses. Very many men and horses fell in the dust, and, with men and horses being hit, many chariots were wrecked. Everywhere blood was flowing in abundance like rain, for a deadly Fate was moving through the conflict.

So the Trojans, pierced with swords or spears, lay beside one another like scattered timbers, when on a beach of the thundering sea men loosen the great fastenings from the strong pegs and scatter here and there long timbers and the wood of a tall raft, and the broad beach is filled up everywhere, and the dark ocean swell washes over them; so the dead lay in the dust and blood, war and its weeping all forgotten.

A few escaped from the pitiless fighting and went into the citadel, avoiding heavy disaster. Their wives and children took from their bloody frames all their armor, wet with foul gore, and warm baths were prepared for all. Through the entire city, doctors hurried to the homes of wounded men and busied themselves with healing the wounded. When these came from war, their wives and children lamented around them, and they called to many who were not there. Some men, struck to the heart with loathsome suffering, lay groaning heavily at their pain; others turned to dinner after toil. The swift horses were noisy, whinny-

---

rescue him at dangerous moments, and this is the second time in this book that Quintus has kept him safe by supernatural intervention.

[3] Quintus is referring to the episode in book v. of the *Iliad*, where Athena helps Diomedes. Near the end of the book, she actually takes Sthenelus' place as Diomedes' charioteer, causes Ares' spear to miss Diomedes, and wounds Ares with Diomedes' spear (835–63).

ing over their abundant fodder. Over on their side, the Greeks were busy with the same activities as the Trojans.

When the Dawn drove her shining horses over the streams of Ocean, and the tribes of men awoke, then some of the soldier sons of the powerful Greeks went against Priam's lofty town, while others stayed at their quarters along with the wounded, lest a fierce army, showing favor to the Trojans, fall upon the ships and capture them. The Trojans fought the Greeks from their towers, and a fierce conflict arose.

Sthenelus, the son of Capaneus, along with godlike Diomedes, was fighting before the Scaean Gates. Above them, Deiphobus, stubborn in war, sturdy Polites, and other comrades were keeping them off with arrows and with stones. The helmets and shields of the men resounded as they were hit, but they protected the warriors from a grim doom and pitiless fate.

Achilles' son was fighting by the Idaean Gates, and all the Myrmidons, experts in vigorous pursuit, were fighting around him.[4] They were being kept away from the wall by the innumerable missiles of brave Helenus and stouthearted Agenor, who were urging the Trojans into conflict. They, indeed, without any urging, were enthusiastically fighting along the walls of their dear native city.

Odysseus and Eurypylus were fighting steadily at the gates facing the plain and the swift ships, but from the high wall noble Aeneas, full of proud thoughts, was keeping them away with stones. Toward the stream of Simois, Teucer of the good ashen spear had his painful task. So one man had his hardship here, another there.

Then it was that the famous men around wise Odysseus arranged their shields for the turmoil of war according to a plan of that man's crafty mind. They flung their shields over their heads, putting them close to one another. They all fitted together into a single unit. You would say it was a tight roof protecting a hall,

[4] No other writer mentions these Idaean Gates of Troy, and Quintus speaks of them only here. Vian (*Recherches*, 117f.) gives some reason for believing that we should read here "Dardanian Gates," which occur in Homer and also twice in Quintus, although in Quintus the phrase is, in both instances, singular.

which neither a great blast of wet-blowing wind could penetrate nor a vast storm of rain from Zeus; so firmly protected by their shields were the ranks of the Greeks. Fitted together into one unit, they had spirits that were uniformly strong. The sons of Troy were throwing down stones from above, but they rolled onto the dry earth, as though from a hard rock. Many spears, cruel arrows, and painful javelins were fixed in the shields, others stuck in the ground, and many were carried useless far away, their points bent back, as the shields were being struck from every side. The Greeks had no fear of the tremendous noise, nor did they give ground, any more than if they were listening to drops of rain. They moved up under the wall all together. Not a one of them stood apart, but they followed along in close formation, just like a dark cloud, a large one that the son of Cronos spreads out from the upper air in midwinter. There was a great din around their ranks, and noise from their feet as they moved. Breezes carried off behind the men the dust that rose just a very little above the plain. There was a sound of indistinguishable speech, like the humming of bees in their hives. Sounds of heavy breathing came pouring out, and gasps from the panting soldiers. The sons of Atreus, of course, were completely delighted and filled with pride in the men, as they saw this bold defense against noisy war.

The Greeks had it in mind to approach in a body the gates of god-descended Priam, break the high walls with their double-edged axes, drag the gates from their hinges, and thrust them to the ground. And there was real hope for this splendid plan. But neither their oxhide shields nor their agile axes protected them when the mighty strength of Aeneas, with eager haste, threw upon them a stone grasped in both his hands. It destroyed with a wretched fate the men whom it caught among the shields, just as in the hills the might of a shattered crag catches goats who are feeding under a cliff, and all those pasturing nearby are afraid; so the Greeks were filled with amazement. Aeneas continued to throw down stones one after another from above, and the ranks were utterly confused. Just as when Olympian Zeus shatters with thunderbolts and

400

bright lightning from heaven crags that cluster at various points around a single peak, and the flocks roundabout are afraid and run off in all directions; so the sons of the Greeks were frightened because Aeneas quickly confounded the protection in war that they had fashioned with their strong shields. A god had given him enormous strength. No one was able even to cast a glance at him in the conflict, because his equipment gleamed on his sturdy frame like divine lightning flashes. Close to him, and with his body cloaked in darkness, stood dreadful Ares, who directed all of Aeneas' missiles, that were bringing either doom or terrible fear to the Greeks. He fought just as when Olympian Zeus from heaven in his anger killed the proud race of terrible giants, shook the vast earth, Tethys, Oceanus, and heaven, when all around, under the onset of unwearying Zeus, the limbs of Atlas were shaken; so the ranks of the Greeks were struck down in the conflict by Aeneas. He rushed everywhere around the wall, wrathful at the enemy, and he threw from his hands everything he lighted upon as he pressed on in the fighting. Many defensive weapons of evil war lay on the steadfast Trojans' walls. With these, Aeneas, raging in his great strength, was keeping off the numerous army of the enemy.

The Trojan resistance stiffened around him. All the soldiers around the city were in serious difficulty, and many were killed, both among the Greeks and among the Trojans. There were great shouts from both sides—Aeneas ordering the warlike Trojans to fight zealously for their city, their wives, and themselves, and the son of the stubborn fighter Achilles ordering the Greeks to stand fast by the famous walls of Troy until they took the town and burned it with fire. The loud, grim battle cry surrounded them both as they fought in the turmoil all day long. There was no respite from battle, either for the Greeks, whose hearts longed to take the citadel by war, or for the Trojans, who longed to save it.

Fighting at some distance from stouthearted Aeneas, Aias was hurling evil dooms upon the Trojans with his missiles. Sometimes an arrow flew straight from him through the air, and then again cruel javelins, and he killed one man after another. The Trojans, cowering before the might of this noble man, no longer stood steadfast for battle, but the soldiers left the wall.

Then it was that Aias' attendant, spirited Alcimedon, far the best of the Locrians in battle, confident of his king, his own strength, and the boldness of youth, and full of eagerness for battle, set his nimble foot upon a scaling ladder to make a path for the men into the unhappy city. Placing his shield over his head as a protection, and with fearless courage in his breast, he mounted the grim path. Sometimes he brandished his pitiless spear in his hand, and then again moved upward, going quickly on his airy road. He would have brought grief to the Trojans, except that, just as he was bending over and inspecting the town for the first and last time from the high wall, Aeneas rushed upon him. Far away though he was, he had not failed to note Alcimedon's move. He hit him on the head with a broad stone. The hero's great strength broke the ladder as well. Alcimedon darted from his lofty place like an arrow from the bowstring. As his body whirled down, fatal doom followed him, and his groaning spirit was quickly mingled with the air before he reached the hard earth. He fell to the ground in his breastplate; his stout spear, wide shield, and strong helmet had been thrown from him. The Locrian troops groaned around him, when they saw the man destroyed in evil ruin. The brain from his shaggy head was spattered here and there, and all his bones and his swift limbs were crushed and spattered with grisly gore.

Then it was that Philoctetes, godlike Poeas' noble son, quickly fired an arrow, aiming it at Aeneas, when he saw the famous hero moving eagerly about the walls with the strength of a wild beast. He did not miss him, but his arrow quite failed to pierce the strong shield and reach his handsome flesh. Cytherean Aphrodite and his shield protected him, and the arrow barely grazed the skin of the oxhide shield. It did not, however, fall fruitless to the earth, but hit Mimas between his shield and his crested helmet. He fell from the tower just as a wild goat falls from a crag, when a man has hit it with a cruel arrow; so he fell and lay stretched out, and his life left him. Aeneas, angry because of his comrade, threw a stone and killed Philoctetes' brave comrade Toxaichmes. The stone shattered his head and broke all the bones along with the helmet, and his glorious heart was stopped. The son of famous Poeas raised a great shout over him:

"Aeneas, you imagine in your heart that you are the bravest of men, while you fight from a tower, where weakling women fight their foes. If you amount to anything, come outside the wall in your armor and learn the skill of Poeas' brave son with spears and with arrows."

So he spoke. The brave son of Anchises did not say anything to him, although he wanted to, because the grim battle was going on continuously about the high walls and the city. They had no rest from evil turmoil. Even though they had been oppressed by battle for a very long time, they had no release from weariness, but the work of war went on without accomplishing anything. 500

BOOK TWELVE

✽ ✽ ✽

The Wooden Horse

WHEN AT LAST the Greek soldiers had worked to utter weariness around the walls of Troy without bringing the war to an end, then it was that Calchas called a meeting of the princes. By the promptings of Apollo, he had an expert knowledge of the flights of birds, the stars, and all the other signs that exist for men through the will of the gods. When they had come together, he spoke to them like this:

"Work no more at war, settled down beside the walls, but contrive some other contrivance in your minds, and a trick which will profit the soldiers and ourselves. I assure you that yesterday I personally saw a sign here: a hawk was chasing a dove. She, hard pressed, went down into a hole in a rock. The hawk was extremely angry and waited for a very long time close to the hole, but she kept out of his way. Then, still full of terrible anger, he hid under a bush. She rushed out in her folly, thinking that he was gone. The exultant hawk then brought a cruel death to the wretched dove. So now let us not attempt any longer to sack the city of Troy by force, but see if trickery and contrivance may perhaps accomplish something."

So he spoke, but none of the princes was able to devise in his mind anything to save them from miserable fighting, although they tried to discover a means. Only Odysseus, the son of Laertes, in his wisdom had an idea, and he spoke out to Calchas:

"My friend, greatly honored by the heavenly gods, if it is really fated that the brave soldiers of Greece sack Priam's town by trickery, we will make a horse, and we Greek princes will gladly go into it as an ambush. The soldiers must go away to Tenedos with the ships, and they must all set fire to their barracks, so the Trojans will pour out fearlessly into the plain, when they have seen this from the city. One courageous man, whom no one among the Trojans knows, should stay behind outside of the horse, steeling his soldier's heart. He must cower under the well-built horse and pretend that he has escaped the proud might of the Greeks, who had been strongly desirous of sacrificing him on behalf of their return. 'This horse they made for Pallas Athena, who was angry on account of the Trojan soldiers.' He must stick to this story during their long questioning until, stubborn though they are, they believe him and take the wretched fellow at once into the city. This is necessary so that he may make for us a grim sign for war. For the men on Tenedos, he should quickly raise a bright torch, and he should urge the men in the great horse to come out, when the sons of Troy are in carefree sleep."

So he spoke, and they all approved. Above all, Calchas marveled at him and at the way he had suggested to the Greeks a contrivance and good trick, which was going to protect the Greeks' victory and be a great disaster for the Trojans. He spoke, therefore, among the brave princes:

"Spend no more time now contriving another trick in your minds, my friends, but be persuaded by brave Odysseus. The idea that he has suggested in his wisdom will not turn out to be useless, because the gods are already accomplishing the Greeks' wish, and signs that will lead to something are appearing in various places: Zeus's thunders, accompanied by lightning, are roaring loudly through the air on high; birds are darting by the troops on the right and shrieking with loud voices. We must not stay for a long time around the city now. Necessity has breathed great boldness into the Trojans, which rouses even a worthless man to war. Then it is that men are strongest in fighting, when they stake their lives and are careless of painful death. So now the sons of Troy are fighting fearlessly around their city, and their hearts are in a real frenzy."

When he had said this, Achilles' sturdy son said to him:

"Calchas, strong men fight their enemies face to face. Those whose minds are harried by fear, worthless men, shun their enemy and fight inside from their walls. Let us not now, therefore, think up any trick or any other contrivance. It is proper for princes to show themselves men in battle and with the spear. Courageous men are better in a fight."

When he had said this, strong Odysseus Laertesson said to him:

"Stouthearted child of fearless Achilles, you have made all these statements as befits a noble and brave man, courageously putting your trust in your hands. But not even the fearless strength of your mighty father had the power to sack Priam's wealthy city, nor have we, even though we have fought very hard. Come, let us, in accordance with Calchas' suggestions, proceed quickly to our swift ships and construct a horse, using the hands of Epeius, who is far the best among the Greeks in carpentry. Athena taught him his trade."

So he spoke, and all the princes were persuaded by him, except brave Neoptolemus. Odysseus did not win over Philoctetes either, whose noble mind was set on deeds of strength. These two were still not sated with wretched war. They were planning to continue the fight in the field, and they gave orders to their own soldiers to bring to the vast wall all the things that prosper fighting in battles. They hoped to sack the strong citadel, because both of them had come to the conflict through plans of the gods. And they would soon have accomplished all that their spirits desired, except that Zeus in the upper sky grew indignant at them; so he made the earth quiver under the Greeks' feet and shook all the air above them, too, and threw a mighty thunderbolt in front of the heroes. All Dardania resounded from it. Their brave thoughts were quickly converted to fear. They quite forgot their strength and splendid

might and, even against their will, gave their allegiance to famous
Calchas. They came to the ships along with the other Greeks,
marveling at the prophet, who, they said, was descended from
Zeus—from Zeus or Apollo—and they obeyed him in everything.

When the shining stars were moving in their course around
the heaven, all gleaming everywhere, and man forgot his trouble,
then it was that Athena left the high dwelling place of the blessed
ones and came to the ships and the army. She looked in every way
like a tender girl, and she stood over the head of Epeius, dear to
Ares, in a dream.[1] She ordered him to make the wooden horse and
said that, while he was busy with it, she would work with him her-
self and stand close beside him, encouraging him in his work.
When he heard the goddess' speech, he leapt from carefree sleep
with exultation in his heart. He knew she was a deathless divine
god, and he had no other thought in his heart, but he kept his mind
constantly on the wonderful work, and his shrewd skill possessed
his thoughts.

When the Dawn came, after pushing the thick shadows aside
into outer darkness, and a sparkling gleam came through the air,
then it was that Epeius told his divine dream among the eager
Greeks, what he had seen, what he had heard. And they felt the
greatest pleasure as they listened. Then the sons of Atreus sent
swift men to go into the flourishing glens of wooded Ida. They
assailed the fir trees in the forest, felling the tall trees. The valleys
re-echoed roundabout as the trees were struck. Long ridges in the
high mountains were robbed of their forest; a whole valley was
revealed, no longer so well-liked by wild animals as before. The
felled trees were withering, missing the force of the wind. The
Greeks cut these up with their axes and carried them quickly from
the wooded mountain to the shores of the Hellespont. Men and
mules alike put their hearts into the work. The soldiers were ex-
tremely busy, serving Epeius on every side. Some cut timbers with
the saw and measured off planks; some with their axes trimmed off

[1] In describing this scene, Quintus may have been inspired by Homer's ac-
count in the *Odyssey* of how Athena, disguised as a girl, appeared to the sleeping
Phaeacian princess Nausicaa, "stood over her head"—the words are almost identical
in both poets, and spoke to her (vi. 13–23).

branches from the logs that were still unsawed. Every man found something to work at and was busy. Epeius made the feet and legs of the wooden horse and then the belly. Above this he fastened the back and flanks, a throat in front, and on top of the lofty neck he fitted a mane that moved as though it were real. He put on a shaggy head and a flowing tail, ears, transparent eyes, and everything else with which a horse is equipped.[2] The holy work grew just as if it were a living horse, because the goddess had given to the man a splendid skill. With the inspiration provided by Pallas Athena, everything was finished in three days. The great army of the Greeks were delighted with it and marveled how spirit and speed of foot had been worked out in wood and how it looked as if it were neighing. Then Epeius offered up a prayer on behalf of the huge horse, stretching out his hands to tireless Tritonian Athena:

"Listen, O goddess great of soul, keep safe me and your horse."

So he spoke, and the goddess, wise Athena, listened to him, and she made what he had created an object of wonder to all men upon the earth, those who saw it, and those who heard about it thereafter.

While the Greeks were enjoying the sight of Epeius' work, and the frightened Trojans were staying inside their walls, avoiding death and pitiless doom, then it was that proud Zeus left the other gods and went to the streams of Ocean and the caverns of Tethys. With his departure, strife fell upon the immortals. In their agitation, their spirits were divided two ways. They mounted upon the blasts of the winds and were soon carried from heaven to earth, and the air roared as they passed. They went to the river Xanthus and took up positions opposite each other, some favoring the Greeks, some the Trojans, and a yearning for battle fell upon their hearts.[3] Along with them those gods were gathered who had

---

[2] This passage may be taken as an illustration of the very few instances in which I have abandoned Zimmermann's text for some other reading. The reading in the manuscripts and in Zimmermann should mean something like "all the other things on which a horse moves." The addition of a single letter to the verb (suggested by C. L. Struve) produces the much more suitable meaning given in the translation.

[3] Quintus got the idea of a battle on the plains of Troy between two factions

received as their portion the wide sea. Some of the gods in their anger were eager to destroy the crafty horse along with the ships, others wanted to destroy lovely Ilios. But wily Fate restrained them and turned the mind of the blessed ones to conflict. Ares began the fighting by leaping against Athena, and then the rest fell upon one another. Their divine golden armor rang loudly as they moved. The broad sea roared in answer, and the dark earth trembled beneath the immortals' feet. All of them at once raised a loud cry, and the terrible din reached all the way to broad heaven and as far as the abyss of proud Hades. The Titans far below were terrified. From around them came groans from all of lofty Ida, the noisy streams of her ever-flowing rivers, the long ravines, the ships of the Greeks, and the famous city of Priam. Human beings, however, felt no fear. Through the will of the gods themselves, they were not even aware of the divine quarrel.

The gods were now breaking off with their hands peaks from Mt. Ida and throwing them at one another. But the peaks were easily scattered here and there like grains of sand, broken into bits about the gods' invincible frames. All this did not remain hidden from the noble mind of Zeus at the ends of the earth. He left Oceanus' streams at once and went up into the broad heaven. Eurus and Boreas together with Zephyrus and Notus carried him. Bright Iris brought them under the marvelous yoke of the everlasting chariot that divine Aeon had made of indestructible adamant with his tireless hands. He reached the great ridge of Olympus. In his anger, he made all the air shake beneath him. Thunder and lightning roared loudly on all sides. Thunderbolts poured out thick and fast to earth. The air was ablaze beyond telling. Terror fell upon the hearts of the immortals. The limbs of 200 all trembled, immortal though they were. Glorious Themis, terrified for them, leapt like a thought through the clouds and soon reached them. (She alone had stayed out of the painful conflict.) She spoke to them like this to check them from fighting:

"Hold back from this noisy tumult. It is not right, when Zeus

of gods from Homer's account of such a battle in the twenty-first book of the *Iliad*.

is angry, for creatures who are forever to quarrel for the sake of short-lived men. You will all soon be made to disappear, because he will crush all the mountains into one mass up there to use against you and will not spare either his sons or his daughters. He will cover you all alike with a vast mound of earth. There will be no way for you to escape into the light, but wretched darkness around you will always keep you in."

So she spoke, and they were persuaded, fearing Zeus's attack. They checked their conflict, cast away their anger, and arranged harmonious friendship. Some of them returned to heaven, some went into the sea, and some stayed on the earth.

Then the shrewd planner Odysseus, the son of Laertes, spoke to the brave Greeks:

"Glorious Greek commanders, stout of heart, now give proof, when I want it, who among you are wonderfully strong and noble. For the task assigned us by necessity is certainly upon us. Let us give our thoughts to fighting and go into the polished horse, to find an end to hideous war. This will be the better way, if by trickery and cruel cunning we sack the great city for whose sake we came here and have suffered many pains, far away from the land we love. Now put into your hearts noble courage and strength. Many a man forced by harsh necessity in battle has put boldness into his spirit and killed a better man, when he was by nature inferior. Boldness gives one a much better spirit. It is boldness more than anything else that is a glory to men. Come, you princes, prepare a good ambush. You others go to the holy city of Tenedos and stay there, until the enemy drag us to the town, imagining that they are bringing a gift to Athena. Let some brave young man whom the Trojans don't know well stand close by the horse, steeling his heart. He must take very great care of all that I said before, and have no other thought in mind, so that what we Greeks are doing will not be revealed to the Trojans."

So he spoke. The others were afraid, but the famous man Sinon answered him. He was about to perform a really great deed, and the vast army marveled at him and his ready spirit. He spoke among them:

"Odysseus and all you excellent sons of the Greeks, I will carry out this task in answer to your desires, if they actually torture me and decide to throw me alive into the fire. This is my spirit's pleasure: to bring to the Greeks the great glory that they desire, whether I die at the hands of our enemies or escape."

So he spoke, boldly, and the Greeks were greatly pleased. And one among them said:

"What great courage a god has given this man today. He was not courageous before. A supernatural power is urging him on to become a mischief for all the Trojans or for ourselves. Now I think the cruel war doubtless will soon reach its destructive end."

So one of the warlike Greeks in the army spoke. Then Nestor, on the other side, spoke encouragingly among them:

"Now, my dear children, you need your strength and noble courage. For now the gods are bringing into our hands the end of labor and the noble victory we desire. Come, proceed courageously into the vast horse. Courage brings great glory to men. How I wish I still had in my limbs such great strength as when Jason, Aeson's son, was summoning the princes to go into the swift ship Argo. I was planning to be the first of the princes to go down into her, but godlike Pelias checked me against my will. As things are, lamentable old age comes upon me. But even so, like a young man in his prime, I will go boldly down into the horse. Boldness gives courage and glory."

When he had said this, the son of brown-haired Achilles said to him:

"Nestor, in intelligence you are the best of all men, but pitiless old age has you in its grip, and, much as you want to participate in the work of war, your strength is not unimpaired. You, therefore, must go to the shores of Tenedos. We young men, who still have not had our fill of battle, will go into the ambush. You, sir, ordered it so, and this also suits our own wishes."

So he spoke, and Nestor Neleusson came close to him and kissed both of his hands and his head as well, because he undertook to go first into the huge horse and ordered the older man to stay outside with the other Greeks, revealing thus his eagerness for the work of war. And he spoke to Neoptolemus, who was longing for battle:

"In strength and sensible speech you are a true son of your famous father, godlike Achilles. I have hopes that the Greeks will sack Priam's famous city by your hands. Although late and after labor, great glory will be ours, who have endured many grim pains in fighting. Pains the gods put before men's feet, but good things far away, and they put labor in between. Because of this, the way to wretched trouble is easy for men, while the way to glory is difficult, until a man forces his way through the painful labor."

So he spoke, and Achilles' famous son answered him:

"Sir, I hope that in answer to our prayers we achieve the hopes of your heart. This is far the better way. But if the gods will otherwise, so be that, too. I should wish to die gloriously in war rather than acquire the great disgrace of running away from Troy."

With these words, he put upon his shoulders the immortal armor of his father. The best of the heroes, all whose spirit was bold, were quick to arm themselves, too. Now in answer to my question, tell me, Muses, accurately and one by one, all those who went down into the vast horse. You put all song in my heart, before the down was spread over my cheeks. I was pasturing my fine sheep in the plains of Smyrna, three times as far from the Hermus as one can hear a man shouting. It was by a temple of Artemis, in the garden of Zeus the Deliverer, on a hill neither particularly low nor very high.

First of all there went down into the hollow horse Achilles' son Neoptolemus, and with him sturdy Menelaus, Odysseus, Sthenelus, and godlike Diomedes. Philoctetes went and Anticlus and Menestheus, and with them spirited Thoas, brown-haired Polypoetes, Aias, Eurypylus, and godlike Thrasymedes. Meriones went, too, and Idomeneus, distinguished men both, and with them Podalirius of the good ashen spear, and Eurymachus, godlike Teucer and stouthearted Ialmenus, Thalpius, Antimachus, and the stubborn fighter Leonteus. With them went godlike Eumelus, Euryalus, Demophoon, Amphimachus, and sturdy Agapenor, and also Acamas, and Meges, son of sturdy Phyleus. All the others, too, who were outstandingly excellent went down into it—all whom the polished horse could contain within it. The last man to go down among them was glorious Epeius, the man who had actually made the horse. He knew in his spirit how to open up the horse's doors and how to close them. For this reason, he went in the last of all. Then he drew inside the ladders on which they had mounted, and, after he had closed everything very carefully, he sat down there beside the bolt. All the heroes sat there in silence, just halfway between victory and death.

When the others had burned the quarters in which they had formerly slept, they sailed in their ships over the wide sea. In command of them, two strong-minded men were giving orders, Nestor and the warrior Agamemnon. They had wanted to go down inside the horse too, but the Greeks checked them, so that they might stay with the ships and give orders to the army. Men proceed to a task much better when lords are in charge. On this account, they stayed outside of the horse, most excellent men though they were. They quickly reached the shores of Tenedos, threw the anchors down in deep water, and speedily disembarked. They fastened the cables to the shore and remained there at ease, waiting for the desired torch to shine.

The men in the horse were close to the enemy, sometimes doubtless expecting to die, and sometimes expecting to destroy the sacred city. These were their expectations as Dawn came upon them.

The Trojans noticed the smoke still rising swiftly through the air on the shores of the Hellespont. They did not, of course, see the ships that had brought them terrible destruction from Greece. All of them ran joyfully onto the beach, first putting on their armor, because fear still enveloped their spirits. They noticed the polished horse, and they naturally stood around it and marveled that so very great a thing had been made. Then they noticed the luckless Sinon close by. They surrounded him in a circle and asked questions about the Greeks from every side. First they questioned him with soft words, but then they used terrible threats and continued for a long time to employ great violence on the crafty man. But he was steadfast as a rock, and his body was clothed in firmness. At last they cut his ears off and his nose as well, using every sort of maltreatment to make him say truthfully where the Greeks had gone with their ships and what the horse really had inside it. But his heart was full of courage, and he showed no concern for the hideous outrage, but his spirit bore up under the blows and even when he was painfully tortured with fire, for Hera inspired him with great strength. And such were the things he said among them, his mind full of guile:

"The Greeks have run away over the sea with their ships, worn out by the long war and their troubles. On the advice of Calchas, they built the horse for wise Athena Tritogeneia, in order to avoid the goddess' wrath, since she is extremely angry because of the Trojans. At the suggestion of Odysseus, they planned destruction for me for the sake of their return. They were going to kill me by the roaring ocean as an offering to the divinities of the sea. But I found out about it, quickly escaped from the cruel libations and offerings of barley meal, and threw myself at the feet of the horse, through the plans of the immortals. They were forced to leave me there, although they didn't want to, out of fear of great Zeus's strong-minded daughter."

So he spoke in his cunning, and his spirit was not exhausted by his pains. It is characteristic of a strong man to endure harsh necessity. Some of the Trojans in the army believed him, while others said that he was a wily deceiver, and Laocoon's plan, of course, appealed to them: he spoke sensibly and said this was a terrible trick devised by the Greeks. He urged them all to set fire to the horse immediately and find out if the wooden horse concealed anything.

They would have obeyed him and escaped destruction, if Athena Tritogeneia, extremely angry at him, the Trojans, and the city, had not shaken the earth miraculously under Laocoon's feet. Fear fell upon him at once, and a trembling shattered the strength of the proud man's limbs. Black night poured over his head, and a

400

loathsome pain fell upon his eyelids, and the man's eyes under his shaggy brows were thrown into disorder. The pupils were pierced with terrible pains and agitated right from their roots, and his eyeballs rolled with all this internal distress. The awful anguish reached even to the membranes and base of the brain. His eyes were at times bright and suffused with blood, at times they had a blind glare of severe pain. There was frequently a discharge from them, like the water mixed with snow that flows sometimes from a rough rock in the mountains. He was like a madman, saw everything double, and groaned dreadfully. Yet he kept giving his orders to the Trojans and disregarded his misery. Then the divine goddess deprived him of his eyesight, and his eyes stood out white under his eyebrows as a result of the destructive blood.

The people groaned around him, pitying the man they loved and fearing Athena, the immortal goddess who drives off the booty, lest in his folly he had committed some wrong against her. Their own thoughts, too, were turned toward terrible destruction, because they had outraged the body of wretched Sinon, hoping in their hearts that he would tell the whole truth. And so with good will they led him into the Trojan city, pitying him very belatedly. At the same time they all got together and quickly threw a rope around the huge horse, fastening it from above. Able Epeius had put smooth-running wooden wheels under its great feet, so that it might follow the young men to the citadel, dragged by the hands of the Trojans. They were all dragging at it, applying their strength as a group. Just as men work hard to drag a ship into the noisy sea, and the strong rollers groan under the friction, and the keel squeaks terribly as it goes sliding down into the swell of the sea; so they were working hard all together dragging Epeius' work into their town for their own ruin. They put around it a splendid decoration of lavish garlands, and they put garlands on their own heads. The flutes sounded loudly, as the men called to one another. Enyo laughed when she saw this harsh end to the war, and up above Hera rejoiced, and Athena was glad at it. When they reached the city, they broke down battlements of the great town and brought in the ruinous horse. The Trojan women shouted, and they all stood around the horse and looked with wonder at the great work of Epeius. Their ruin was hidden within it.

Laocoon still stood firm and urged his companions to destroy the horse with blazing fire. But they were not persuaded at all, because they were afraid of the rebuke of the immortals. The goddess, proud Athena, had another still more abominable plan, this one directed against Laocoon's luckless sons. There was somewhere under a rocky crag a dark cavern where mortals could not go. Terrible wild animals of the deadly stock of Typhon still lived in it. It was in a cleft of the island in the sea off Troy that people call Calydna. The goddess roused mighty dragons from this cave and called them to Troy. Set into quick motion by the goddess, they made the island quake terribly. The sea roared as they moved, and the waves parted before them. While they rushed along, they flicked their tongues dreadfully, and the creatures of the sea shuddered. The nymphs, daughters of Xanthus and Simois, groaned loudly, and on Olympus Cyprian Aphrodite was filled with sorrow.

They came quickly to the spot where the goddess had ordered, whetting their teeth on their grim jaws, preparing ruin for the luckless boys. Cowardly flight came upon the Trojans, when they saw the terrible monsters in the town. Not a one of the men, not even if he had been fearless before, ventured to stand his ground. Absolute terror possessed them all, as they tried to get away from the beasts. There, too, the women wailed in anguish. Some women doubtless forgot their children in their own efforts to get away from a loathsome doom. As her people rushed away, Troy groaned roundabout. Many persons, as they hurried into one place, had the skin torn from their limbs. They packed the streets, cowering down everywhere.

Laocoon was left apart, alone with his sons. Destructive Doom and the goddess bound them fast. The dragons seized both the sons in their deadly jaws, frightened of death and stretching out their hands to their dear father, but he had no strength to protect them. The Trojans, watching from a distance, wept with wonder in their hearts. When the snakes had zealously carried out Athena's command, so hostile to the Trojans, they both disappeared underground. There is still a marker indicating where they entered Apollo's shrine in holy Pergamum. In front of this shrine, the sons of Troy gathered together and built a cenotaph for Laocoon's sons, mercilessly killed, and their father shed upon it tears from his blind eyes. Their mother, wailing about the cenotaph, raised many a cry over it, expecting something else still worse. She groaned for her husband, ruined by his folly, and was afraid of the blessed ones' wrath. Just as in a shadowy glen a nightingale, filled with great misery, wails around her ravaged nest, when a grim snake has destroyed in its strong jaws her still-helpless young before they had their full power of song and so brought pain to the mother bird, and she, grieved beyond telling, wails with many a cry around her empty home; so this mother groaned over the hideous fate of her sons and wailed around their empty tomb. She had, too, the other terrible disaster of her blinded husband.

So she kept up a lament for her dead sons and her husband— the sons dead, the husband with no share in the sunlight. The Trojans, however, were busy with sacrifices to the gods, pouring libations of choice wine, because their hearts were convinced that they would escape from the heavy might of wretched war. But the sacrifices would not burn, and the flame of the fire went out, as though a roaring storm of rain had swooped down from above. Bloodstained smoke rose up from the sacrifices, and all the thigh pieces fell quivering to the ground. The altars collapsed, and the libations turned to blood. Tears flowed from the statues of the gods, the temples became wet with gore, groans came from unexpected places, the high circling walls shook, and the towers gave loud roars, as if they were in pain. The bars of the gates opened automatically with terrible shrieks, and night birds moaned dismally in answer and gave desolate cries. All the stars above the city that gods had built were covered with a mist, even though the sky was bright and cloudless. The laurels by the temple of Phoebus Apollo withered, although they had previously been most flour-

500

ishing. Wolves and fierce jackals howled inside the gates. A thousand other portents appeared, bringing ruin to the Trojans and their city. But no troublesome fear came into the Trojans' hearts, as they saw all the troublesome portents in the city. Fates drove all of them out of their minds, so that they might meet their doom at the banquet table and be destroyed by the Greeks.

Only one person kept a firm heart and an intelligent mind: Cassandra. No word of hers had ever gone unfulfilled; what she said was always true, but through some fate she was always heard without profit, so that griefs might come to the Trojans. When she saw the grisly portents in the town, all leading swiftly to one conclusion, she gave a loud cry, just like a lioness which an eager hunter has stabbed or shot in the woods, and her heart rages within her [from pain, and she runs roaring][4] everywhere on the high mountains, and her strength is beyond holding; so Cassandra's prophetic heart was frantic within her. She went from the hall, and her hair poured about her silver shoulders and down her back. Her eyes glared terribly, and her neck quivered like a tree in the wind. With a deep groan the noble girl cried out:

"My miserable people, now we are for the dark. Our city is full of fire and blood and hideous doom. Everywhere the immortals are showing portents full of tears, and ultimate doom is before our feet. You poor fools, you do not understand at all your evil fate, but all of you alike are rejoicing, still acting senselessly regarding what has your complete destruction hidden within it.[5] You pay no attention to me, no matter how much I tell you, because the Furies are filled with anger because of Helen and her dreadful marriage, and the pitiless Dooms are darting everywhere through the citadel. At a banquet full of pains, you eat your last feast, food defiled with evil gore, and you are already setting foot on the road used by ghosts."

And one of them, sneering at her, made this pernicious speech:

[4] A guess to fill a gap.
[5] Many editors and commentators have found it odd that the prophetess is not more clear and specific about the horse, and many have suspected that there is something wrong with the text and possibly something lost.

"Daughter of Priam, why do your mad tongue and your folly command you to speak this windy nonsense? No pure, maidenly modesty clothes you, but a fatal madness possesses you. So every human being always dishonors you for talking so much. Go and make your evil predictions to the Greeks, or to yourself. An even more painful trouble awaits you than disrespectful Laocoon's. Because it isn't right to destroy in one's folly the dear gifts of the immortals."

So one of the Trojans spoke in the town. Others, also, blamed the girl in the same way, and said her talk was unsuitable. This was, of course, because ruin and the terrible might of Fate had taken their stand close to the Trojans. They jeered at her, with no thought of destruction, and diverted her from the vast horse. She was bent on shattering all the wood or burning it up with blazing fire. And so she had taken from the hearth a stick of pine that was still burning, and with it she rushed on. She carried in her other hand a double ax and was making her way toward the grim horse, so that the Trojans might see clearly the ambush that would bring them sorrow. But they threw the fire and the destructive iron far from her hands and carelessly set about their feast—a grim one, for their last night was truly coming upon them.

The Greeks inside the horse were delighted when they heard the noise of the men banqueting in Troy and paying no attention to Cassandra. They marveled at her themselves—at how she had been endowed with an unerring knowledge of the purpose and plan of the Greeks.

And Cassandra, just as a leopard runs harried in the mountains, one which dogs and hard-working herdsmen chase swiftly, and the leopard, her heart full of savagery, draws back under their pressure, although she keeps turning upon them; so Cassandra ran away from the vast horse, her heart full of grief for the slaughter of the Trojans. She expected a really great disaster.

BOOK THIRTEEN

The Sack of Troy

S O THE TROJANS were feasting in the citadel, and among them
was the loud music of flute and pipe alike. Everywhere there was
song and dancing and a confused noise of banqueters, such as ac-
companies banqueting and wine. Many a man there, taking a full
goblet in his hands, drank with carefree heart. Their wits grew
heavy within them, their eyes rolled. Word after word came from
their lips, as they babbled brokenly. The furniture in the halls and
the building itself seemed to them to be in motion, and they
thought that everything in the town was turning every way. A
mist came over their eyes. The vision and the intelligence of men
are impaired by strong drink when it is taken in quantity and
reaches the mind. This is the sort of thing a man said, his head
heavy with wine:

"The Greeks certainly brought a great army here to no pur-
pose. The wretches did not carry out all the plans they had in
mind, but they just rushed away from our city like foolish children
or women."

So one of the Trojans spoke, his wits in the grip of wine. Poor
fool, he did not notice the ruin at his doors.

When they had sated themselves with abundant wine and

food, and sleep held men everywhere through the town, then it was that Sinon lifted up the shining torch, showing the Greeks the blaze of fire. He had a thousand worries in his heart, afraid that the powerful Trojans might see him and everything be quickly revealed. But they were in their beds, sleeping their last sleep, weighed down by much strong drink. When the Greeks saw the signal, they made ready to sail in their ships from Tenedos.

Sinon himself came close to the horse. He called softly, very softly, so that no one among the Trojans might hear him, but only the Greek officers. They were so eager to be at the work of war that sleep had completely flown from them. And so the men in the horse heard Sinon, and all inclined their ears toward Odysseus. He urged them to go out of the horse quietly and fearlessly. They obeyed his summons to battle and were zealous to move on out of the horse to the ground. But he was wise enough to check them all in their eagerness, and then with his swift hands he personally opened the sides of the wooden horse here and there, working very quietly under the direction of Epeius of the good ashen spear. He raised himself a little above the openings and peered around in all directions to see if any Trojan was awake anywhere. Just as when a wolf, his heart struck by the pain of hunger, comes down from the mountains with a great longing for food and approaches a wide sheepfold and then, avoiding the men and dogs who are eager to guard the sheep, walks unhindered over the fence of the fold; so Odysseus came down from the horse. The other mighty kings of the Greeks followed him, filing down the ladders that Epeius had made as ways for the sturdy princes to enter and leave the horse. They went down along them then, some from one exit, others from another, like bold wasps which a woodcutter disturbs, and they all pour out from the branch with angry spirits, when they hear the noise; so they poured eagerly from the horse into the splendid citadel of Troy, their hearts pounding in their breasts.

They were soon at work killing the enemy, and meanwhile the others were rowing at sea, and the ships moved quickly over the great expanse. Thetis directed their way and sent a breeze after them, and the minds of the Greeks were cheered. They soon reached the shores of the Hellespont, where they halted their ships again. They skillfully collected all the gear that ships always carry, disembarked at once, and hurried toward Troy, making no noise, just like sheep hurrying to the fold from a woodland meadow in an autumn night; so without a sound they moved quickly to the city of the Trojans, all of them eager to help their princes. Just as wolves in a terrible frenzy of hunger attack a sheepfold in the high wooded mountains, when the hard-working shepherd is asleep, and in the darkness they destroy one sheep after another inside the enclosure, and everywhere roundabout [there is death and blood; so the Greek leaders filled Troy with][1] blood and corpses, and a terrible destruction began, even though still more of the Greeks were outside.

But when quite all of them had reached the walls of Troy, then they eagerly and steadily poured into Priam's town, breathing the might of war. They found the whole citadel full of battle and corpses, and everywhere in the unhappy town they found buildings being cruelly burned with fire. Their hearts were greatly pleased, and they themselves rushed upon the Trojans with evil thoughts. Ares was raging among them along with Enyo, goddess of groaning. Everywhere the dark blood flowed, and the earth grew wet, as the Trojans and their foreign allies were destroyed. Some of them, mastered by chill death, lay in their blood in the citadel. Others fell on top of them, breathing out their strength. Others again, holding their entrails clutched in their hands, were wandering piteously in the houses. Some, with both their feet cut off, crawled among the corpses, shrieking terribly. Many who had been eager to fight lay in the dust with their hands cut off and their heads as well. Others were struck as they fled, the spears piercing their backs and going straight through to their breasts, or reaching their waists above their genitals, where the spearpoint of tireless Ares is most full of anguish. Everywhere through the town a wretched howling of dogs arose, and the pitiable groaning of wounded men, and all the rooms were filled with noise beyond telling.

100

[1] A guess to fill a gap.

There was, too, the sad wailing of women. They were like cranes when they see an eagle swooping from above through the air. They have no bold courage in their hearts, but merely chirp loudly in their fear of the eagle, the sacred bird. So the Trojan women were wailing loudly on all sides, some rising up from their beds, some leaping to the ground. They had no concern now for proper dress in their misery, but roamed about after throwing a single garment around them. Some did not stop to take even a veil or a long cloak; in their fear of the attacking enemy, their hearts pounded, they were shackled by helplessness, and, poor creatures, they concealed their nakedness only with their swift hands. Some in their misery were pulling the hair from their heads, beating their breasts with their hands, and groaning loudly. Still others ventured to face the enemy turmoil and forgot their fear in their eagerness to help their husbands and children who were being killed; necessity gave them boldness.

The wailing roused from sleep the children, whose tender spirit had never yet known cares. One after another they breathed their last. Some lay there who had seen their doom simultaneously with their dreams. Grim Fates took delight in the piteous deaths. The Trojans were killed by the thousands, like pigs in the home of a rich man who is preparing a great feast for his people. The wine still left in the mixing bowls became mixed with grisly gore. There was no one who would have kept his cruel iron free from slaughter, not even if he was a complete weakling. The Trojans were being destroyed just as sheep are killed by jackals or by wolves, when excessive heat comes on at midday, and the flocks gather all close together in a shady place, waiting for the shepherd who has gone to the house with milk, [and the wild beasts][2] attack them, fill their capacious bellies, and lap up the black blood, staying to destroy the whole flock and fashion an evil feast for the wretched shepherd; so the Greeks in Priam's town attacked the Trojans in their last battle and killed one man after another. Not a Trojan was left unwounded, every man's limbs were spattered and black with streams of blood.

[2] A guess to fill a gap.

The Greeks did not escape unwounded from the conflict either. Some were hit with goblets, some with tables, some with sticks of wood that were still burning on the hearth. Some died pierced by spits on which hot chitterlings had doubtless been left still sizzling in the warmth of the strong fire. Others, again, writhed in their blood from blows of hatchets and swift battle-axes. Some had their fingers cut from their hands when they threw their hands upon a sword, hoping to keep off a loathsome death. Many a man doubtless hit a comrade with a stone in the confusion and mixed his skull with his brain. Like wild beasts wounded at a shepherd's fold in the country, they raged cruelly in the ghastly night, as their anger was roused. In their great desire for war, they rushed about Priam's palace and routed enemies from everywhere. Many of the Greeks were killed with spears too, because all of the Trojans who were quick enough to lift a sword or a long spear in their hands destroyed enemies, even though they were heavy with wine. A great glare rose up through the city, because many of the Greeks held bright flares in their hands, so that they could clearly distinguish friend from foe in the conflict.

Then the soldier Coroebus, son of famous Mygdon, came against Diomedes, Tydeus' son, in the turmoil, and Diomedes pierced him with his spear through the hollow throat, where are the quick ways of drink and food. He found his black doom on the spear and fell among the black blood and the heaps of other corpses. Poor fool, he got no good of the marriage for which he had come the day before to Priam's town, with the promise to thrust the Greeks from Troy. The god did not fulfill his hope, for the Fates sent doom upon him first. With him Tydeus' son killed Eurydamas, who came against him. He was a spear fighter and a son-in-law of Antenor, who had the highest pre-eminence among the Trojans for his sensible spirit. There, too, Tydeus' son met Ilioneus, an elder of the people, and drew his terrible sword against him. The limbs of Ilioneus' aged body completely collapsed. He held out both his trembling hands, with one grasping the swift sword, and with the other taking hold of the murderous hero's knees. And Tydeus' son, rushing into battle though he was, whether because he put off his anger, or at the bidding of some god, held his sword away from the old man for a little, so that he might say something, beseeching the swift and mighty man. Ilioneus, in the grip of loathsome fear, quickly gave a miserable cry:

"I beseech you, whoever you are of the sturdy Greeks, have respect for my arms, as I fall before you, and stop your harsh anger. A man wins great glory, if he kills a man who is young and strong. But if you kill an old man, no praise of your strength will follow you. Turn your hands, therefore, away from me and against the young men, hoping some day to reach an old age like mine."

In answer to his words, the son of mighty Tydeus said to him:

"Sir, I hope to reach a good old age, but while my strength is still growing I will not spare any enemy of my person. I will send 200 them all to Hades. He is a good man who defends himself against an enemy."

With these words, the fearful man drove his deadly sword through Ilioneus' throat and directed it to where the doom of life is swiftest for mortals, and the terrible paths of the blood lie. And so a terrible doom shattered Ilioneus, destroyed by Tydeusson's hands. Diomedes continued to slaughter Trojans, rushing up through the citadel and raging terribly in his strength. He killed noble Abas, and he hit with his long spear the son of Perimnestus, famous Eurycoon. And Aias killed Amphimedon, Agamemnon killed Damastorson, Idomeneus killed Mimas, and Meges killed Deiopites.

Achilles' son, for his part, destroyed with his invincible spear glorious Pammon and struck Polites as he attacked, and with them he killed Antiphonus, all of them alike sons of Priam. As glorious Agenor came against him in the conflict, he cut him down. He dispatched one hero after another. Everywhere there was apparent the black doom of dying men. Wearing his father's strength, he eagerly butchered all whom he met. His mind was filled with evil thoughts when he came upon the enemy king himself beside the altar of Zeus of the courtyard. When Priam saw Achilles' son, he recognized at once who he was, and he felt no fear, because in his heart he was himself longing to join his sons in death. And so, in his eagerness to die, he said to him:

"Stouthearted son of the good soldier Achilles, kill me in my misery and feel no pity for me. Personally, after such great and such terrible sufferings, I have no desire to look upon the light of the all-seeing sun. I want to die now, along with my sons, and quite forget my dismal troubles and the hideous confusion of war. I wish your father had killed me before I saw Ilios in flames, killed me when I brought him the ransom for dead Hector, my son whose life your father took. But the Fates, I suppose, spun it this way. Sate your mighty heart in my slaughter, so that I may forget my sorrows."

In reply to him, Achilles' mighty son said:

"Sir, you command a man who is ready and eager. I will not leave you who are my enemy among the living, for nothing is dearer to men than life."

So speaking, he cut off the old man's grey head, easily, just as if someone were reaping an ear of grain from a dry field in the season of warm summer. The head, with a deep moan, rolled a considerable distance away from the rest of the body. And so he lay in the black blood and gore of the other men, [Priam, once renowned][3] for wealth and noble birth and numerous children. Glory does not for long increase for human beings, but disgrace comes on unexpectedly. Yet, while doom overtook Priam, he did forget all his troubles.

The Greeks of the swift horses also threw Astyanax from a high tower. In their anger at Hector, who had caused troubles for them when he was alive, they snatched his dear child from its mother's arms and took its life. They hated Hector's stock, and they threw the boy down from the high wall, just a baby, with no knowledge yet of the conflict of war. Just as wolves in need of food cut off a calf from its mother and her milky udders and evilly drive it over an echoing cliff, and the cow, moaning for its dear calf, runs here and there with loud laments, and later another

[3] A guess to fill a gap.

evil comes upon her, when the cow herself is snatched by lions; so hostile men took, along with the other captive women, noble Eëtion's daughter Andromache, wild with grief for her son and crying out dreadfully. She, Andromache of the fair ankles, when she thought of the terrible slaughter of her son, her husband, and her father, wanted to die. It is better for royal persons to die in war than to serve their inferiors. With deep grief in her heart, she uttered this sad cry:

"You Greeks, come now and throw my body quickly down from the dreadful wall, or down from crags, or into the fire, for my troubles are truly beyond telling. Achilles, Peleus' son, killed my noble father in holy Thebe, and in Troy my famous husband, who was to me absolutely everything that my heart desired. He left to me in our halls a son, still small, in whom I took infinite pride, for whom I had many hopes. An evil and monstrous doom has cheated me of him. And so take from me quickly in my sorrow a life with so much misery. Don't bring me to your homes along with those your spears have won. My spirit finds no pleasure any longer in being with humankind, because a supernatural power has destroyed my family. Besides my other hateful sufferings, a terrible pain awaits me if I am left alone and without the Trojans."

So she spoke in her desire to be dead and buried. It does not befit those persons to remain alive whose great glory has been swallowed up by disgrace, for it is a terrible thing to be looked down upon by others. But the Greeks, much against her will, dragged her forcibly away to the day of slavery.

Men were losing their lives in various other houses, and very melancholy cries arose in them, but not in the halls of Antenor, because the Greeks remembered his charming hospitality. He had previously entertained as his guests in the town godlike Menelaus and Odysseus, when they came together, and he had kept them safe. Out of kindness to him, the excellent sons of the Greeks spared his life and left his property unharmed, showing regard both for all-seeing Themis and for a man who had befriended them.

Then it was that the brave son of noble Anchises, after much   300 courageous labor with his spear about the city of Priam, child of gods, and after having taken the life of many, gave up hope in his heart of looking any longer upon his strongly fortified city. And when he saw that the grim hands of the enemy had set fire to the citadel, that people were dying in great numbers, that vast treasure as well was being destroyed, that wives with their children were being dragged from their homes, he made plans to escape from the great disaster. Just as when on the deep sea a man controlling the rudder of a ship skillfully avoids wind and wave that rush at him from every quarter in the hateful season of winter, and then his hand and his spirit alike grow weary, and when the ship, breaking up, begins to sink, he abandons his rudder and transfers to a small skiff, no longer giving his concern to the merchant ship; so the brave son of wise Anchises left to the enemy his city, blazing with sheets of fire. He snatched his son and his father and took them with him. With his strong hands, he set his father, suffering from the many miseries of old age, on his broad shoulders; the boy he allowed to walk and, holding him by his soft hand, led him away from the noisy fighting. The little boy was frightened by the deeds of destructive turmoil and had to hang clinging to him, with tears flowing on his tender cheeks. Aeneas leapt with swift feet over many dead bodies, and many, too, he trampled on in the darkness without meaning to. His mother, Cyprian Aphrodite, led the way, carefully saving from the terrible disaster her grandson, son, and husband. As Aeneas rushed on, the fire yielded everywhere beneath his feet, the blasts of raging flame parted, and the spears and arrows of men which the Greeks hurled at him in the cruel battle all fell fruitless on the ground. Then it was that Calchas gave a great shout to hold the army back:

"Stop hurling your cruel arrows and destructive spears at mighty Aeneas. It is decreed for him by the splendid plan of the gods to go from Xanthus to the broad stream of Tiber. There he shall fashion a sacred city, an object of wonder for future generations, and he shall himself be lord of a widespread people. The stock born from him shall thereafter rule all the way from the rising to the setting sun. Moreover, it is decreed for him to take a place among the immortals, because he is the son of fair-haired Aphrodite. And let us, in any case, keep our hands away from this man, because in preference to gold and all his other possessions, things that preserve a man when he goes as an exile to a foreign land, in preference to all this, he has chosen his father and his son. A single night has revealed to us a son marvelously kind to his old father, a noble father marvelously kind to his son."

So he spoke, and they all listened to him and looked upon Aeneas as a god. He was quickly gone from his city to the place where his busy feet carried him, while the Greeks continued the sack of the splendid citadel of Troy.

Then it was that Menelaus killed with his cruel sword Deiphobus, having found the luckless wretch drowsing by Helen's bed. (She had run and hid in the house.) As the blood poured out, Menelaus rejoiced at the killing and spoke like this:

"You dog, this day I have given you a painful death. The divine Dawn will not find you still alive among the Trojans, even if you are proud to be the son-in-law of Zeus, the loud thunderer. Black destruction has found you, overcome pitilessly in the halls of my wife. How I wish that before now cursed Alexander had come against me in battle, and I had taken his life away too; my sorrow would then have been easier to bear. But by now he has paid all the penalties he owed and has gone underneath the chill darkness. It is now clear, too, that my wife was not to bring you any profit. Sinful men do not ever escape pure Themis. She watches them night and day, and she flits everywhere through the sky over the races of men, punishing along with Zeus those who participate in evil deeds."

When he had said this, he continued his merciless destruction of the enemy. The jealous spirit within him was raging and grew steadily more impassioned. His bold mind was full of evil intentions toward the Trojans, intentions that now the goddess, revered Justice, executed. The Trojans had been the first to do wrong in connection with Helen, they had been the first to break their oaths —wicked men, because in their minds' transgressions they completely forgot the black blood and the other rites of the immortals.

243

For this reason, the Furies created sorrows for them thereafter. And this is why, of course, some of them died in front of the wall, and others inside the city while enjoying themselves with feasting and with their fair-haired wives.

At last, in the innermost parts of the house, Menelaus found his wife. She was fearful of this attack by the firm-minded husband of her youth. When he caught sight of her, he was planning to kill her in the jealousy of his mind, but lovely Aphrodite restrained his strength, knocked the sword from his hand, and checked his attack. She removed his black jealousy from him and roused sweet desire in his heart and eyes. An unexpected amazement came upon him, and when he saw Helen's conspicuous beauty, he could no longer bring himself to strike her neck with his sword. He stood like a dead tree on a wooded mountain, which neither the swift blasts of Boreas nor of Notus can shake as they rush through the air upon it; so he stood for a long time, lost in wonder. His strength was shattered as he looked upon his wife, and he immediately forgot all the wrongs she had done to him and to their marriage bed. Everything was effaced by the goddess Cyprian Aphrodite, the goddess who conquers the mind of all immortals and mortal men. Even so, however, he lifted his swift sword again from the ground and charged upon his wife. But his mind within was planning other things as he rushed at her: he was, of course, beguiling the Greeks with a trick. And then his brother Agamemnon held him back, for all his zeal, and with gentle words gave him much earnest advice, because he was afraid that all they had done might become useless:

"You have gone far enough, Menelaus, angry though you are. It isn't proper to kill the wife of your youth, for whose sake we endured many sorrows and made evil plans against Priam. Helen is not to blame, as you think, but Paris, who forgot Zeus, the god of guest and host, and forgot what he owed your table. A supernatural power has therefore brought him to painful punishment."

So he spoke, and Menelaus was prompt to obey him. The gods then covered glorious Troy in dark clouds and mourned for it, except for fair-haired Tritonian Athena and Hera. Their minds were filled with exultation when they saw the famous city of god-descended Priam being sacked. But no, not even wise Athena Tritogeneia herself was wholly tearless when within her temple Aias, the strong son of Oïleus, defiled Cassandra. He was a man deranged in mind and spirit, and the goddess afterward cast upon him a terrible disaster and punished him for the outrage. She did not look upon his disgraceful deed, but shame and anger enveloped her. She turned her grim eyes to her high temple, the divine image resounded, and the floor of the temple shook vigorously. But Aias did not stop his hideous outrage, because Cyprian Aphrodite had infatuated his mind.

All over the town, tall buildings were falling down on every side, and a choking dust mingled with the smoke. A terrible noise arose, and the streets quaked. Aeneas' home was burning, and all the rooms of Antimachus' house. The great city height was ablaze around lovely Pergamus, the shrine of Apollo, the holy temple of Tritonian Athena, and the altar of Zeus of the Courtyard. The lovely rooms of Priam's grandsons were burning up, and the whole city was being completely destroyed.

As for the Trojans, some fell beneath the sons of the Greeks, some were killed by the ghastly fire and their own homes, which became at once their evil death and their tomb; others drove swords through their own throats, when they saw fire at the door along with the enemy. Still others killed their wives and children and then, completing a monstrous deed forced upon them by necessity, fell dead upon them. One man, thinking the enemy was fighting far off, quickly took up a jar from the fire and was planning to go for water. But he was heavy with wine, and a Greek, anticipating him, struck him with a spear and took away his life. He fell inside his house, and the empty water jar fell down beside him. A burning beam fell upon another while he was running through his great hall and brought quick death as it crashed upon him. Many women, too, who had hurried off in wretched flight, remembered their dear children whom they had left in bed at home. Running back at once, they were killed along with the children, when the buildings fell upon them. Horses and dogs were rushing in terror through the city, running from the force of the hideous fire. With their feet they trampled upon men who had been killed and frequently brought death to the living by crushing them. Shrieks resounded through the city. One young man was rushing through the flames [. . . a gap of unknown length . . .] as he spoke, and pitiless doom destroyed those inside. Various were the ways of cruel death that carried men off. The blaze rose up into the divine sky, and a brightness beyond telling spread abroad. The neighboring peoples saw it, all the way to the high peaks of the Idaean hills, Samothrace, and the island of Tenedos. And a man on shipboard out at sea said:

"The strong-minded Greeks have done a deed beyond telling, after their many toils for Helen of the glancing eyes. All Troy, vastly rich before, is now being consumed with fire, and no god defended them, for all their longing. Irresistible Fate looks upon all the works of men, and many things that have been undistinguished and inconspicuous she makes famous, and lofty things she brings low. Very often good comes out of evil, and out of good comes evil, as our miserable life keeps changing."

So some man spoke, as he looked from a distance on the brightness beyond telling. Painful anguish still held the Trojans, but the Greeks were spreading confusion through the town. Just as the blustering gales when they have been roused drive the boundless sea wildly, when opposite to Arcturus, star of evil winds, the Altar rises into the starry threshold, turned to the murky south wind, and at its rising many ships are overwhelmed in the sea and sunk as the winds increase; like them the sons of the Greeks were sacking lofty Ilios, and it was burning in the vast fire. Just as a mountain covered with dense woods burns quickly when fire is roused by the winds, and the tall hills roar, and all the wild creatures are in pitiful distress in it, as they are driven in circles through the forest by the force of the fire; so the Trojans were being killed in the town. No one of the heavenly ones protected them, because the Fates had set their high nets around them everywhere, those nets which no mortal has ever escaped.

And then Aethra, mother of great Theseus, met in the city

Demophoon and the stubborn fighter Acamas.[4] She was eager to meet some Greek, and one of the blessed gods had led her and brought her face to face with them. She had been running in terror from the fighting and the fire. When in the bright glare they saw   500 the build and size of the woman, they thought she was the godlike wife of Priam, son of gods. Immediately and enthusiastically, they laid hands on her, eager to take her to the Greeks. But she gave a terrible cry and said:

"You glorious sons of the warlike Greeks, don't take me to your ships by dragging me away like an enemy. I make no boast of Trojan stock, but I am of good Greek blood and very famous too. Pittheus begot me in Troezen, and glorious Aegeus took me in marriage, and from me was born a famous son: Theseus. Please, by great Zeus and your happy parents, if the sons of noble Theseus have really come here with the Atreussons, show me to his dear sons in the army. I think they are of the same age as you. They are eager to see me, and my heart will have relief if I see them alive and both of them princes."

So she spoke, and as they listened they remembered their father: all that he had done in connection with Helen, and how her brothers, Castor and Polydeuces, sons of Zeus the thunderer, had in other days sacked Aphidnae, while they were themselves still babies, and their nurses had hidden them away from the fighting. And they remembered illustrious Aethra and all she had suffered under the hardships of slavery, when she became at once the mother-in-law and the maidservant of divine Helen. They were so delighted they could hardly speak. And then excellent Demophoon spoke in answer to her eager request:

"Well, the gods are quick to fulfill the wish of your heart. You see in us the sons of your noble son. We'll lift you in our loving arms and carry you to the ships, and we'll gladly bring you to

---

[4] "Aethra, daughter of Pittheus," is mentioned in the third book of the *Iliad* as one of two servants of Helen (144). Quintus himself gives most of her history. He does not mention that when Helen's brothers rescued her from her kidnapper Theseus, they took Theseus' mother Aethra and made her Helen's slave.

the holy soil of Greece, the very place where before you were a queen."

When he had said this, the mother of his great father flung her arms about him and pressed him to her, and she kissed his broad shoulders, his head and chest, and his bearded cheeks. Then she kissed Acamas in the same way, and sweet tears flowed down from their eyes as they wept. Just as when people spread a report about the death of a man who has been in foreign lands, and he returns to his home from somewhere, and his sons cry with great joy at the sight of him, and he in his turn weeps himself in his halls on his sons' shoulders, and around the house there hovers a mournful cry of men who are sweetly wailing; so as they wept there arose a lamentation that was pleasant to hear.

And then it was, I fancy, men say that Laodice, daughter of long-suffering Priam, lifted her arms to the sky, praying to the tireless blessed ones that the earth might swallow her before she put her hand to slavish tasks.[5] And one of the gods heard her and immediately caused the great earth to break beneath her. At the request of the god, the earth received the glorious girl within the hollow gulf, as Troy was being destroyed.

Men say that because of Troy, too, long-robed Electra herself hid her body in mist and clouds and left the chorus of the other Pleiades, who are her sisters. They rise in a troop into heaven, visible to toiling mortals, but she alone hides ever unseen, because the holy city of her noble son Dardanus fell in ruins. Not even Zeus himself, most high, brought her any help from heaven, because even the might of great Zeus yields to the Fates. This destruction, I fancy, was probably brought about by the good purpose of the gods and by the Fates themselves.

The Greeks, meanwhile, were still stirring up their spirit against the Trojans everywhere in the citadel, and Eris, goddess of strife, held in her hands the conclusion of the conflict.

---

[5] Laodice, daughter of Priam and Hecabe, is twice mentioned in the *Iliad* (iii. 124; vi. 252) and is both times called the most beautiful of their daughters. It should be noted, however, that Homer gives this same high praise to Cassandra.

BOOK FOURTEEN

The Departure for Home

THEN DAWN, the goddess of the golden throne, leapt up into heaven from the streams of Ocean, and chaos took night. The Greeks violently wrecked the well-walled city of Troy and took for themselves infinite booty. They were like rivers in winter, which rush roaring down from the mountains in the driving rain and carry into the sea many tall trees and everything that grows in the mountains along with the mountain crags themselves; so the Greeks, when they had destroyed the Trojan city with fire, carried all of the treasure to the bounding ships. Along with the treasure, of course, they brought down from their various homes the Trojan women, some of them still virgins and knowing nothing of marriage, some of them recently brought to the joys of husbands' love, others, again, with grey hair, and some, younger than these, whose children were snatched from their breasts as their eager lips sought their mother's milk for the last time.

Among them Menelaus, too, brought his wife from the blazing city. His great task was done, and he felt at once pleasure and shame. Agamemnon of the good ashen spear brought Cassandra, and Andromache was brought by Achilles' noble son. Odysseus, though, forcibly dragged Hecabe. Tears poured in floods from her eyes, as though from a spring. Her limbs were trembling, her heart was distracted with fear, and she had torn hair from her grey head. Thick ashes covered her, which her hands had doubtless taken from the hearth and poured down over her when Priam was being killed and her city was blazing. She groaned loudly because the day of slavery had seized in her an unwilling victim. So the Greeks led by force to their several ships their various wailing Trojan women. And they cried out their loud wails from every side, lamenting most pitifully along with their little children. Just as when men drive the bright-tusked swine and the young piglets from their former station to a new one, when winter comes on, and they set up a pitiful, confused, and steady squealing; so the Trojan women who had been conquered by the Greeks were groaning. Queen and slave now endured the same necessity.

Helen, however, showed no signs of lamenting. But shame sat upon her dark eyes and reddened her beautiful cheeks. The heart within her was troubled by a thousand worries, and she was afraid that when she went to the dark ships the Greeks would abuse her. On this account her spirit was fearful and trembling. So she covered her head with a veil and followed the footsteps of her husband, her cheek red with shame. She was like Cyprian Aphrodite when the heavenly ones saw her in the arms of Ares, openly shaming her marriage bed. She was caught in the close-set chains of clever Hephaestus and lay in them with pain in her heart and full of shame before the race of the blessed ones who gathered in a troop and before Hephaestus himself.[1] It is a terrible thing for a woman to be seen in open shame by her husband's eyes. With an appearance and an utter shame like hers, Helen went along with the captive Trojan women to the well-equipped ships of the Greeks. The soldiers standing around looked with amazement on the splendor and lovely beauty of the faultless woman. Not a man ventured to assail her with insults, either secretly or openly. They

---

[1] The story of this celestial adultery is told in the eighth book of Homer's *Odyssey* (266–366), where Demodocus, the court bard in Phaeacia, uses it as the theme of one of his songs.

found pleasure in looking at her, as though looking at a goddess. She stood visible before them, a sight they had all longed to see. Just as when men have been roaming through the restless sea, and after a long time their native country comes in sight in answer to their prayers, and, escaped from the sea and from death, they stretch out their hands to their native land, with infinite joy in their hearts; so all the Greeks were full of joy. No longer did they remember their painful labors or fighting. This was the sort of mood Cytherean Aphrodite produced in them all, showing favor to the bright-eyed Helen and to Father Zeus.

And then the river Xanthus, still recovering from the bloody confusion, when he saw that his beloved city was destroyed, wept along with the nymphs, because evil from somewhere had fallen upon Troy and leveled Priam's town. Just as when a storm of hail falls upon a field of ripe grain and cuts it to bits, its evil onset destroys all the ears of grain, and the stalks fall useless to the earth, and the crop lies on the ground badly spoiled, and the owner's grief is great and terrible; so grief came to Xanthus' heart when Ilios was abandoned. His sorrow was continuous, immortal though he was. Great Ida, too, groaned, and Simois, and, far away, all the streams of Ida wept, bewailing Priam's town.

The Greeks went to their ships with loud laughter, singing about the mighty force of their glorious victory, then again of the holy race of the blessed ones, and again of their own bold spirit and Epeius' immortal work. Their song went through the air to heaven, like the vast clamor of jackdaws when a fine clear day comes after a hard winter, and the air is calm; so, beside the ships, from these men with deep joy in their hearts, [a great clamor went up to heaven and] the immortals [when they heard it][2] were joyous in heaven, all those, that is, who were enthusiastic protectors of the war-loving Greeks. The others, though, all those who had been defending the Trojans, were full of anger as they saw Priam's citadel in flames. But they had no power to defend Troy contrary to Fate, much as they wanted to. For no, not even Zeus Cronosson himself can easily thrust Fate aside beyond what is destined,

[2] A guess to fill a gap.

100 although his strength is supreme among all the immortals, and all things come from Zeus.

The Greeks, of course, put many thigh pieces of oxen on the fire and burned them with kindling and, moving quickly around the altars, poured fine wine over the blazing sacrifices, doing honor to the gods because they had accomplished a great deed. At the pleasant feast, they enthusiastically acclaimed all those whom, with their arms, the wooden horse had received. They admired famous Sinon, too, because he had endured the painful outrages of the enemy, and they all kept honoring him with song and with enormous gifts. He was deeply pleased in his enduring spirit at the Greek victory and felt no grief at the outrages to himself. For a wise and sensible man, glory is far better than gold and beauty and all the other good things there are and will be among men. So the Greeks, their hearts free of fear, banqueted beside the ships, constantly saying to one another:

"We brought the long war to an end. We have won glory far and wide by killing our enemies and taking their great citadel. But, O Zeus, grant us in answer to our desires a return home as well."

So they spoke, but the father did not grant a return to all of them.

Among them a man skilled [at playing the lyre sang the end of the long conflict, and they listened with pleasure,]³ for they no longer had any fear of noisy war, but turned to things of an orderly world and lovely gaiety. The singer sang first to his eager listeners how the host gathered at the holy soil of Aulis; how the great strength of tireless Peleusson sacked twelve cities by sea and eleven more on the broad earth; all that he did in connection with lord Telephus and mighty Eëtion; how he killed proud Cycnus; all the difficulties the Greeks had had as they fought during the wrath of Achilles; how he dragged Hector around the walls of his city; how he killed Penthesileia in battle; how he laid low the son of Tithonus; how sturdy Aias killed Glaucus of the good ashen spear; how the son of swift Achilles killed the glorious man Euryp-

³ A guess to fill a gap.

ylus; how the arrows of Philoctetes destroyed Paris; how many men went inside the horse of trickery; and how, after having sacked the city of Priam, son of gods, the Greeks feasted far from evil tumults. Other men sang other songs—whatever pleased their hearts.

But when midnight came round to the banqueters, then it was, I fancy, that the Greeks abandoned their feasting and their strong drink and took the sleep that brings forgetfulness of cares. The hard work of the day before had overpowered them all, and so, much as they longed to feast the whole night through, they stopped. Sleep checked them, no matter how hard they fought against it. They slept, one man here, one there. But Menelaus Atreusson talked in his quarters with his fair-haired wife. Sleep had not yet fallen upon their eyes, but Cyprian Aphrodite hovered about their hearts, so that they might remember their marriage bed of long ago and throw grief far from them. Helen spoke first, addressing him in words like these:

"Menelaus, do not be putting in your heart anger against me. I did not voluntarily leave your home and your bed, but strong Alexander and the sons of Troy came and snatched me away while you were gone. And when I was constantly desirous of dying a pitiful death with the painful noose or the cruel sword, they held me back, encouraging me in their halls with talk, while I was suffering because of you and our dear daughter. I beg you, by her, by our marriage with its many joys, and by yourself, forget the hateful trouble you had because of me."

When she had said this, sensible Menelaus replied:

"Think of these things no more now, but check the sorrows in your heart. I hope the black hall of forgetfulness may shut all this somewhere deep within. It is not proper to remember evil things any longer."

So he spoke, and joy took hold of her, and the fear swept from her heart. She was sure her husband had put an end to his painful wrath. She threw both her arms around him, and tears of sweet lamentation poured from the eyes of them both. Gladly they lay beside each other, and their hearts recalled their marriage.

Just as when ivy and a vine intertwine about a stump, and no power of wind is able to force them apart; so these two clung together, longing for love.

But when kindly sleep came at last even upon them, then it was that the mighty spirit of godlike Achilles stood above the head of his son, looking just as he was when alive, when he was a bane to the Trojans and a joy to the Greeks. He kissed with delight his son's neck and bright eyes and, encouraging him, said such things as these:

"Greetings, my son. Do not harry your spirit with sorrow at all because I am dead; now I share the hearth of the blessed gods. Check your heart from its oppression on my account, and put my great strength in your spirit. Always stand in the forefront of the Greeks, and yield to no one in manliness, though in council give heed to older men. Then everyone will say that you are sensible. Honor all noble men whose minds are firm. A good man is friend to the good and harsh to the bad. If the thoughts within you are good, you will produce good deeds as well. That man never reaches the goals of Excellence whose mind is not honorable. The base of the tree of Excellence is hard to climb, and her branches extend far up into the air. But all those whom strength and labor accompany, they climb up the famous tree of Excellence with her beautiful crown and reap the delightful fruit after their work. Be noble, and in your sensible heart do not harry your spirit overmuch with anguish at disaster, and do not rejoice greatly at good fortune. Let your mind be gentle to the comrades you love, to your sons, and to your wife, remembering in your heart that the gates of fated doom and the halls of the dead stand close by for humankind. The stock of men is like the flowers in the grass, the flowers of spring: some waste away, and some grow. For this reason be kindly.

"And tell the Greeks, and especially Agamemnon Atreusson, if they have any recollection in their hearts of all the work I did around Priam's town, and all the booty I won before we reached the land of Troy, then let them, in answer to my desires, bring to my tomb from Priam's booty Polyxena of the lovely robe to sacrifice with speed. Because I am still even more angry with them than I was over Briseis. I will set in motion the swells of the sea and send storm upon storm so that they may stay here wasting away for a long time in their folly, until, out of eagerness for a return, they pour libations to me. The girl's body, when they have taken her life, I do not begrudge their burying—at some distance from me—if they want."

When he had spoken thus, he hurried off like a swift breeze and quickly came to the Elysian plain in the place where there has been made for the blessed immortals a way down from heaven most high and a way up. When sleep left Neoptolemus, he remembered his father, and his noble mind was cheered.

When the early-born Dawn had gone up to broad heaven, after having scattered the night, and earth and sky were clearly visible, then it was that the sons of the Greeks leapt from their beds, longing for return. With laughter in their hearts, they would have dragged the ships into deep water, except that the mighty son of Achilles checked the eager men, called them to an assembly, and told them his father's command:

"Hear from me, dear sons of the Greeks who are firm in battle, the order of my glorious father which he gave me yesterday when I was asleep on my bed in the darkness. He said that he was with the eternal deathless ones, and he ordered you and king Atreusson to bring to his broad tomb the beautiful prize of war, Polyxena of the fine robe. He said, too, that when you had sacrificed her you should bury her at a distance from him. And if, disregarding him, you should sail on the sea, he threatened to raise opposing waves on the deep and keep army and ships as well here for a long time."

They were persuaded by what he said and prayed to Achilles as though to a god. For already on the sea the waves, driven by a storm, were getting larger and wider and were coming more frequently than before, and the wind was raging. The great ocean was being stirred up by Poseidon, because he was showing favor to mighty Achilles. All the winds, too, rushed swiftly upon the sea. The Greeks, as they prayed earnestly to Achilles, were all alike saying things like this to one another:

"Achilles was certainly descended from great Zeus. And so he is now a god, too, even though he was previously with us. Everlasting time does not destroy the stock of the blessed gods."

With these words, they went to Achilles' tomb. They led Polyxena, just as herdsmen tear a heifer away from its mother in the scrub and lead it to the sacrifices being made to a god, and the heifer bellows loudly and moans with stricken heart; so on this day the daughter of Priam wailed in the hands of her enemies, and floods of tears flowed from her. Just as when in a strong press olives not yet blackened by winter rains pour out abundant oil, and the long beams creak under the ropes as men apply pressure; so, as the daughter of long-suffering Priam was dragged to the tomb of pitiless Achilles, groans came from her, and there was a terrible flow of tears from her eyes. The tears filled her bosom and made wet her skin that was truly like precious ivory.

Then a still more abominable grief fell upon the spirit of suffering Hecabe and added to her dismal sorrows. The heart within her recalled the sad and painful dream she had had while asleep on the night just passed. She thought she was standing sorrowfully at the tomb of godlike Achilles. Her hair streamed from her head all the way to the ground, and from both her breasts red blood flowed to the ground and made wet the tomb. She was wailing terribly around the tomb, full of fear and foreboding a great disaster, and in her lament she raised a loud cry. Just as when a dog, whimpering in front of a house and newly swollen with milk, sends out a loud barking, but the masters have thrown away her puppies before their eyes were open to be a find for birds, and the dog whimpers and barks and howls, and her hideous cry goes up through the air; so Hecabe in her sorrow cried aloud for her daughter:

"Overwhelmed with many evils and with anguish in my heart, what shall I lament first, what last? My sons, or my husband, who suffered terrible fates they did not foresee, my city, or my disgraced daughters, or my own day of constraint and slavery? The cruel Fates have hemmed me in with many evils. And, my child, they have spun for you, too, terrible sorrows you did not expect to see. You were near your wedding day, and they have flung you far from marriage and have brought about your death, a death inevitable, terrible, and unspeakable. Clearly Achilles, even as a corpse, cheers his spirit still with our blood. How I wish, dear child, the earth had this day gaped open and covered me   300 along with you, before I saw your fate."

As she said this, the tears poured steadily down from her eyes, because she had a dismal sorrow added to her sorrows.

When the Greeks reached the tomb of divine Achilles, then his dear son drew a swift sword and, checking the girl with his left hand, with his right he touched the tomb and addressed it like this:

"Listen, my father, to your son as he prays, and to the other Greeks, and do not continue any longer with your cruel anger at us. Now we have done everything that your heart desires. Become merciful to us and create quickly for us, in answer to our prayers, a return that will please our spirits."

With these words, he drove his deadly sword through the girl's neck. She raised a pitiful wail on this last day of her existence, and her lovely life left her at once. She fell prone on the ground, and all the flesh below her neck grew red. It was like snow on the mountains, which grows red quickly with dark blood, when a wild boar or a bear has been stabbed with the javelin. The Greeks immediately handed her over to be carried to the house of godlike Antenor in the city, because he among the Trojans had been taking care of her in his halls as a wife for his glorious son Eurymachus. When he had buried Priam's famous daughter near his own home beside the holy monument of Ganymede and opposite the temple of Athena Atrytone, then the waves stopped, the terrible gale died down, and a calm made the sea smooth.

The Greeks went quickly to their ships, with loud laughter and singing the praises of the gods' holy stock and of Achilles. After they had cut off the thigh pieces of oxen for the gods, they at once had a feast, and there was splendid sacrificing everywhere. They drew off the fine wine and drank it, I fancy, in goblets of silver and gold. Full of desire as they were to reach their own country, their spirit was glad. When they had had their fill of eating and feasting, then it was that Nestor the son of Neleus spoke to the eager army:

"Listen to me, my friends, now that you have escaped from the attacks of protracted war, that I may speak out words that will suit your longing hearts. Now is the season for a return to please our spirits. Let us be on our way. Achilles' mighty heart, I think, has now stopped its wretched anger, the Earthshaker Poseidon has checked the mighty waves, the winds blow soft, and the waves no longer rise in great crests. Come, let us drag the ships into the sea's swell and think of our return."

So he spoke to the eager men, and they made ready for sailing. Then a portent appeared, an object of wonder to earthly creatures: the wife of most unhappy Priam changed from a human being to a wretched dog. The people gathered around her and marveled. A god turned her entire frame to stone, a wonder even for human beings yet to be. At the suggestion of Calchas, the Greeks put her on a swift ship and took her across the Hellespont.

Speedily then the Greeks dragged their ships into the sea and put on board all the possessions they had taken as booty earlier on their way to Troy, when they had overcome the neighboring peoples, and all they had brought from Troy herself. They took especial delight in this latter, because the amount of it was so vast. Along with the other booty, many captive women followed with deep sorrow in their hearts. Then the men themselves got on board the ships.

Calchas, however, did not follow the eager army into the sea. On the contrary, he even tried to hold the other Greeks back, because he was afraid that a terrible destruction was rushing upon the Greeks in the vicinity of the Capherean Rocks. But they paid no attention to him at all; an evil Fate had beguiled the minds of the men. Amphilochus alone, swift son of noble Amphiaraus, and a man skilled in prophecy, stayed with wise Calchas. They were both fated to go to the citadels of the Pamphylians and the Cilicians, far from their own country.

But these were matters that the gods arranged later. The Greeks now untied the cables of their ships from the land and speedily drew up the anchor stones. The Hellespont re-echoed the sounds of their haste, and the waters of the sea washed round the ships. Everywhere in the prows lay piles of armor taken from men who had been killed, and up above there hung thousands of signs of victory. They crowned with garlands the ships, their heads, and the spears and shields with which they had fought against the enemy. From the prows, the lords poured into the dark blue sea libations of wine, with many a prayer to the blessed gods to grant a return free from trouble. But their prayers were mingled with the winds, and far from the ships were carried fruitlessly along with the clouds and the air.

The captive women, sad of heart, kept gazing at Troy and giving many a wail and groan (concealed from the Greeks) because of the great sorrow they had in their breasts. Some of them had their hands clasped about their knees, some poor wretches had their heads resting on their hands, and some held children in their arms. The children were not yet groaning over their day of slavery or at their country's disasters. Their desires were fixed on their mother's breast; the childish heart is far from cares. All the women's hair hung loose, their unhappy breasts were torn with their fingernails, and tears flowed thick and fast from their eyes over the tears dried on their cheeks. They gazed at their suffering city, still blazing fiercely and sending up clouds of smoke. Looking at famous Cassandra, they all remembered her dismal prophecy as they gazed at her. She, unhappy as she was at the hideous disasters of her country, laughed at the groaning women.

All the Trojans who had escaped from the pitiless war gathered in the city and went busily to work burying the dead. 400 Antenor led them to this melancholy task. They put many on the same pyre.

The Greeks, their hearts full of constant laughter, sometimes made their way through the black water with oars, sometimes in eager haste spread the sails on the ships. All Dardania and the tomb of Achilles were speedily left behind. For all the good cheer in their hearts, they felt the pangs of sorrow when they remembered comrades killed in action, and they cast their eyes at the foreign land that they could see withdrawing far from the ships. Quickly they were carried by the shores of the island of Tenedos. Then they passed by Chryse and the seat of Sminthian Apollo and holy Cilla, and windy Lesbos began to appear. Speedily they rounded the headland of Lectus, where there is the last ridge of Ida. The full sails hummed, the dark swells roared about the prows. The long waves grew dark with shadows, and their paths over the sea showed white with foam.

The Greeks would have reached the sacred soil of Greece, all going safely over the depths of the sea, if Athena, daughter of Zeus the loud thunderer, had not become indignant at them. She had in mind a heavy and merciless doom for Aias, the king of the Locrians, against whom she was uncontrollably angry. And so, when the Greeks were close to windy Euboea, she stood beside Zeus, lord of the gods, and spoke to him apart from the other immortals. Her spirit could not contain her wrath.

"Zeus, my father, men are contriving things against the gods that are no longer tolerable. They have no concern in their hearts either for you or for the other blessed ones, because punishment no longer follows close upon wretched men, but frequently a good man actually suffers more pains than a bad one and has sorrow without end. On this account, no one has any respect for justice any more, nor is there any sense of decency among men. I personally shall no longer be on Olympus nor continue to be called your daughter, if I do not punish the wanton insolence of the Greeks. Why, actually within my temple, Aias, son of Oïleus, did a most evil deed. He showed no pity for Cassandra, did not heed her innocent hands stretched out again and again to me, had no fear of my power, showed no realization in his heart that I was an immortal goddess, but committed his uncontrollable act. Do not, therefore, in your immortal heart, begrudge me the right to do as my spirit wills, so that other men, too, may fear the manifest attack of the gods."

In answer to her speech, her father replied with gentle words: "My child, I shall not in any way oppose you for the Greeks' sake, but I shall even put into your eager hands all the weapons which in time gone by the Cyclopes, showing favor to me, contrived with their tireless arms. Do you with your own vigorous spirit stir up a fierce storm against the Greeks."

With these words, he placed close beside his fearless girl the swift lightning, the deadly thunderbolt, and the grim thunder, and the spirit in her heart was greatly cheered. Quickly she put on the gleaming aegis, shield for swift fighting, unbreakable, stout—a marvel even to immortals. The terrible head of grim Medusa had been worked on it, and above this there were powerful snakes breathing out a rushing blast of dancing flame. The whole aegis resounded about the breast of the queen, just as when the great air re-echoes from lightning. Then she took her father's weapons, those which no god lifts except great Zeus, and she made huge Olympus shake. She threw into confusion the clouds and all the air above them. Night was shed about the earth, and the sea grew dark. Zeus looked on with great delight, as the broad heaven moved about the feet of the goddess. The air roared around her, as though unwearying Zeus were rushing into battle.

Athena at once sent immortal Iris from heaven to fly over the dark sea to Aeolus, ruler of the winds, so that he might send the winds to come crashing down all together, keep steadily close to the crags of rocky Caphereus, and, raging with hideous blasts, raise the sea in swells.[4] When Iris heard, she swooped away in a

[4] Quintus' description of Aeolia, although it reproduces some of the features described in Homer's *Odyssey* (x. 1–22), in some points diverges from it. In Homer, as in Quintus, Aeolus is the son of Hippotas, lives with his wife and twelve children, and is steward of the winds. But Homer says nothing about any caves, or about Aeolus striking the mountain with a trident, or about any steady roaring in the neighborhood. It is true that in Homer Aeolus is not engaged in stirring up a storm. He is portrayed doing this in the first book of Virgil's *Aeneid*, and un-Homeric features of Quintus' narrative appear there. Scholars interested in the question of Quintus' sources argue either that Quintus was influenced by Virgil or that both poets followed a common source now lost.

curving course in the clouds. You would say that she was fire mixed with air and dark water. She arrived at Aeolia, where the caves of the strong-blowing winds are, vaulted, noisy caves with rough rocks all around. Very close are the halls of Aeolus Hippotasson. She found him inside with his wife and his twelve children. She told him all that Athena had in mind in connection with the Greeks' return. He did not disobey, but went out from his halls and, with a trident held in his tireless hands, struck the great mountain where the noisy blustering winds bivouac in a hollow lair. There is always a sound of terrible roaring in the neighborhood. The force of Aeolus' blow broke the hill, and the winds poured out at once. He ordered them all to unite in forming a dark tempest and to blow until the swelling sea rose so terribly that it covered the crags of Caphereus. They rushed off immediately, before they had heard all that their king had to say.

The sea roared uncontrollably as they swooped over it, and waves like steep mountains ran in all directions. The spirit of the Greeks was shattered in their breasts, since the waves carried their ships now high in the air and now, as though they were rolling down a cliff, carried them into a dark abyss. A kind of uncontrollable force kept causing the sand to boil up as the waves parted. They were overcome with helplessness and, in their state of shock, had no power to put hand to oar, nor, much as they wanted to, did they have the strength to furl about the yards the sails that were being torn by the winds, nor, on the other hand, could they arrange them for sailing, because the terrible storm blasts drove them violently on. The helmsmen, too, no longer had the strength to manipulate the ships' rudders nimbly with their expert hands, for the evil gales were scattering everything in all directions. They had no hope of saving their lives, assailed as they were simultaneously by dark night, the great storm, and the dreadful wrath of the immortals. For Poseidon, showing favor to his brother's glorious daughter, was stirring up the pitiless sea, and she herself up above, in her merciless rage, was swooping with lightning. From heaven Zeus sent thunder in accompaniment, glorifying his child in his heart. All the islands roundabout and the mainland

500

were being deluged by the sea. And not far away was Euboea, where, most of all, the merciless supernatural power was fashioning for the Greeks troubles added to troubles. Throughout the ships there rose the groaning and wailing of dying men and the crashing of timbers as the ships broke up, for they were continually colliding with one another.

The work the men did accomplished nothing. Some poor wretches, eager to thrust away with oars ships that were rushing at them, fell into the great depths, oars and all, and died a pitiful death as long timbers from other ships assailed them from every side, and the bodies of all were horribly crushed. Some fell in the ships and lay there like dead men. Others, embracing polished oars, swam under pressure of necessity. Others, again, floated along on planks. The sea roared from its depths, and it seemed as if ocean, heaven, and earth were all confounded together.

Athena Atrytone, thundering loudly from Olympus, did not in any way shame her father's might; the air resounded about her. Bringing upon Aias wrath and ruin, she struck his ship with a thunderbolt and immediately broke it into small pieces that scattered in all directions. Earth and air resounded, and all the encircling sea rose in high surges. The men fell all together out of the ship, and the high waves encompassed them. About the lightning of the queen, a flashing brightness darted through the clouds. The men gulped the froth of the roaring brine that no man can drink, breathed out their life, and were swept over the sea. Joy came to their captive women even as they died themselves. Some of them, poor wretches, flung their arms about their children and sank into the brine, but others flung their hands upon the luckless heads of their enemies. Grim though their own lot was, they were eager to take their enemies with them in death and punish the Greeks for their outrages. Glorious Athena Tritogeneia watched from above and was delighted in her heart.

Aias swam for a time supported on a ship's timber, and then propelled himself with his arms through the briny depths, seeming like a tireless Titan in his defiant strength. The briny swell was cut by the bold man's mighty arms, and the gods marveled as they looked upon his manliness and power. Now a vast wave would carry him up through the air as though to the summit of a tall mountain, and now from this high point would hide him as though in a mountain chasm. But his tough arms did not grow weary. Many thunderbolts crashed here and there and were quenched in the sea. The daughter of loud-thundering Zeus was not planning in her heart to destroy him yet, angry though she was, before he had endured many evils and suffered extremities of pain. On this account, his misery was long in subduing him in the sea, even though he was assailed from every side, for the Fates of death set round him a thousand evils. But necessity breathed strength into him, and he thought he would escape, even if all the Olympians should, in their anger, come to one place and overturn the whole sea.

But he did not at all escape the attack of the gods. Poseidon, the mighty Earthshaker, grew indignant at him when he noticed him laying hands on the Gyraean rock. Filled with a great anger at him, he simultaneously shook the sea and the vast earth, and all around the slopes of Caphereus quaked and fell, and the beaches, vigorously struck by the furious waves sent by the angry lord, roared at the blustering swell. He split off and sent into the sea a broad rock, the very one that Aias' hands were grasping. As Aias spun for a long time about the rocky crag, his hands were torn, and the blood ran up under his nails. He was continually tossed in the boiling waves, and the floods of foam whitened his head and his shaggy beard.

He would have escaped from his evil doom, except that [the Earthshaker, still angry][5] at him, shattered the supporting land and hurled a hill upon him. Just as long ago wise Pallas Athena had lifted up the island of Sicily and thrown it down upon great Enceladus, and it still burns continuously because the tireless giant inside the earth breathes out a smoky flame; so the mountain crag fell upon the lord of the Locrians from above and covered the wretch. It weighed heavily on the mighty man, and the black

[5] A guess to fill a gap.

doom of death came to him, subdued at once by land and in the restless sea.

So, too, the other Greeks were being carried over the great gulf of the sea, some of them panic-stricken in the ships, and some thrown out of the ships. A grim misery possessed them all. Some of the ships were drifting in the sea, some had capsized and moved along keel uppermost. The masts of others, I think, had been broken away from the timbers by the rushing wind, and the swift blasts had entirely scattered the planks of others. Some had sunk into the great depths, as the floods of rain assailed them, unable to withstand the raging water of the sea, the winds, and the rain of Zeus all compounded together. For the sky was flowing steadily like a river, and the divine sea below was raging. And some man said:

"Such a storm as this probably assailed men when the rain came beyond telling in Deucalion's day, the earth was turned to sea, and deep water covered everything."

So one of the Greeks spoke in his heart, panic-stricken by the dreadful storm. Many men died. The wide surface of the sea was full of corpses, and all the shores were thickly strewn with them, for the waves had spewed up many onto the dry land. Quantities of ship timbers covered the whole of roaring Amphitrite, and in their midst the waves showed.

One man met with one evil doom as his lot, another with another: some on the broad deep, where the sea was stirred up uncontrollably; some died miserably when their ships were shattered on rocks, in accordance with the plan of Nauplius. He was very angry because of his son Palamedes, and when the storm rose, and the Greeks died, sorrowful though he was, he found great pleasure in it, because a god had been quick to give him vengeance and he saw the hated crowd suffering on the sea. He prayed earnestly to his father Poseidon to sink their ships and drown them all. His father was glad to hear him and carried them all close along the black swells. And Nauplius, like a watchman, lifted up in his hand a blazing torch of pine. His trick deceived the Greeks, who believed they had arrived at a place with harbors that offered good

600

anchorage, but they and their ships were terribly damaged on the rough rocks, and on top of this evil they suffered a still worse grief when their bodies were shattered on the cruel rocks in the swift-falling night. Only a few escaped, men saved either by a god or some helpful supernatural power.

Athena, however, while she sometimes felt great joy in her spirit, at other times felt sorry for intelligent Odysseus, because he was destined to endure many griefs from Poseidon's attack. At the moment, Poseidon was directing the full force of the grudge in his tireless heart against the walls and towers which the powerful Greeks had made to protect them against the Trojans' hateful onset. He quickly swelled to overflowing all the sea that comes down from the Euxine along the Hellespont and drove it against the shores of Troy. Up above, Zeus sent rain, showing favor to the glorious Earthshaker. Nor did Apollo the far-worker fail to share in the effort. He brought into one place quite all the streams from the hills of Ida and deluged the Greek work. The sea rose in waves, and still the noisy torrents came on, tremendously increased by the rain from Zeus. The black swells of Amphitrite's roaring sea kept the rivers from emptying into the ocean until they had by their effort leveled all the walls of the Greeks. Poseidon himself cracked the ground under them and caused water beyond telling to gush out along with mud and sand. With his mighty strength, he caused Sigeum to shake. The shores and the foundations of Dardania roared loudly. The vast fortification was hidden out of sight under the sea and sank down into the ground, which opened wide. When the sea withdrew, only sand was still visible, stretching out from the thundering cliffs all the way to the distant shore.[6]

These deeds doubtless were done by the immortals' evil purpose. But all the Greeks whom the storm had scattered were sailing on in their ships. All those who had escaped the grim storms on the sea went to their several lands, where a god led each one.

[6] In the twelfth book of the Iliad, Homer describes how Poseidon and Apollo destroyed the Greek wall after the capture of Troy and the Greeks' departure (3–33).

***
Index

The index does not aim at mentioning every occurrence of every name, but contains references to most characters who participate in important events. Though I have included characters who appear once, only to be killed, I have merely given their nationality and the pages on which they die. Their relatives are merely identified and given a page reference. A few words, especially geographical names, are merely defined, no page reference being given. I have not tried to be exhaustive in listing characters, events, places, and objects which, though mentioned by Quintus, lie outside the action of his story, and I have not ordinarily listed his personifications. The transcription of the Greek names is not, and is not meant to be, consistent, and some are Latinized, some are not—F. M. C.

Morys, Trojan ally: 164

Mosunus, a Greek: 140

Muses: leave Helicon and come to mourn Achilles, 82

Mygdon, father of Coroebus: 238

Myrmidons, Greek troops of Achilles: mourn for Achilles, 77; cut their hair and put it on Achilles' body, 84; quench Achilles' pyre and gather his bones, 85

Nastes: Trojan ally from Miletus: 31

Nauplius, father of Palamedes: raises false signal light to destroy Greeks, 265

Neleusson, *see* Nestor

Nemean lion: on Eurypylus' shield, 129

Neoptolemus, son of Achilles and Deidameia: in Quintus' poem, 12; greets Odysseus and Diomedes, 146–47; agrees to join the Greek forces, 148; eagerness to be off to Troy, 150; his appearance as he marches to the ship, 151; puts on his father's arms, 153; helps in repulse of Eurypylus, 154; fights long without weariness, 156–57; kills twin sons of Meges (3), 157–58; greeted by Phoenix, 158–59; entertained and honored by Greeks, 159–60; goes to his quarters and sees his father's treasures and captives, 160; exhorts the Myrmidons and leads out the Greeks to battle, 162–63; kills many Trojans, 164; fights with Eurypylus and kills him, 165–67; routs the Trojans, 168; kills many Trojans, 169; is not afraid of Ares, 170; leads Greeks in driving Trojans into Troy, 171; at his father's tomb, 176–77; slaughters Trojans, 179–80; drives to meet Deiphobus, 180; leads Greeks towards Scaean Gates, 182; kills twelve Trojans, 192; kills Laodamas and others, 204–205; rallies the retreating Greeks and kills many Trojans, 209–10; fights at the Scaean Gates, 213; urges on the Greeks at the walls of Troy, 215; rejects the idea of taking Troy with a trick, refuses to abandon effort to take Troy by force, but frightened by Zeus, 220;

reminds Nestor of his age and keeps him out of the horse, 225; enters the horse, 226; kills many Trojans, 239; kills Priam, 240; brings Andromache from Troy, 249; sees Achilles' ghost at night, 254–55; reports Achilles' demand of Polyxena's sacrifice, 255; sacrifices Polyxena to Achilles, 257

Nereids (daughters of Nereus): come from the sea to mourn for Achilles, 82

Nessus: on Eurypylus' shield, 13

Nestor Neleusson, aged Greek leader: in Quintus' poem, 12; saddened by Antilochus' death, incites Thrasymedes to fight Memnon, 54–55; resolves to attack Memnon, 55; complains of old age and abandons idea of attacking Memnon, 56; kills Meneclus and begs Achilles to rescue Antilochus' body, 57; delivers opening oration at funeral games, 91–93; receives Telephus' horses as prize, 93; declares wrestling match a draw, 95; urges the young men to enter the boxing contest, 96–97; advises that Trojans decide the contest for Achilles' armor, 109; urges Greeks to proceed with Aias' funeral, 121–22; comforts Podalirius, 143–44; recognizes that Zeus is at work, urges withdrawal to the ships, 173–74; urges the princes into the horse and volunteers to go himself, 225; praises Neoptolemus, 226; with Agamemnon, leads Greek army to Tenedos, 227; proposes departure, 258

Nesus, a Greek: 140

Niobe: turned to stone, 32

Nireus, handsome Greek: killed by Eurypylus, 133–34; his burial, 142

Nirus, a Trojan: 205

Nissus, a Trojan: 72

Nychius, companion of Memnon: 57

Ocyroe, mother of Hippomedon: 205

Ocythous, a Trojan: 72

Odysseus Laertesson: in Quintus' poem, 12; kills Alcon, kills many in fight by Achilles' body, 74; kept by wounds from participating in the funeral